Best of
SALADS
and
BUFFETS

Christian Teubner
&
Annette Wolter

HPBooks

ANOTHER BEST-SELLING VOLUME FROM HPBooks®

Executive Editor: Rick Bailey
Editorial Director: Helen Fisher
Editors: Veronica Durie, Retha M. Davis
Art Director: Don Burton
Book Design: Dana Martin
Typography: Cindy Coatsworth, Michelle Claridge
Photography: Christian Teubner

NOTICE: The information contained in this book is true and complete to the best of our knowledge. All recommendations are made without any guarantees on the part of the authors or HPBooks®. The authors and publisher disclaim all liability incurred in connection with the use of this information.

Published by HPBooks®, P.O. Box 5367, Tucson, AZ 85703
602/888-2150
ISBN 0-89586-255-7
Library of Congress Catalog Card Number 83-80083

© 1983 Fisher Publishing, Inc. Printed in the U.S.A.

Cover photo: Italian Buffet, page 212.

First published under the title
Kalte Kostlichkeiten wie noch nie
© Gräfe und Unzer GmbH, München, 1980

English edition published by
The Hamlyn Publishing Group Limited, 1982

Contents

Introduction 5
Party Drinks 7
Basic Recipes 10
Party Sandwiches 20-33
   Open Sandwiches 20
   Sandwiches & Rolls 23
   From the Smörgåsbord 26
   Sandwich Snacks 32
Spreads & Fillings 34-37
   Super Spreads 34
   Special Fillings 36
For Cocktail Parties 38-51
   Canapés & Snacks 38
   More Party Canapés 47
The First Course 52-61
   French-Style Hors d'Oeuvres . . . 52
   Antipasti from Italy 54
   Party Starters 56
Pâtés & Pies 62-67
   Pâtés en Croûte 62
   Terrines & Galantines 65
Salads 68-117
   Crudités 68
   Light Salads 71
   Nouvelle Cuisine 78
   Salads as Main Meals 80
   Party Specials 95
   Fruit Salads 106
Aspic Dishes 118-123
   Seafood Molds 118
   Seafood in Aspic 119
   Vegetable Molds 120
   Party Dishes 122
Egg Dishes 124-129
   Stuffed Eggs 124
   Egg Specialties 126

Vegetable Dishes 130-135
   Stuffed Vegetables 130
Exotic Fruits 136-139
   For the Gourmet 136
Fish 140-155
   Shellfish 140
   Fish Specialties 144
Cold Meats 156-165
   Roast Meats 156
   Game 159
   Poultry 160
   For the Epicure 162
Cheese from Many Lands 166-167
   The Cheeseboard 166
Party Extras 168-175
   Herb Oils & Vinegars 168
   Butters with Herbs & Spices . . . 170
   Special Sauces 172
   Dips 174
Soup Selection 176-183
   Heartwarming Soups 176
   Cold Savory Soups 178
   Dessert Soups 181
Party Baking 184-189
   Crisp Savories 184
   Pies & Pastries 186
For Two 190-199
   Light Meals 190
Special-Occasion Buffets 200-217
   Party Buffets 200
   Cold Platters 202
   The Cold Table 208
Index 218

Introduction

Best of Salads and Buffets introduces over 325 of the best and most original ideas for dishes and garnishes. Each has a full-color picture, and is explained in detail to ensure success for everyone, from the aspiring amateur cook to the accomplished professional.

The selection and organization of our recipes has come about through careful consideration. We looked at all the different occasions on which a choice of cold dishes would be appropriate. We begin with open sandwiches and rolls which can be adapted to any purpose, from lunchtime snacks to party canapés. Then there's a comprehensive selection of salads, first as crisp accompaniments, then as satisfying meals and also as colorful party platters. Next, we feature a wealth of egg, vegetable, fish and meat dishes. Ideas for entertaining family and friends alike abound here.

For really festive occasions, we can offer the finest pâtés and terrines, rich recipes for all types of fish and seafood and simple to sophisticated suggestions for cold-meat platters. For the gourmet, there are luscious concoctions of exotic fruits, or delicate aspic creations featuring fish, shellfish, chicken and vegetables.

And as well as the traditional savory soups, both hot and cold, we have brought you some delicious continental ideas. You can enjoy cold soups for the dessert course, such as Apricot & Cherry, and Orange Soup with Vanilla Ice Cream.

Finally, there's a section packed with ideas for many different occasions. These range from a children's party to a classic cold buffet, taking in Danish, Swedish, Swiss and Italian specialties on the way. The buffets culminate in a full-scale festive spread for a special celebration.

The extra sections at the front of the book deal in detail with the basic recipes. Those who love every aspect of party catering: homemade breads and mayonnaises, pastries, stocks and aspics, will find the information invaluable. Our detailed instructions and clear line drawings put them well within the reach of any amateur cook. A chapter on drinks gives lots of ideas for what to serve with any kind of buffet food, formal or informal. We feel sure this is the most comprehensive handbook available for anyone wishing to create beautiful and delicious salads and buffets.

We hope you enjoy preparing, serving and eating these dishes. We know the results will win compliments from everyone around you.

Christian Teubner and Annette Wolter

Party Drinks

One of the most important and enjoyable aspects of planning any party buffet is deciding on what to drink with the food. From having a few friends for supper to throwing a huge summer party, your meal should be complemented by the drinks you serve. Wines and spirits are popular, but there is a whole range of fruit juices to buy or make yourself, as well as still and sparkling mineral waters.

Aim to suit your drink to the occasion—tall, cool drinks and a fruit cup on summer evenings, hot mulled wine at a Christmas party. Even a simple family meal can be given a special touch if accompanied by a delicious fruit cocktail. Here we give enough suggestions for drinks to match every possible occasion. For information on mixed drinks, refer to *The Cocktail Book* by Michael Walker, published by HPBooks. Or, for information on other spirits, refer to *Spirits & Liqueurs* by Rosalind Cooper, published by HPBooks.

Soft Drinks

Soft drinks are all too rarely offered at parties. Yet there are bound to be some guests who prefer something non-alcoholic. Contrary to popular opinion, soft drinks do not have to be boring and you'll find a wide variety of refreshing alternatives to alcohol. Tomato, orange, grapefruit, pineapple and apple juices are the standard alternatives, but you can now find grape, peach, tropical-fruit and mixed-flavor juices on the market. Only products with no additives—not even sugar or water—are entitled to the name *fruit juice*. If you buy fruit drinks under any other name, you are not obtaining pure fruit juice.

You can of course make your own. There is nothing to beat 1 or 2 freshly squeezed oranges or lemons, served with ice and a twist of the fruit itself on a hot summer day. If you really enjoy pure fresh fruit juices, then it is definitely worth investing in a juicer. One of these opens a whole new range of possibilities because juice can be obtained from all kinds of fruits and vegetables—apples, carrots, cucumbers and celery, to name a few.

Freshly squeezed juices are full of vitamins. They make healthy and appetizing aperitifs, delicious summer cocktails and are favorites with waistline-watchers. Here are some unusual ideas, each of which makes 1 glass:

Cucumber Cocktail

1/4 cup cucumber juice
1/4 cup apple juice
1 tablespoon celery juice
1 teaspoon lemon juice
Pinch each salt and freshly ground black pepper
1 teaspoon chopped parsley

In a tall glass, combine cucumber, apple and celery juices. Season to taste with lemon juice, salt and pepper. Serve sprinkled with parsley.

Carrot & Apple Juice

1/4 cup carrot juice
1/3 cup apple juice
1 teaspoon lemon juice
Pinch each salt and pepper
1 teaspoon finely chopped dill, if desired

In a tall glass, combine carrot and apple juices. Season to taste with lemon juice, salt and pepper. Serve sprinkled with dill, if desired.

Tomato & Celery Juice

1/4 cup tomato juice
3 tablespoons celery juice
1 teaspoon lemon juice
3 tablespoons dairy sour cream
Pinch each salt, pepper and paprika
1 teaspoon chopped parsley

In a small bowl or blender, beat together tomato, celery and lemon juices and sour cream. Season to taste with salt, pepper and paprika. Transfer to a tall glass. Serve sprinkled with parsley.

Finally, one of the most sophisticated and refreshing drinks is simply clear spring water, still or sparkling. Serve it chilled with ice and a twist of lemon or lime.

Wine

The choosing and serving of wine deserves a book to itself. A recommended reference is *The Wine Book*, by Rosalind Cooper, published by HPBooks. Here are some points to remember when handling wines and tips on the correct type of wine to serve with each course.

Handling

Correct handling of wine begins when it is bought. Wine is a living thing and reacts to vibration and temperature changes. Buy it, if possible, a few days before your party. If you have to buy it on the day itself, carry the bottles home as carefully as you can.

Wine is best stored in a cellar, if you are lucky enough to have one. This is because a constant temperature can usually be maintained in a cellar. Otherwise, store your wine in a cupboard in a room where you know the temperature is not likely to vary much. Always lay the bottles on their sides so the wine is in contact with the cork. If stored upright, the cork dries out and shrinks. The bottle is then no longer completely airtight.

The temperature at which wine is served has a great effect on the bouquet or aroma of the wine. For the connoisseur, each wine has its optimum serving temperature. But as a rule, white wines are served chilled and red wines at room temperature. The exception among red wines is Beaujolais which should be lightly chilled. Sparkling wines should be served as cold as possible. However, genuine champagne should be only slightly chilled or it will lose its bouquet and some flavor. You will know the temperature is correct if your glass mists up when the champagne is poured in. As for sweet white wines, these should be served ice-cold, because they taste warm and syrupy at room temperature.

Red wine which has been stored in a cool place needs to be warmed slowly before drinking. Place the bottles in the room where they are to be served early on the day of your party, or even the night before. Never try to warm them up quickly in the oven or near a heater, because this kind of shock treatment will impair the wine. Many young red wines taste better if you remove the cork about an hour before serving. The oxygen in the air can then bring out their full bouquet.

Old red wines often contain a black sediment which, if shaken up when the wine is poured, makes the wine cloudy. It is therefore a good idea to decant these a couple of hours before serving. Carefully remove the cork, holding the bottle as near as possible to the flat position in which it has been stored. This will prevent the sediment from being disturbed. Slowly and evenly pour the wine into a decanter or a glass jug. Before the sediment reaches the neck of the bottle, stop pouring. This will keep the wine clear when serving.

There is an established custom of serving white and red wine and champagne in different glasses, but not everyone has a full range to choose from. The shape of the glass in no way affects the taste of the wine. What is important is that the glass should be large enough. White wine should fill the glass no more than two-thirds full, and red wine should fill it only to half full. This is to allow the scent and flavor of the wine to develop to its best. To keep the bouquet, the glass should be round or tulip-shape, tapering at the top. It should have a stem so the heat of your hand holding the glass does not change the temperature of the wine. Finally, part of the enjoyment of wine is its color. This can be anything from pale gold to deep ruby, with an infinite variety of shades in between. Do not spoil the effect by serving it in tinted glasses.

Once you have your basic glass, you can use it for all kinds of wine, even champagne, the only exceptions being sherry and port.

Serving Wine

Nowadays it does not matter if you break the rules and serve a heavy wine at the beginning of the meal or a white wine with game. You should serve whatever you feel goes best with each course. If you are not sure other people will share your taste, it might be safer to follow some traditional rules:

As an aperitif, serve a dry sparkling wine or champagne, sherry or vermouth.

With an hors d'oeuvre of artichokes, avocados, tomatoes, cucumber, eggs or smoked fish, serve a dry sherry, especially if the hors d'oeuvre contains vinegar.

With pork, veal, pâtés and continental sausages, serve dry, not-too-young wines, red or white. These can be Beaujolais and Alsace wines from France, and Soave and Frascati from Italy. Almost any wine from southern Germany would also be appropriate.

Oysters and shellfish are best eaten with very dry white wines. The classic accompaniments to oysters are Chablis and dry champagne. Moselle and dry Orvieto are also good.

Fish tastes much better served with white rather than red wine. The sharpness of white wine seems to tone down any excessively fishy taste. Serve white wines such as Rhine and Alsace, white Côte-du-Rhône and Muscadet.

Hot or cold beef, lamb or game dishes traditionally require full-bodied red wines. These can range from Bordeaux, a comparatively light wine, to the richer Burgundy. Other good choices include Valpolicella and Chianti from Italy and Rioja from Spain. You can also serve good, full-flavored, even slightly sweet white wines such as Rhineland Palatinate, which goes especially well with venison.

Chicken is the perfect dish for the indecisive because red and white wines go equally well with it. You can serve almost any wine you like, according to taste. Turkey follows the same rule. But wild duck, partridge, quail and pheasant, being game birds, really do need red wine.

Cheese is usually eaten with red wine, as you simply continue drinking whatever wine you have had with the main course. If you are serving Stilton, however, there can be no better way of rounding off a meal than with a glass of vintage port.

Punches

Making a punch is a good and convenient way of serving drink at a party. Once you have made the basic mixture, you can just keep adding to it as it is drunk. Punch can be adapted to different times of the year. There is a whole wealth of different recipes to choose from. Here is a sample, with one or two general points to bear in mind when making them.

While a lot of punches contain spirits, these do not have to be included. In fact, punches are more economical without. Resist the temptation to use inexpensive wine in the mixture. Your guests may not be able to taste it, but they will certainly feel the effects the next day. For the same reason, be careful when sweetening with sugar, as sugar increases the effects of alcohol. Try to use a sweet white wine or sparkling wine instead.

If you are putting fruit in your punch, use only fresh or frozen fruit, not canned or bottled. Preserving syrup will affect the taste without making it particularly fruity.

Punch is best served chilled, but not overchilled. Never add ice cubes to the punch bowl to chill it unless you are making Sangria. Instead, stand the bowl itself in crushed ice.

If you have no punch bowl, use a large soup tureen or earthenware pot. Use a ladle to transfer the drink to tumblers or wine glasses, half-filling them each time. Replenish the glasses regularly so cold punch does not become too warm in the glass nor hot punch too cool.

Mock Champagne

2 standard (25-oz.) bottles chilled white wine
1 lemon
1 (16-oz.) bottle chilled soda water,
 sparkling mineral water or sparkling wine

Pour white wine into a large jug or bowl. Thinly pare lemon making a very thin spiral of peel. Place peel in wine; let stand 15 minutes. Remove lemon peel. Add soda or mineral water or sparkling wine. Stir well. Remove pith from lemon. Slice lemon very thinly, discarding seeds. Place a lemon slice in each glass. Pour in wine mixture. Makes 6 to 8 servings.

Strawberry Cup

1 small basket fresh strawberries
1/2 cup water
3 tablespoons sugar
2 standard (25-oz.) bottles light white wine
1 standard (25-oz.) bottle sparkling wine

Chill a punch bowl. Hull strawberries; rinse quickly in cold water and place in chilled punch bowl. In a small saucepan, combine water and sugar. Heat over medium heat until sugar dissolves; cool slightly. Pour over strawberries. Add 1 bottle white wine. Cover and let stand in a cool place 1 hour. To serve, add the second bottle of white wine and sparkling wine. Serve immediately. Makes 6 to 8 servings.

Pineapple Cup

1 medium pineapple
1/2 cup water
2 to 3 tablespoons sugar
2 standard (25-oz.) bottles light white wine
1 standard (25-oz.) bottle sparkling wine

Chill a punch bowl. Slice pineapple in half lengthwise. Scoop out flesh and cut it in 1/2-inch cubes. Discard any hard core. Place pineapple pieces in chilled punch bowl. In a small saucepan, combine water and sugar. Heat over medium heat until sugar dissolves. Pour into punch bowl, followed by 1 bottle white wine. Cover and let stand in a cool place 1 hour. To serve, add the second bottle of white wine and sparkling wine. Serve immediately. Makes 6 to 8 servings.

Sangria

This refreshing punch from Spain has many variations. It works on a balance between lemon juice and sugar, so take care to adjust one if you alter the other. Serve as a tall drink with plenty of ice.

1/2 cup sugar
1 qt. plus 1 cup chilled Spanish red wine
1 cinnamon stick
5 whole cloves
3 oranges
3 lemons
1 qt. chilled water or mineral water

In a large bowl, combine sugar and red wine. Stir until sugar dissolves. Stir in cinnamon stick and whole cloves. Pare 1 orange and 1 lemon in a thin spiral. Place peel in wine. Thinly slice all the oranges and lemons, both peeled and unpeeled. Add fruit slices to wine. Cover and let stand in a cool place several hours. To serve, add water and ice cubes. Serve immediately. Makes 6 to 8 servings.

Mulled Wine

3 standard (25-oz.) bottles red wine
8 cinnamon sticks
10 blades mace
16 whole cloves
Peel and juice of 4 oranges
1 tablespoon freshly grated nutmeg
1 cup sugar

In a large saucepan, combine all ingredients. Heat over low heat. Remove from heat; let stand 1 to 2 hours. Strain wine mixture. Reheat until just below boiling point. Ladle into suitable serving glasses. Never allow mulled wine to boil, as this will ruin its delicate spicy flavor. Makes 6 to 8 servings.

Basic Recipes

Although the range of ready-prepared basic foods you can buy is wider now than ever before, there is still plenty of scope for the home cook. This ranges from making crusty loaves and creamy mayonnaises to real vanilla ice cream. And there are certain essential cold buffet ingredients which cannot readily be bought, such as good meat stocks and aspics. On the following pages you will find all these necessities, plus a selection of recipes for the basics most frequently used in cold-table preparation. For convenience, they can be bought, but they taste much better if they are homemade.

Homemade Bread

Baking your own bread is time-consuming, but it is one of the most enjoyable processes in cooking. Once you have tasted a loaf fresh from the oven, you will be sold on the idea.

The most important ingredient in any bread recipe is the leavening agent, which in most cases is yeast. Yeast is sold either as a compressed cake or dried granules. Cake yeast is sold foil-wrapped. It is perishable and should be stored in the refrigerator. Dried yeast is sold in little packets or jars of granules. Dried yeast stays fresh for several months in a cool, dry place. Be sure to check the date on the yeast before using. Yeast needs a warm environment if it is to work most effectively. The room temperature of most kitchens should be warm enough to allow yeast to rise, while too hot a temperature will kill the yeast cells and prevent the bread from rising. Dried or compressed yeast can be used interchangeably.

Whole-Wheat Bread

3/4 cup milk
3 tablespoons sugar
2 teaspoons salt
1/3 cup margarine
1/3 cup molasses
1-1/2 cups warm water (110F, 45C)
2 (1/4-oz.) pkgs. active dry yeast (2 tablespoons)
  or 2 cakes compressed yeast
4-1/2 cups unsifted whole-wheat flour
About 2-3/4 cups unsifted all-purpose flour

Grease 2 (9" x 5") loaf pans. In a small saucepan, scald milk over low heat. Stir in sugar, salt, margarine and molasses; cool to lukewarm. Measure warm water into a large warm bowl. Sprinkle or crumble in yeast; stir to dissolve yeast. Stir in lukewarm milk mixture, 2 cups whole-wheat flour and 2 cups all-purpose flour. Beat until smooth. Add enough of the remaining flours to make a soft dough. Turn out on a lightly floured board. Knead until smooth and elastic, about 8 to 10 minutes. Place in a greased bowl, turning to grease top. Cover and let rise in a warm place until doubled in bulk, about 1 hour. Punch down dough and divide in half. Shape into 2 loaves. Place in greased pans. Cover and let rise in warm place until doubled in bulk, about 1 hour. Preheat oven to 400F (205C). Bake about 25 to 30 minutes. Loaves are done when they sound hollow when tapped on the bottom. Remove from pans and cool on racks. Makes 2 loaves.

French Bread

2-1/2 cups warm water (110F, 45C)
2 (1/4-oz.) pkgs. active dry yeast (2 tablespoons)
  or 2 cakes compressed yeast
2 teaspoons salt
1 tablespoon melted margarine
7 cups all-purpose flour
Cornmeal
1 egg white
1 tablespoon cold water

Lightly grease 2 baking sheets. Measure warm water into a large warm bowl. Sprinkle or crumble in yeast; stir to dissolve yeast. Add salt and margarine. Add flour, stirring until well blended. Dough will be sticky. Place in a greased bowl, turning to grease top. Cover and let rise in a warm place until doubled in bulk, about 1 hour. Turn out dough onto a lightly floured board. Divide into 2 equal portions. Roll each portion into a 15" x 10" rectangle. Beginning at long side, roll up dough tightly toward you. Seal edges by pinching together. Taper ends by rolling gently back and forth. Lightly sprinkle greased baking sheets with cornmeal. Place loaves on prepared baking sheets. Cover and let rise in a warm place until doubled in bulk, about 1 hour. Preheat oven to 450F (230C). Using a sharp knife, make 4 diagonal cuts on top of each loaf. Bake in hot oven 25 minutes. Loaves are done when they sound hollow when tapped on the bottom. In a small bowl, combine egg white and water. Remove loaves from oven; brush tops and sides with egg-white mixture. Bake 5 minutes longer. Remove from sheets; cool on racks. Makes 2 loaves.

Garlic Bread

You can make garlic bread with purchased or homemade French loaves. Either way, the taste of the hot, savory, crisp garlic bread straight from the oven is irresistible. It goes especially well with a fresh green or mixed salad.

1/2 cup butter
3 garlic cloves, more if desired
Generous pinch salt
1 tablespoon each chopped parsley and chives or
  other fresh herbs
1 (1-lb.) loaf French bread

Preheat oven to 375F (190C). In a small bowl, beat butter until light and fluffy. Peel and crush garlic. Beat garlic, salt and chopped herbs into butter. Season to taste. Using a sharp knife, make diagonal cuts at 1-inch intervals along the French loaf, stopping short of cutting through the base. Spread cut surfaces with butter mixture. Wrap loaf in foil. Place on a baking sheet. Bake 15 minutes or until heated through. Makes 1 loaf.

Rye Bread

1/4 cup cornmeal
1 cup milk
2 tablespoons honey
1 tablespoon sugar
1 tablespoon salt
1 tablespoon margarine
3/4 cup warm water (110F, 45C)
1 (1/4-oz.) pkg. active dry yeast (1 tablespoon) or
   1 cake compressed yeast
2-1/2 cups unsifted rye flour
1 tablespoon caraway seeds, if desired
About 2-1/2 cups unsifted all-purpose flour
1 egg white
2 tablespoons water

Lightly grease 2 baking sheets; sprinkle sheets lightly with cornmeal. In a small saucepan, scald milk over low heat. Stir in honey, sugar, salt, and margarine; cool to lukewarm. Measure warm water into a large warm bowl. Sprinkle or crumble in yeast; stir to dissolve yeast. Stir in lukewarm milk mixture. Add rye flour and caraway seeds, if desired. Beat well. Add enough all-purpose flour to make a soft dough. Turn out dough onto a lightly floured board. Knead until smooth and elastic, about 7 minutes. Place in a greased bowl, turning to grease top. Cover and let rise in a warm place until doubled in bulk, about 1-1/2 hours. Punch down dough and turn out onto a lightly floured board. Divide dough in half. Shape each portion into a smooth ball. Cover and let rest 10 minutes. Flatten each piece slightly. Roll lightly on board to form tapered ends. Place loaves on baking sheets. In a small bowl, combine egg white and water. Brush tops and sides of loaves with egg-white mixture. Let rise, uncovered, in a warm place about 35 minutes. Loaves are done when they sound hollow when tapped on the bottom. Preheat oven to 400F (205C). Bake 25 minutes. Remove from sheets; cool on racks. Makes 2 loaves.

Mayonnaise Variations

Although you can buy many kinds of good-quality ready-made mayonnaises and salad creams, there is still nothing to beat the homemade variety. Here is a basic recipe for mayonnaise, together with some ideas for different flavorings.

Classic Mayonnaise

2 egg yolks
Generous pinch each salt and sugar
Pinch pepper
1 teaspoon Dijon-style mustard
1 teaspoon lemon juice
1 cup vegetable oil
1 tablespoon wine vinegar
1 tablespoon warm water

Make sure all ingredients are at room temperature. In a small bowl or blender, beat together egg yolks, salt, sugar, pepper and mustard until frothy. Add lemon juice; let stand a few minutes. Then, whisking constantly, add oil a few drops at a time until mixture thickens. Stir in a little vinegar, continuing to add oil in a slow steady stream, whisking constantly. Keep adding a few drops of vinegar whenever mayonnaise becomes thick, so it can absorb more oil. Continue until all the oil is incorporated. Then gradually whisk in warm water. Mayonnaise mixtures will curdle easily if oil is poured in too quickly or if too much oil is added in relation to vinegar. You can remedy this by beating another egg yolk in a separate bowl and gradually whisking in the curdled mixture. Makes about 1-1/2 cups.

Quick Mayonnaise

1 tablespoon cornstarch
2/3 cup water
1 egg
1 teaspoon Dijon-style mustard
Generous pinch each salt and sugar
Pinch pepper
2/3 cup vegetable oil
2 to 3 tablespoons wine vinegar

In a medium saucepan, combine cornstarch and water. Bring to a boil. Reduce heat and simmer a few minutes, stirring constantly. Cool slightly. In a small bowl, whisk together egg, mustard, salt, sugar and pepper until frothy. Gradually pour in oil, whisking constantly. Stir in cooled cornstarch mixture, a spoonful at a time. Season with vinegar. Add additional salt, sugar and pepper to taste. Makes about 1-1/2 cups.

Rémoulade Sauce

3 hard-cooked eggs
1 onion
1 teaspoon capers
2 canned anchovy fillets
1 dill pickle
Bunch fresh mixed herbs
1-1/2 cups Classic Mayonnaise, opposite

Finely chop eggs and onion. Drain capers, anchovies and pickle; finely chop. Finely chop herbs. In a small bowl, combine all ingredients. Stir to blend. Makes about 2 cups.

Mushroom Mayonnaise

4 oz. mushrooms
1-1/2 teaspoons butter
Salt
2 hard-cooked eggs
1 bunch parsley
1/2 cup Classic Mayonnaise, opposite
Generous 1/2 cup plain yogurt
1 to 2 teaspoons lemon juice
Pinch each pepper and grated nutmeg

Trim, clean and chop mushrooms. Melt butter in a small skillet. Add mushrooms and salt. Sauté mushrooms 2 to 3 minutes or until slightly soft. Finely chop eggs and parsley. In a small bowl, beat together mayonnaise, yogurt, lemon juice, pepper and nutmeg. Stir in sautéed mushrooms, chopped eggs and parsley. Makes about 1-1/2 cups.

Tomato Mayonnaise

2 tomatoes
1/2 cup Classic Mayonnaise, opposite
Generous 1/2 cup plain yogurt
1/4 cup tomato paste
Salt and pepper
1 teaspoon paprika

In a medium saucepan, bring 4 cups water to a boil. Plunge tomatoes in boiling water 10 to 15 seconds. Remove tomatoes; plunge in cold water. Peel and quarter tomatoes. Remove tomato seeds; dice tomatoes. In a small bowl, beat together mayonnaise, yogurt and tomato paste. Season to taste with salt, pepper and paprika. Stir in diced tomatoes. Makes about 2 cups.

Olive Mayonnaise

1/2 cup Classic Mayonnaise, opposite
Generous 1/2 cup plain yogurt
1 teaspoon lemon juice
1 teaspoon paprika
Pinch pepper
10 pimiento-stuffed olives
1 garlic clove

In a small bowl, beat together mayonnaise, yogurt, lemon juice, paprika and pepper. Slice olives in half. Crush garlic. Stir olive slices and garlic into mayonnaise. Makes about 1-1/2 cups.

Anchovy Mayonnaise

1/2 cup Classic Mayonnaise, opposite
Generous 1/2 cup plain yogurt
6 canned anchovy fillets

In a small bowl, beat together mayonnaise and yogurt. Drain anchovy fillets; finely chop fillets. Stir chopped anchovies into mayonnaise mixture. Makes about 1-1/2 cups.

Curry Mayonnaise

1 crisp apple
1 banana
1/2 cup Classic Mayonnaise, opposite
Generous 1/2 cup plain yogurt
2 teaspoons curry powder

Peel and finely shred apple. Cut banana in half lengthwise; thinly slice banana halves. In a small bowl, beat together mayonnaise, yogurt and curry powder. Stir in shredded apple and sliced banana. Makes about 1-1/2 cups.

Herb Mayonnaise

1/2 cup Classic Mayonnaise, opposite
Generous 1/2 cup plain yogurt
Pinch pepper
Generous pinch garlic salt
About 1/4 cup alfalfa sprouts
1 bunch fresh mixed herbs (parsley, dill, chives)

In a small bowl, beat together mayonnaise and yogurt. Season to taste with pepper and garlic salt. Finely chop sprouts and herbs. Stir chopped sprouts and herbs into mayonnaise. Makes about 1-1/2 cups.

● French Dressing and vinaigrette dressings are, like mayonnaise, classic accompaniments to salads and other cold dishes. Recipes are on pages 116 and 173.

Pâtés, Terrines & Galantines

Some confusion exists over these terms and it is true to say that their traditional meanings have changed over the years. Here is the main difference between a *pâté* and a *terrine*. A true pâté, literally translated as *pastried,* should always have a pastry crust, although nowadays they are often made without. A terrine is baked sealed in an ovenproof earthenware dish from which it takes its name. The dish stands in a large container, such as a roasting pan, filled with hot water. This is known as a *bain-marie*. The bain-marie allows the terrine to cook gently at an even temperature without baking or drying out. In all other respects, pâtés and terrines are made in the same way, except that the filling for a pâté tends to be smooth whereas a terrine can contain chunks of meat. Today, the term *pâté* is often applied to both dishes, but we have kept the traditional distinction for the purpose of this book.

Galantines are made from poultry, game or meat, boned out, stuffed and served cold. The stuffing itself is prepared in a similar way to that for pâtés and terrines.

The pie crust for pâté can be made from brioche dough or puff pastry, but the classic and most popular dough is a basic pie-crust pastry.

Pie-Crust Pastry

The quantity below is enough to line a round 10-inch cake pan or a 9" x 5" loaf pan, including a pastry lid and trimmings. It will also make 8 pastry tartlet cases or 12 pastry boats.

3 cups all-purpose flour
1 teaspoon salt
1 cup vegetable shortening or margarine
10 to 12 tablespoons water
1 egg yolk

Sift flour and salt together in a medium bowl. With a pastry blender or fork, cut in shortening or margarine until pieces are the size of small peas. Add the smaller amount of water. Toss with a fork until flour is moistened and mixture starts to form a ball. If necessary, add remaining water to crumbs in bottom of bowl. Gather dough in your hands and gently shape in a flat ball. Wrap dough in waxed paper or plastic wrap. Refrigerate 30 minutes. Grease a cake or loaf pan. Divide dough in the number of pieces you need for base, sides, and top of pâté, depending on the kind of pan being used. Roll out these pieces in turn on a lightly floured surface. Leave portions you are not using in refrigerator. Line pan, opposite, if used, with pastry pieces. Spoon in filling. Alternatively, if you are not using a pan, wrap filling in pastry. Pinch edges together to seal. Roll out any leftover pastry until quite thin. Cut out decorative shapes such as leaves, rings and crescents. Beat egg yolk. Use half to brush top of pastry. Arrange decorations on pâté. Brush surface again with egg yolk. Bake as directed in recipe.

Brioche Pastry

2 tablespoons warm water (110F, 45C)
1-1/2 (1/4-oz.) pkgs. active dry yeast or
  1-1/2 cakes compressed yeast
4 cups all-purpose flour
7 to 8 eggs
2 teaspoons salt
3 tablespoons sugar
1-1/2 cups unsalted butter
1 egg
1/2 teaspoon salt

Place water in a medium bowl. Sprinkle or crumble in yeast. Add a little flour. Let stand 5 to 10 minutes. Sift remaining flour into a large bowl. Add 7 eggs, 2 teaspoons salt and sugar to yeast mixture; mix lightly. Pour egg mixture into flour. Using a mixer fitted with a dough hook, beat mixture to a soft sticky dough. If dough is dry, beat last egg and add it little by little. Pound butter with your fist or a rolling pin to soften. Beat butter into dough using dough hook until completely mixed in. Place dough in a lightly oiled bowl. Turn dough to oil all sides. Cover bowl with a damp cloth; place in a warm place. Let rise 2 hours or until doubled in bulk. Turn out dough on a lightly floured board. Fold a third of the dough over the middle third and the remaining third over all, patting to work out air. Return to bowl; cover with a damp towel. Let rise until doubled in bulk or place in refrigerator overnight. Brioche dough is much easier to handle if refrigerated. Preheat oven to 425F (220C). Grease 15 (3-inch) brioche pans or 2 (6-inch) brioche pans. Knead dough gently to work out air. Divide dough in 15 pieces for individual brioches or in half for large brioches. Pinch off a third of each piece of dough and shape both large and small pieces into balls. Place a large ball in each brioche pan. Cut a deep cross on top and crown it with a smaller ball of dough. An alternate method is to make holes in the larger balls and place the smaller balls on the holes. Let small brioches rise in a warm place 15 minutes and large brioches 20 to 25 minutes or until pans are almost full. In a small bowl, combine 1 egg and 1/2 teaspoon salt. Brush risen dough with egg mixture. Bake small brioches 15 to 20 minutes or until browned. Baked brioches will sound hollow when tapped on bottoms. Bake large brioches 15 minutes, then reduce oven temperature to 375F (190C). Bake 30 to 40 minutes longer until brioches begin to pull away from sides of pans and sound hollow when tapped on bottoms. Turn out onto a rack to cool. Brioches can be stored 1 to 2 days in an airtight container but are best eaten the day they are baked. Makes 15 small or 2 large brioches.

Puff Pastry
Cook's Tips

Making your own puff pastry is time-consuming and you can produce almost as good a result with ready-made frozen puff pastry unless you are an expert cook. Here are some general points to help you when using frozen puff pastry.

● Always thaw at room temperature before use. This should take 1 to 2 hours.

● Roll out puff pastry on a very lightly floured surface. Remember never to roll in 1 direction only but from top to bottom as well as from left to right. If rolled only in 1 direction, the pastry will not rise evenly during baking.

● Cut puff pastry with a very sharp pastry wheel or a thin sharp knife to avoid pressing down on the layers and causing the edges to stick together during baking. If you are using a pastry cutter, dip it in cold water before cutting out the pastry.

● When brushing the surface of the pastry with egg, keep this away from the cut edges as beaten egg will also make the layers stick together and prevent pastry from rising.

● Any leftover pieces of puff pastry can be gathered together and rolled out again. This pastry will not rise as well, but is ideal for cutting out decorations.

● Always place puff pastry on a baking sheet or in a pan which has been lightly sprinkled with cold water. Let stand in a cool place 15 minutes before baking.

Pies & Pastries, by Janet Pittman, published by HPBooks is an excellent source for pastry recipes.

Lining a Pâté Pan

Flour work surface generously before rolling out pastry to 1/8 inch thick. Place pan in the center and mark out base in pastry, either by lightly drawing round it with the point of a knife or pricking out the shape with a pin or the end of a fine skewer. Turn pan over on its side and mark measurements in pastry in the same way, allowing an extra 1 inch along top edge. Do this with each side. Using a sharp knife or a pastry wheel, cut along outside edge of pattern. Place pan upside down on remaining pastry and cut all around shape of pan to make a lid. Set aside.

Grease pan. Lightly sprinkle main piece of pastry with flour. Fold sides gently together and place in pan. Open pastry again. Using a small ball of dough, press each pastry side into the corresponding side in pan. Press edges and corners firmly together to seal. Trim all around upper edge of pastry with scissors, leaving an even border of about 3/4 inch.

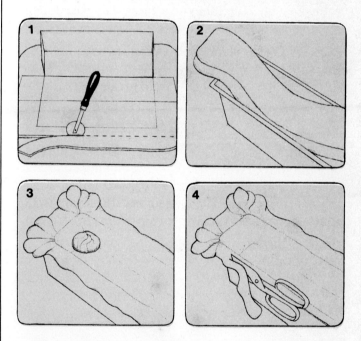

1/Mark shape of pan in pastry and cut it out, allowing 1 inch extra on top edge.

2/Lightly fold sides of pastry together and place in greased pan.

3/Open pastry out and press sides into sides of pan, using a ball of dough.

4/Trim round upper edge to leave a 3/4-inch border.

Spoon pâté filling into pastry case, pressing it well into corners and smoothing over top. Fold edges of pastry over filling; press down lightly. If you wish, fill small gap between pastry edges with an extra strip of pastry, as shown, but this is not essential because the lid should be enough to seal the pâté. Top with pastry lid. Press edges firmly together. Seal pâté well by pressing all along edges of the lid with the tip of a spoon.

Prick surface all over with a skewer to allow steam to escape or, cut 1 to 2 holes through pastry down to filling, using a knife or small pastry cutter. Fold a double thickness of foil around your finger to make a chimney. Insert it into opening. Chimney prevents meat juices from spilling out onto top of pie and spoiling its appearance. It is also useful for testing whether pâté is cooked or not. Insert a thin skewer through chimney into center of pâté and leave for 30 seconds. If when you remove skewer it feels hot to the touch, pâté is ready. If cold, pâté is not yet done. If burning hot, it is overcooked. For round pâtés, 1 chimney in center will be enough; rectangular pies will need two.

Finish pâté by brushing top with beaten egg yolk and decorating it with pastry shapes. Brush top again with egg before baking.

When pâté is baked, remove foil. If desired, pour a little hot aspic, page 18, through chimney. This will fill gap which sometimes appears between filling and pastry case during baking.

Lining & Cooking a Terrine

A classic rectangular terrine mold should be lined with thin slices of fresh white pork fat or bacon. Cut slices large enough—or use enough of them—to leave a generous margin above edges of terrine. Line base and sides of dish as shown. The slices should overlap to create an unbroken layer. Spoon in filling. Fold over top edges of fat or bacon to cover filling completely. Garnish surface with herbs and spices. Place lid on terrine.

You can make a terrine without either fat or bacon if you grease inside of mold thoroughly and cover filling with a double sheet of waxed paper brushed with oil. However, you will inevitably lose some flavor.

The lid of the terrine should fit tightly with a hole both to allow steam to escape and for the terrine to be tested with a thin skewer in the same way as pâté. To ensure terrine is thoroughly sealed, it is a good idea to fill all around crack between lid and terrine mold with Luting Paste, opposite, a simple mixture of flour and water.

To cook the terrine, place it in a large bain-marie, page 14. Fill bain-marie with boiling water to 1 inch below top of terrine. Cook on the lowest shelf of a preheated 350F (180C) oven for time indicated in the recipe.

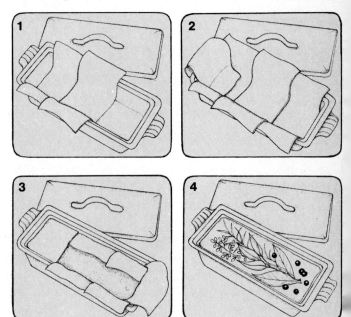

1/Line base and sides of terrine with pork fat or bacon slices.

2/Make sure slices overlap to give an unbroken lining of fat.

3/Place filling in terrrine and fold over edges of fat to cover filling completely.

4/Garnish surface with spices and sprigs of herbs.

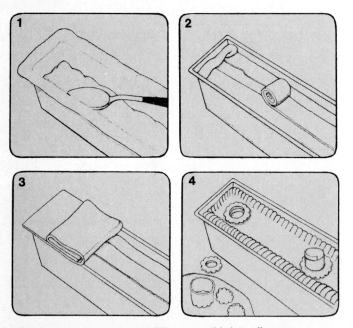

1/Use a spoon to press pâté filling smoothly into all corners.

2/Fold pastry edges over filling. If desired, seal center with a pastry strip.

3/Top whole pâté with pastry lid.

4/Decorate holes for escape of steam with pastry trimmings. Insert foil chimneys to protect the surface.

Luting Paste

1-3/4 cups all-purpose flour
1 to 1-1/4 cups water

Sift flour into a medium bowl. Make a well in the center. Pour in 1 cup water. Mix with your fingers to form a smooth paste firm enough to shape. Add more water, if necessary. Place paste on a floured surface. Roll out paste in a rope long enough to fit around top of mold. Lay rope all along crack between mold and lid, pressing down firmly. Paste will harden and provide an effective sealing agent.

Cooking a Galantine

Galantines are cooked on top of the stove in a rich meat, poultry or game stock, at a constant temperature of 175F (80C). First heat stock. Add galantine; cook in an uncovered pan for time given in the specific recipe. Do not allow to boil. Let galantine cool in stock.

Stocks & Aspics

While a rich stock is the classic basis of all good cooking, in buffet cookery it plays a special role in making aspic, a vital ingredient of dishes for the cold table. Not only does aspic allow you to prepare dishes in advance without the danger of their drying out, it also gives the food a succulent and appetizing appearance.

Aspic takes time to prepare, but it's time well spent if you want to make a particularly attractive party dish, or serve the more familiar smoked fish, cold meats and vegetables in an unusual way. You can make aspic from any kind of meat or fish stock, but the result will be especially good if you use beef or veal bones, or even a calf's foot or pig's feet for a meat stock. Bones, particularly those from young animals, contain a rich store of flavor and gelatin. Ask the butcher to chop the bones for you.

Basic Fish Stock for Aspics

Melt 1 tablespoon butter in a large saucepan. Add 1-1/2 pounds rinsed white-fish bones, a sliced onion, a few white peppercorns, the juice of 1/2 a lemon and a little salt. Simmer, covered, over low heat 10 minutes. Add 1-1/2 quarts water. Bring to a boil. Skim surface until surface is clear. Reduce heat and simmer gently 20 minutes. Strain stock; cool slightly if not for immediate use. Refrigerate until needed.

To clarify fish stock, bring stock to a boil. Add 1 whisked egg white. Simmer 2 minutes. Remove from heat and let stand until egg white gathers on surface of stock. Strain through a piece of cheesecloth or a sieve lined with 3 thicknesses of paper towel. Use as directed in specific recipe.

Light Meat Stock for Aspics

2 lbs. chopped beef or veal bones
1 lb. beef shanks
Pinch salt
About 4 qts. water
2 leeks
1 carrot
1 celery stalk
1 onion
4 whole peppercorns
1 bay leaf

Place bones in a large saucepan with cold water to cover. Bring to a boil over high heat. Drain; rinse bones and saucepan thoroughly. Fill pan with fresh water. Add bones, beef shanks and salt. Again, bring to a boil over high heat. Reduce heat and simmer 1-1/2 hours. Skim foam from surface occasionally until surface is clear. Wash, trim and chop leeks, carrot and celery. Add chopped vegetables, onion, peppercorns and bay leaf to bones. Simmer, uncovered, 1-1/2 hours. Strain off stock. Makes about 1 quart stock.

● Stock for making aspic should be entirely fat-free. Skim surface of stock with a spoon and use paper towel to soak up any fat that rises to the top. If time permits, chill stock thoroughly. Then lift congealed fat from surface. Strain stock through a fine sieve to collect any remaining pieces of fat.
● This rich stock can be used for soups and sauces as well as aspic. Vary ingredients according to type of stock needed in each recipe, using chicken meat and bones for a chicken stock, fish and fish bones for a fish stock and so on.
● If you reduce stock by further simmering, it will eventually jellify as it cools, especially if veal bones are used.

White-Wine Aspic

Egg whites in the following recipe clarify stock, making it crystal clear and suitable for aspic. Use this method whenever clarified stock is specified. You may not always have time to simmer it as long as is necessary, in which case 5 to 10 minutes simmering should be enough to absorb most impurities. A really clear stock does not require the full cooking time.

2 egg whites
1 small onion
1 leek
1 celery stalk
1 sprig parsley
Pinch salt
8 white peppercorns
1/2 bay leaf
4 cups fat-free clear meat stock
1/2 cup white wine
1/2 oz. gelatin

Beat egg whites until thick and frothy but not too stiff. Finely chop onion, leek, celery and parsley. Stir chopped vegetables into egg whites along with salt, peppercorns and bay leaf. In a large saucepan, heat meat stock and wine. Stir in egg-white mixture. Bring to a boil over high heat, whisking vigorously to prevent egg white from sticking to bottom or sides of pan. As egg white rises to surface, it will collect all impurities in stock. When egg white has risen to top of pan, stop whisking. Continue to simmer stock over very low heat 40 to 50 minutes but do not boil. Strain stock carefully through a sieve lined with a double thickness of paper towel. Pour 3 tablespoons stock into a small bowl. Stand bowl in a saucepan of hot water. Sprinkle gelatin over stock. Stir until dissolved. Return gelatin mixture to remaining stock. If stock has cooled too much during filtering, heat it again before adding gelatin without letting it boil. Stir well; cool, stirring occasionally. Wait until aspic is just beginning to set, then use as directed in specific recipe or let set completely in refrigerator until it can be chopped and used as a garnish.

• An occasional recipe requires you to line a mold with a thin layer of aspic. To do this, chill mold. Pour in aspic when it is just on the point of setting. Turn mold slowly around between your fingers to coat each side. Chill to set before arranging a filling on top.
• This basic method can be adapted to make port, sherry, muscatel or Madeira aspic, using meat, chicken, game or fish stock depending on the recipe.

For Madeira Aspic, substitute 1/2 cup Madeira wine for the white wine in the basic recipe.
For Muscatel Aspic, substitute 1/2 cup Muscatel wine for the white wine in the basic recipe.
For Port Aspic, substitute 1/2 cup port wine for the white wine in the basic recipe.
For Sherry Aspic, substitute 1/2 cup dry sherry for the white wine in the basic recipe.

Making Chaudfroid

This is a savory jelly similar to aspic, except that being based on a sauce it is opaque rather than clear. Like aspic, it protects meat and poultry dishes from drying out, makes them look attractive and adds a very special flavor. Use a light chaudfroid to cover cold roast or boiled veal and poultry, and a dark one for beef and game. The following recipe makes about 1 quart sauce.

Light Chaudfroid

7 cups fat-free light veal, chicken or fish stock
3 tablespoons cornstarch
1 tablespoon dry white wine
3 tablespoons warm water
3/4 oz. gelatin
1-1/4 cups whipping cream
Salt and white pepper

In a medium saucepan, bring stock to a boil. Simmer over medium heat until reduced by half. Whisk cornstarch into white wine. Pour cornstarch mixture into stock. Bring to a boil again. Simmer over medium heat, stirring constantly, 1 minute. Pour warm water into a bowl; set bowl in a saucepan of hot water. Sprinkle gelatin over water. Stir until gelatin dissolves. Stir gelatin mixture into stock. Stir in cream. Strain stock mixture through a fine sieve. Season to taste. Let cool. Use as it is beginning to set, as you would an aspic.

Dark Chaudfroid

3 tablespoons butter
1 small onion
1/4 cup all-purpose flour
1 tablespoon tomato paste
2/3 cup water
2/3 cup red wine
3 tablespoons imported beef extract
Salt and pepper
7 cups fat-free game or meat stock
1 tablespoon Madeira wine
3 tablespoons warm water
1/2 oz. gelatin

Melt butter in a deep heavy skillet. Finely dice onion. Sauté onion in butter until golden brown. Sprinkle flour over onion; brown over heat, stirring constantly. Stir in tomato paste, water and wine. Bring to a boil. Simmer brown sauce over low heat 10 minutes, stirring constantly. Stir in beef extract. Season with salt and pepper. In a medium saucepan, bring game or meat stock to a boil. Simmer over medium heat until reduced by half. Remove from heat and pour in Madeira. Gradually stir hot stock into brown-sauce mixture. Bring stock mixture to a boil. Remove from heat. Pour warm water into a bowl. Set bowl in a saucepan of hot water. Sprinkle gelatin over water. Stir until gelatin dissolves. Stir gelatin mixture into hot stock. Strain mixture through a fine sieve. Adjust seasonings as needed. Cool slightly. Use as it is beginning to set.

For Dessert

Finally, 2 classic extras for the dessert course.

Sweet-Wine Sauce

This rich, foamy sauce is delicious poured over both hot and cold desserts. Serve it as a special accompaniment to fruit salads.

4 eggs
1/2 cup sugar
1 teaspoon cornstarch
1 cup sweet white wine
Juice of 1 lemon

Separate eggs. Whisk egg whites until very thick but not stiff. Stir in 1 tablespoon sugar. Continue whisking until completely stiff. Beat egg yolks in a separate bowl with remaining sugar. Dissolve cornstarch in a little cold water. Stir cornstarch mixture into egg yolks along with white wine and lemon juice. Set bowl in a saucepan of hot water. Stir sauce over a gentle heat until it thickens and turns creamy. Remove from hot water. Fold in egg whites. Serve hot or cold. Makes about 1-1/2 cups.

Vanilla Ice Cream

1-1/3 cups sugar
1 tablespoon cornstarch
1/4 teaspoon salt
3 cups whole milk
2 egg yolks
1 (5.33-oz.) can evaporated milk
1 cup whipping cream
1 tablespoon vanilla extract

In a medium saucepan, combine sugar, cornstarch and salt. Stir in whole milk. Stir over medium heat until mixture begins to simmer. Simmer 1 minute over low heat; set aside. In a small bowl, lightly beat egg yolks. Stir about 1 cup milk mixture into egg yolks; stir egg-yolk mixture into remaining milk mixture. Cook and stir over low heat 2 minutes or until slightly thickened. Stir in evaporated milk, whipping cream and vanilla. Cool to room temperature. Pour into ice-cream canister. Freeze in ice-cream maker according to manufacturer's directions. Makes 2 quarts.

Ham & Egg

For each:
1-1/2 teaspoons soft butter
2 oz. smoked ham, finely chopped
Pinch curry powder
1 slice whole-wheat bread
1 hard-cooked egg
1 teaspoon chopped fresh mixed
   herbs or a generous pinch dried
   mixed herbs
1 tablespoon mayonnaise
Parsley sprig

In a small bowl, combine butter, ham and curry powder. Spread mixture on bread. Slice egg; arrange over top of ham mixture. In a small bowl, combine herbs and mayonnaise. Spoon mixture over egg slices. Garnish with parsley sprig.

Cheese Salad

For each:
1-1/2 teaspoons soft butter
1 slice whole-wheat bread
2 to 3 endive leaves
3 oz. Edam cheese
1/2 hard-cooked egg
2 tablespoons chopped walnuts
1 teaspoon chopped chives
1 tablespoon mayonnaise
1 teaspoon plain yogurt
Salt and pepper
2 to 3 grapes for garnish
2 walnut halves

Spread butter on bread. Cut endive in thin strips; scatter over bread. Dice cheese and egg. In a small bowl, combine diced cheese and egg, walnuts, chives, mayonnaise and yogurt. Season with salt and pepper. Spread cheese mixture over endive. Garnish with grapes and walnut halves.

Sausage & Peppers

For each:
1-1/2 teaspoons soft butter
1 slice whole-wheat bread
1/2 green bell pepper
1/2 red bell pepper
1 small onion
3 oz. ham loaf
1 tablespoon vegetable oil
1 teaspoon vinegar
1 teaspoon chopped parsley
Salt and pepper

Spread butter on bread. Slice green pepper in rings. Arrange pepper rings on bread. Finely dice red pepper. Slice onion in rings. Cut ham loaf in small strips. In a small bowl or jar, combine oil, vinegar, parsley, salt and pepper. Stir or shake to blend. In a small bowl, combine diced red pepper, onion rings and ham-loaf strips. Pour oil mixture over red-pepper mixture. Toss lightly to coat. Spoon red-pepper mixture over green-pepper rings.

Salami & Egg Salad

For each:
1-1/2 teaspoons soft butter
1 slice whole-wheat bread
6 thin slices salami
1 lettuce leaf
1 hard-cooked egg
3 mushrooms
1/2 tomato
1 teaspoon mayonnaise
1 tablespoon whipping cream
Dash of lemon juice
Salt and pepper
Capers, if desired

Spread butter on bread. Arrange salami slices on bread. Top with lettuce. Chop egg and mushrooms. Dice tomato. In a small bowl, combine chopped egg and mushrooms, diced tomato, mayonnaise, cream and lemon juice. Season with salt and pepper. Spoon onto lettuce leaf. Sprinkle with capers, if desired.

Mussels & Sprouts

For each:
1-1/2 teaspoons soft butter
1 slice white or whole-wheat bread
1/2 small onion
1/2 small basket alfalfa sprouts
5 canned mussels or smoked
  oysters, drained

Spread butter on bread. Finely chop onion. Sprinkle half the chopped onion over bread. Sprinkle sprouts over onion in a thick layer. Arrange mussels or oysters on sprouts. Garnish with remaining chopped onion.

Smoked Trout

For each:
1 slice white or whole-wheat bread
1-1/2 teaspoons soft butter
1 (3-oz.) smoked-trout fillet
2 thin slices honeydew melon
1 teaspoon mayonnaise
1 teaspoon pickled peppercorns or
  a sprinkling of freshly ground
  white pepper

Lightly toast bread; cool slightly. Spread butter on bread. Cut trout in half; arrange pieces on bread. Remove rind and seeds from melon slices. Place melon slices on trout. Spoon mayonnaise over melon. Sprinkle with peppercorns or white pepper.

Swiss-Cheese Salad

For each:
1-1/2 teaspoons soft butter
1 slice white bread
2 to 3 lettuce leaves
1 teaspoon lemon juice
1/4 teaspoon Dijon-style mustard
1 tablespoon vegetable oil
Salt and pepper
1 small tomato
1/2 small green bell pepper
3 oz. Emmentaler cheese
Parsley sprig

Spread butter on bread. Cut lettuce in strips; arrange on bread. In a medium bowl, combine lemon juice, mustard, oil, salt and pepper. Dice tomato, green pepper and cheese; add to lemon-juice mixture. Toss lightly to coat. Spoon tomato mixture over lettuce. Garnish with parsley.

Tomato & Fish

For each:
1-1/2 teaspoons soft butter
1 slice whole-wheat bread
1 tomato
1/2 teaspoon white pepper
2 canned herring or sardines
1/2 hard-cooked egg, cut
  lengthwise
1 tablespoon mayonnaise
1/2 teaspoon canned lumpfish
  caviar, if desired

Spread butter on bread. Slice tomato; place slices on bread. Sprinkle with white pepper. Place herring or sardines on top. Remove yolk from egg. In a small bowl, combine egg yolk and mayonnaise. Spoon yolk mixture into egg white. Place egg on herring or sardines. Garnish with caviar, if desired.

Vegetarian Special

For each:
1/2 cup frozen peas and carrots
1 tablespoon vegetable oil
1 teaspoon wine vinegar
1 teaspoon chopped parsley
Salt and pepper
1/4 teaspoon hot mustard
1-1/2 teaspoons soft butter
1 slice whole-wheat bread
2 leaves red endive or red cabbage
1 teaspoon whipped cream

Cook peas and carrots according to package directions; drain well. In a small bowl or jar, combine oil, vinegar, parsley, salt and pepper. Pour oil mixture over cooked peas and carrots. In a small bowl, combine mustard and butter. Spread mustard mixture on bread. Place endive or cabbage on bread. Spoon seasoned peas and carrots over endive or cabbage. Top with whipped cream.

Mushroom with Egg

For each:
1 teaspoon lemon juice
1 teaspoon vegetable oil
Salt and pepper
3 oz. mushrooms
1 slice white bread
1/2 garlic clove, crushed
1 tablespoon soft butter
1/2 hard-cooked egg
1 teaspoon chopped fresh herbs

In a small bowl or jar, combine lemon juice, oil, salt and pepper; blend well. Thinly slice mushrooms; place in a small bowl. Pour lemon-juice mixture over sliced mushrooms. Rub 1 side of the bread with garlic. Melt 1-1/2 teaspoons butter in a small skillet over medium heat. Place bread, garlic-side down, in skillet. Brown bread slightly. Cool. Spread unbrowned side of bread with remaining 1-1/2 teaspoons butter. Arrange mushrooms on buttered side of bread. Chop egg; sprinkle chopped egg and herbs over mushrooms.

Pinwheels

1 loaf white bread, unsliced
1 (8-oz.) can tuna
1 small onion
3 tablespoons grated fresh horseradish or prepared creamed
  horseradish
1/4 cup whipped cream
1/4 teaspoon salt
1/4 teaspoon pepper
1/4 cup soft butter
6 cherry tomatoes
6 lemon twists
Alfalfa sprouts

Remove crusts from bread. Cut loaf lengthwise in 6 slices. Stack bread slices, placing a piece of waxed paper between each slice. Using a rolling pin, roll bread out until 1/4 inch thick. Roll up each slice lengthwise, jelly-roll fashion. Drain tuna well. Finely chop tuna and onion. In a blender or food processor, combine chopped tuna and onion, horseradish and whipped cream. Blend well. Season with salt and pepper. Unroll bread slices; spread evenly with butter. Spread tuna mixture on bread. Re-roll bread. Wrap each roll in waxed paper, then wrap in foil. Refrigerate 1 hour. To serve, cut each roll in slices. Arrange slices in a circle on individual plates. Garnish each plate with a cherry tomato, a lemon twist and a small bunch of alfalfa sprouts. Makes 6 servings.

Danish Salami & Cucumber

For each:
1 tablespoon soft butter
1 slice whole-grain bread
Top half of 1 sesame roll
1/4 cucumber
Salt and pepper
6 to 8 thin slices salami
Chopped parsley

Spread butter on bread and sesame-roll half. Thinly slice cucumber; season with salt and pepper. Arrange half the cucumber slices on bread. Top cucumber with salami slices and remaining cucumber slices. Sprinkle with parsley. Top with buttered sesame-roll half.

Cook's Tip

This refreshing and satisfying roll makes an ideal snack for summer. For an outing, wrap rolls in plastic wrap or foil. An equally delicious variation would be sliced apple and cold roast pork, garnished with horseradish sauce.

Corned Beef & Egg

For each:
1 Kaiser roll
1 tablespoon soft butter
1-1/2 teaspoons cheese spread
2 to 3 lettuce leaves
2 slices canned corned beef
1 hard-cooked egg
1/2 dill pickle

Cut roll in half; spread each half with butter. Spread buttered halves with cheese spread. Place lettuce and corned beef on bottom half of roll. Cut egg in lengthwise slices. Cut pickle in thin strips. Arrange egg slices and pickle strips on corned beef. Top with remaining roll half.

Cook's Tip

These rolls are great for picnics. As a variation, substitute cold pork or ham for corned beef.

Brunch Slices

For each:
1/4 teaspoon salt
Pinch each pepper and paprika
4 oz. pork tenderloin
2 tablespoons bacon drippings
2 slices white bread
1 tablespoon soft butter
2 to 3 lettuce leaves
1 hard-cooked egg
1 small onion
1 strip canned pimiento
3 tablespoons whipping cream
1 tablespoon whipped cream
1 teaspoon curry powder
1 dill sprig, if desired

Rub salt, black pepper and paprika into pork. Heat bacon drippings in a small skillet over medium heat. Brown pork in hot drippings, turning frequently. Reduce heat to low; cook 10 minutes. Let pork stand 5 to 10 minutes to cool. Evenly slice pork. Spread butter on bread. Arrange lettuce on 1 bread slice. Top with sliced pork. Finely chop egg. Finely dice onion and pimiento. In a small bowl, combine chopped egg, diced onion and pimiento, whipping cream, whipped cream and curry powder. Adjust seasonings, if desired. Spoon egg mixture over pork slices. Top with remaining slice of bread. Garnish with dill, if desired.

Club Sandwich

For each:
2 slices white bread
1 slice liver sausage
1 slice whole-wheat bread
1 tablespoon mayonnaise
1 slice ham
2 to 3 lettuce leaves
1 slice Cheddar or Edam cheese
1 small bunch radishes

Lightly toast white bread. Place liver sausage on 1 slice of toast. Cover with whole-wheat bread. Spread mayonnaise on top of whole-wheat bread. Top with ham slice, lettuce and cheese. Place second slice of toast on top. Using a sharp knife, cut sandwich diagonally in half. Secure each half with a wooden pick. Serve with radishes.

Cook's Tip

As a variation, use a slice of cooked chicken instead of liver sausage, and replace cheese with a few tomato slices, sprinkled with freshly ground black pepper.

Baked Roquefort Slices

4 slices white bread
6 tablespoons butter
8 slices smoked ham
4 oz. Roquefort or other blue cheese
1/2 red bell pepper
1/2 green bell pepper

Preheat oven to 475F (245C). Cut bread slices in half. Melt butter in a large skillet over medium heat. Fry bread in melted butter until golden brown on both sides. Let bread stand 5 to 10 minutes to cool. Arrange bread pieces on a baking sheet. Top each piece with a slice of ham. Cut cheese in 4 equal slices. Place a slice of cheese on each ham slice. Bake a few minutes until cheese begins to melt but not brown. Cool slightly. Cut red and green pepper in thin strips. Top each serving with pepper strips. Makes 8 servings.

Cook's Tip

Unless you are baking large quantities of these slices at a time, using the oven may prove uneconomical. The same delicious result can be achieved by cooking in the microwave oven.

Tuscan Crostini

8 slices white bread
1-1/2 oz. canned anchovy fillets
3 tablespoons capers
2 garlic cloves, crushed
1/2 cup olive oil
Parsley sprigs
1/4 teaspoon freshly ground white pepper
1 (4-oz.) pkg. sliced mozzarella cheese
Black olives

Preheat oven to 475F (245C). Remove crust from bread. Cut each slice in half. In a blender or food processor, combine anchovy fillets, capers and garlic. Process to make a smooth paste. Stir 5 tablespoons olive oil into anchovy mixture. Finely chop parsley; add to anchovy mixture. Season with white pepper. Spread half the bread with anchovy mixture. Top with cheese. Cover with remaining bread slices. Brush both sides of sandwiches with remaining 3 tablespoons oil. Place on a baking sheet. Bake a few minutes until golden brown. Turn once during baking. Remove from oven. Let stand to cool slightly. Serve with black olives. Makes 8 servings.

Smörgåsbord Favorites

For each:

Egg & Tongue
1-1/2 teaspoons soft butter
1 slice whole-wheat bread
1 hard-cooked egg
2 to 3 lettuce leaves
2 oz. sliced smoked tongue
2 pimiento-stuffed olives
1/4 teaspoon capers

Spread butter on bread. Cut egg in crosswise slices. Top bread with lettuce, smoked tongue, sliced egg, olives and capers.

Roast Beef & Egg
1-1/2 teaspoons soft butter
1 slice whole-wheat bread
2 to 3 lettuce leaves
2 slices cold roast beef
1 wedge hard-cooked egg
1/2 teaspoon grated fresh horse-radish, if desired
Parsley sprig

Spread butter on bread. Top with lettuce, roast beef, egg and horseradish, if desired. Garnish with parsley.

Prawn & Mock Caviar
2 oz. frozen or canned prawns or medium shrimp
1-1/2 teaspoons soft butter
1 slice white bread
2 to 3 lettuce leaves
Twist of lime
1 teaspoon lumpfish caviar

Allow frozen prawns or shrimp to thaw. Drain prawns or shrimp. Spread butter on bread. Top with lettuce. Arrange prawns or shrimp on lettuce. Garnish with lime and caviar.

Mariners's Breakfast
2 tablespoons soft butter
1 slice whole-wheat bread
2 smoked-trout fillets
1 egg
1 teaspoon whipping cream
Salt and pepper
Chopped fresh parsley

Lightly butter bread. Top bread with trout fillets. In a small bowl, beat together egg, cream, salt and pepper. In a small skillet, melt remaining butter over low heat. Add egg mixture, stirring until just cooked. Spoon scrambled egg over trout. Sprinkle with parsley.

Rollmop Herring
1-1/2 teaspoons soft butter
1 slice white bread
2 to 3 lettuce leaves
2 rollmop herring
1/2 onion, cut crosswise
4 to 5 capers

Spread butter on bread. Top with lettuce and rollmop herring. Slice onion in rings. Place onion rings on herring. Garnish with capers.

Pâté & Bacon
1-1/2 teaspoons soft butter
1 round slice white bread
2 to 3 lettuce leaves
2 slices smooth līver pâté
1 crisp-fried bacon slice

Spread butter on bread. Top with lettuce and liver pâté. Garnish with bacon slice.

Blue Cheese & Walnut
1-1/2 teaspoons soft butter
1 large crispbread cracker
1 large tomato
Salt and pepper
2 small slices Stilton cheese
2 walnut halves

Spread butter on cracker. Slice tomato; arrange slices on cracker. Season with salt and pepper. Arrange cheese on tomato. Garnish with walnut halves.

Cook's Tip

Rollmop is a herring fillet rolled around a pickle, onion or other tidbit, then steeped in a pickling liquid. It can be homemade or commercially prepared.

Smoked Mackerel

For each:
1-1/2 teaspoons soft butter
1 slice rye bread
2 to 3 lettuce leaves
2 oz. farmer's cheese or ricotta cheese
1 tablespoon whipping cream
Pinch each salt, sugar and white pepper
1/2 small pear
1/2 small banana
Few drops lemon juice
4 oz. smoked-mackerel fillet
Coarsely ground black pepper
Dill sprig, if desired

Spread butter on bread. Top with lettuce. In a small bowl, combine cheese, cream, salt, sugar and white pepper. Coarsely shred pear; dice banana. Add shredded pear, diced banana and lemon juice to cheese mixture. Stir well; spoon onto lettuce. Cut mackerel in thick slices. Arrange mackerel on cheese mixture. Sprinkle with black pepper. Garnish with dill, if desired.

Cook's Tip

Substitute cold roast pork, rolls of smoked tongue or diced smoked ham for mackerel.

Spicy Chicken Livers

For each:
4 oz. chicken livers
2 tablespoons soft butter
1/4 teaspoon salt
1 slice white bread
1 large lettuce leaf
1 tablespoon mayonnaise
2 teaspoons red wine
1 teaspoon cranberry sauce
1/2 red apple
Few drops lemon juice
1/4 teaspoon sugar
1 lemon wedge

Wash chicken livers in cold water; drain well and trim. In a medium skillet, melt 1 tablespoon butter over medium heat. Add livers; fry 8 minutes, turning constantly. Season with salt. Let stand 10 minutes to cool. Cut livers in equal slices. Toast bread. Spread remaining 1 tablespoon butter on bread. Top with lettuce. Arrange sliced liver on lettuce. Spoon mayonnaise on liver. In a small bowl, combine wine and cranberry sauce; spoon over mayonnaise. Coarsely shred apple; sprinkle with lemon juice and sugar. Arrange shredded apple around 1 corner of bread. Garnish with lemon wedge.

Prosciutto & Fig

For each:
1-1/2 teaspoons soft butter
1 slice crusty whole-wheat bread
4 slices prosciutto
Freshly ground pepper
1 tablespoon mayonnaise
1 fresh fig, sliced

Spread butter on bread. Place ham slices on a board. Sprinkle ham with pepper. Roll up ham slices; arrange on bread. Spoon mayonnaise onto ham. Top with fig slices.

Asparagus Crispbread

For each:
3 tablespoons vegetable oil
1 tablespoon wine vinegar
Pinch ground ginger
6 to 10 cooked asparagus spears
1-1/2 teaspoons soft butter
1 crispbread cracker
1/2 orange slice
1/2 hard-cooked egg
1 tablespoon whipping cream
1 tablespoon Cointreau
Grated peel of 1/4 orange

In a small bowl, beat oil, vinegar and ginger. Add asparagus; marinate 30 minutes. Drain asparagus well. Spread butter on crispbread. Top cracker with asparagus and orange slice. Chop egg. In a small bowl, combine chopped egg, cream, Cointreau and orange peel. Spoon egg mixture over asparagus.

Breakfast Special

For each:
2 thin bacon slices
1 slice white bread
1 tablespoon mayonnaise
2 to 3 lettuce leaves
1 tomato
1 teaspoon finely chopped fresh chives, if desired

Fry bacon slices in a small skillet over medium heat until crisp. Lightly toast bread; cool slightly. Spread mayonnaise thickly on bread. Arrange lettuce on bread. Slice tomato; arrange over lettuce. Sprinkle tomato with chives, if desired. Top with cooked bacon slices.

Cook's Tip

You can stretch bacon slices to make them thin. Lay bacon flat on a board. Holding bacon down at one end, pull the back of a knife blade along the length of bacon.

New Yorker

For each:
3 tablespoons cream cheese
1 slice rye bread
3 thin slices smoked salmon
1/2 small red onion, cut crosswise

Spread cream cheese thickly on bread. Fold each salmon slice in half. Arrange salmon on bread. Cut onion in rings. Place onion rings over salmon.

Cook's Tip

As an alternative to onions, season cream cheese with freshly grated horseradish. Mix 1/2 to 1 teaspoon horseradish with cream cheese. Spread bread with this mixture.

Beef Mayonnaise

For each:
1 tablespoon mayonnaise
1 thin slice whole-wheat bread
3 slices cold roast beef
1 hard-cooked egg
1/4 dill pickle, sliced

Spread mayonnaise thickly on bread. Fold roast beef slices in half lengthwise. Arrange beef on bread. Cut egg lengthwise in slices; arrange slices on beef. Garnish with pickle slices.

Cook's Tip

Roast-beef sandwiches are just as delicious made with lightly toasted bread. Mix mayonnaise with 1 teaspoon cranberry sauce to spread on toast. Omit pickle.

Smoked Eel & Salmon

For each:
1 egg
1 teaspoon chopped fresh mixed herbs or a generous pinch dried
  mixed herbs
Salt and white pepper
4-1/2 teaspoons soft butter
1 slice whole-wheat bread
2 to 3 lettuce leaves
2 small smoked-eel fillets
1 thin slice smoked salmon

In a small bowl, beat together egg, herbs, salt and white pepper.
Melt 3 teaspoons butter in a small skillet over low heat. Add egg
mixture; stir until just cooked. Cool slightly. Spread remaining
1-1/2 teaspoons butter on bread. Place lettuce on bread. Cut
bread in half with a sharp knife. Spoon egg mixture on both
halves. Remove skin from eel; arrange eel on 1 half-slice of
bread. Roll smoked-salmon slice. Place salmon on other half-
slice of bread.

Cook's Tip

Most kinds of smoked fish can be used in this recipe.

Bavarian Cornets

For each:
1-1/2 teaspoons soft butter
1 slice whole-wheat bread
2 to 3 lettuce leaves
1 small onion
1/2 cup pickled red cabbage
Few drops lemon juice
Pinch sugar
Salt and pepper
2 small slices cold roast pork
1 teaspoon hot mustard
1 tablespoon whipped cream
1/4 teaspoon coarsely ground black pepper

Spread butter on bread. Arrange lettuce on bread. Finely dice
onion. In a small bowl, combine half the diced onion, red cabbage, lemon juice, sugar, salt and pepper. Spoon onion mixture
on lettuce. Form roast pork into cones; arrange cones on onion
mixture. In a small bowl, combine mustard and whipped cream.
Spoon mustard mixture into a pastry bag fitted with a star tip.
Pipe mustard mixture into meat cones. Sprinkle with remaining
diced onion and coarsely ground pepper.

Gourmet's Delight

For each:
1-1/2 teaspoons soft butter
1 slice whole-wheat bread
2 to 3 lettuce leaves
1 cooked chicken-breast half, skinned
1 canned peach half
1 tablespoon mayonnaise
Chopped parsley

Spread butter on bread. Arrange lettuce on bread. Thinly slice chicken. Arrange slices on lettuce. Cut peach half in even slices; arrange in a fan-shape on chicken slices. Spoon mayonnaise into a pastry bag fitted with a star tip. Pipe 2 swirls onto peach slices. Sprinkle lightly with parsley.

Cook's Tip

When peaches are in season, use instead of canned peaches. Scald a fresh peach by placing it in a heatproof bowl. Pour boiling water over peach. Let stand a few seconds. Lift peach out. Remove skin; cut peach in half. Remove pit; slice 1 half as above.

Danish Sandwiches

For each:
2 tablespooons soft butter
1 slice white bread
1 lettuce leaf
1 slice Tilsit or Cheddar cheese
2 canned sardines
2 large tomato slices
1/2 onion
Salt and coarsely ground black pepper
1 teaspoon grated Emmentaler or Edam cheese

Melt butter in a small skillet over low heat. Add bread; cook until lightly browned on both sides. Cool slightly. Arrange lettuce on bread. Top lettuce with Tilsit or Cheddar cheese. Drain sardines; arrange diagonally across cheese. Arrange tomato slices on sardines. Finely dice onion. Sprinkle tomato slices with diced onion, salt, pepper and Emmentaler or Edam cheese.

Cook's Tip

Danish Sandwiches can be topped with canned anchovy fillets cut in strips instead of sardines. To reduce saltiness, soak anchovies in a little milk.

Curried Peaches with Cream Cheese

2 firm fresh peaches or 4 canned peach halves
1 (8-oz.) pkg. cream cheese
1-1/2 teaspoons paprika
1/4 cup milk
1/2 teaspoon salt
1/2 teaspoon white pepper
1/4 cup port
3 tablespoons mild curry powder
4 slices whole-wheat bread
Parsley sprigs

If using fresh peaches, scald by placing in a heatproof bowl. Pour boiling water over peaches. Let stand a few seconds; lift peaches out. Remove skins. Cut peaches in quarters; remove pits. If using canned peaches, drain 4 peach halves. Cut in half again. In a small bowl, cream together cream cheese, paprika, milk, salt, pepper and port. Sprinkle curry powder on a flat dish. Dip rounded outer edges of peach quarters in curry powder, coating as evenly as possible. Remove crusts from bread. Cut slices in half. Place cream-cheese mixture in a pastry bag fitted with a large star tip. Pipe a strip of cheese mixture in center of each slice of bread. Place a peach quarter on each slice, curry-side down. Top with a swirl of cheese mixture. Garnish with parsley sprigs. Makes 8 servings.

Smoked-Eel Salad

1 (6-oz.) smoked-eel fillet
Lettuce leaves
2 slices whole-wheat bread
3 tablespoons farmer's cheese or ricotta cheese
1 tablespoon vegetable oil
1 tablespoon mayonnaise
1/2 teaspoon black pepper
1/2 teaspoon sugar
1 teaspoon wine vinegar
5 pimiento-stuffed olives
20 button mushrooms
3 tablespoons pickled cocktail onions
1 crisp apple
Parsley sprigs

Remove skin from eel; cut eel in 4 equal portions. Arrange lettuce on a plate. Cut bread slices in half. Arrange bread on lettuce. Place a portion of eel on each piece of bread, trimming bread to fit if necessary. In a small bowl, combine cheese, oil, mayonnaise, pepper, sugar and vinegar. Slice olives and mushrooms. Drain and finely chop onions. Peel and coarsely shred apple. Add sliced olives and mushrooms, chopped onions and shredded apple to cheese mixture. Stir to combine. Spoon cheese mixture over eel. Garnish with parsley. Makes 4 servings.

Delicatessen Meat Salads

4 slices whole-wheat bread
1/3 cup farmer's cheese or ricotta cheese
3 tablespoons whipping cream
1 teaspoon paprika
1/4 teaspoon salt
1/4 teaspoon white pepper
8 oz. meat salad (bought ready-made)
1 tomato
8 pimiento-stuffed olives
Dill or parsley sprigs

Remove crusts from bread; cut each slice in 2 equal triangles. In a small bowl, cream together cheese, cream, paprika, salt and pepper. Place cheese mixture in a pastry bag fitted with a small star tip. Pipe cheese mixture around edges of triangles. Fill center of each triangle with a spoonful of meat salad. Cut tomato in 8 wedges. Slice olives. Place 1 tomato wedge on each triangle. Garnish each salad with olive slices and a sprig of dill or parsley. Makes 8 servings.

Cook's Tip

For a change, replace meat salad with crab, chicken or vegetable salad, each made with a mayonnaise dressing.

Hawaiian Ham Rolls

1/4 cup mayonnaise
3 tablespoons farmer's cheese or ricotta cheese
2 teaspoons wine vinegar
1/4 teaspoon salt
1/4 teaspoon white pepper
1/4 teaspoon sugar
2 canned pineapple rings
3 hard-cooked eggs
2 slices dark-rye bread
1 tablespoon soft butter
4 large ham slices
1 tomato
Parsley sprigs
Few lettuce leaves

In a small bowl, cream together mayonnaise, cheese, vinegar, salt, pepper and sugar. Cut pineapple rings in small pieces. Finely chop eggs. Add pineapple and chopped egg to mayonnaise mixture. Remove crusts from bread. Spread butter on bread. Cut each slice of bread in quarters. Trim any fat from ham. Cut each ham slice in half. Spoon an equal amount of mayonnaise mixture on each half-slice of ham. Roll ham slices. Place 1 ham roll on each piece of bread. Cut tomato in 8 wedges; remove seeds. Garnish each ham roll with a tomato wedge and a parsley sprig. Serve on lettuce leaves. Makes 8 servings.

Stilton Spread

6 oz. Stilton cheese or other blue
   cheese
4 oz. sliced salami
3 small sweet gherkins
10 pickled cocktail onions
3 tablespoons chopped walnuts
1 teaspoon grated horseradish
1 tablespoon plain yogurt
1/4 cup mayonnaise
Pinch salt
5 drops Tabasco sauce

Place cheese in a large bowl.
Using a fork, break up cheese.
Cut salami in thin strips. Finely
dice gherkins. Drain and chop
cocktail onions. Add salami
strips, diced gherkins, chopped
onions, walnuts, horseradish,
yogurt, mayonnaise, salt and
Tabasco sauce. Stir until blended. Adjust seasonings, if
desired.

Egg & Pepper Spread

5 hard-cooked eggs
3/4 cup plus 2 tablespoons soft
   butter
1/2 red bell pepper
1 small onion
1/4 teaspoon salt
Pinch each celery salt, white
   pepper, curry powder and red
   (cayenne) pepper

Cut eggs in half; remove yolks.
In a small bowl, combine egg
yolks and butter. Beat until
smooth. Finely dice egg white,
red bell pepper and onion; add
to butter mixture. Stir well.
Season with celery salt, white
pepper, curry powder and red
pepper.

Emmentaler Spread

8 oz. Emmentaler cheese
4 canned baby sweet-corn cobs,
   drained
10 pimiento-stuffed olives
1/2 garlic clove, crushed
Small bunch fresh mixed herbs
   (dill, chives, parsley and
   rosemary) or a generous pinch
   of each herb in its dried form
3/4 cup soft butter
1 teaspoon pickled green
   peppercorns, if desired
Salt and pepper

Finely dice cheese. Finely chop
sweet-corn cobs, olives and
fresh herbs. In a medium bowl,
beat butter until light and
fluffy. Stir in diced cheese,
chopped sweet-corn cobs,
chopped olives, herbs and
garlic. Drain peppercorns. Add
peppercorns, if desired. Season
to taste with salt and pepper.
Cover and refrigerate 1 to 2
hours.

Cook's Tip

These spreads are mildly seasoned. If you prefer hotter, saltier
or sharper spreads, then season
accordingly.

Cottage Cheese with Ginger & Honey

1 cup cottage cheese
1/4 cup whipping cream
1 piece candied ginger
1/4 cup honey
1 oz. cut mixed candied peel

Press cottage cheese through a sieve into a medium bowl. In a small bowl, lightly whip cream. Fold whipped cream into sieved cheese. Stir in ginger and honey. Refrigerate before serving. To serve, garnish with candied peel.

Cottage Cheese with Apple

1 cup cottage cheese
1 crisp apple
1/2 large onion
Salt

Press cottage cheese through a sieve into a medium bowl. Peel and coarsely shred apple. Finely chop onion. Stir shredded apple and chopped onion into sieved cottage cheese. Season with salt. Refrigerate before serving.

Cook's Tip

Serve these spreads as sauces with hard-cooked eggs, page 126, or as tomato fillings, page 210.

Cottage Cheese with Herbs

1 cup cottage cheese
Small bunch fresh mixed herbs (chives, dill and parsley) or 1/2 teaspoon each dried chives, dill and parsley
1 small onion
1 garlic clove
1/4 teaspoon salt
Generous pinch freshly ground white pepper

Press cottage cheese through a sieve into a medium bowl. Finely chop herbs, onion and garlic; stir into cheese. Season with salt and pepper. Refrigerate before serving.

Cottage-Cheese Salad

1 cup cottage cheese
1 small bunch radishes
1 small red bell pepper
1 medium dill pickle
1 small onion
1/4 teaspoon Tabasco sauce
1/4 teaspoon salt

Press cottage cheese through a sieve into a medium bowl. Finely chop radishes, red pepper, pickle and onion; stir into sieved cheese. Season with Tabasco sauce and salt. Refrigerate before serving.

Luxury Party Loaf

1 loaf French bread
6 tablespoons mayonnaise
1 small head lettuce
8 oz. sliced ham loaf
1 carrot
1 celery stalk
1 bunch radishes
1 onion
3 tablespoons wine vinegar
1/3 cup vegetable oil
1 tablespoon chopped parsley
Salt and pepper
1 cup frozen peas
8 oz. sliced salami
4 oz. Edam or Cheddar cheese
3 tablespoons plain yogurt
1/4 teaspoon paprika
4 hard-cooked eggs
Dill and parsley sprigs

Slice outer crust off top of loaf, lengthwise to within 2 inches of each end. Scoop out some of the bread. Coat inside of loaf with 5 tablespoons mayonnaise. Separate lettuce leaves. Line inside of loaf with lettuce. Cut ham loaf and carrot in thin strips. Slice celery and radishes thinly. Cut onion in rings. In a medium bowl, combine strips of ham loaf and carrot, thin slices of celery and radishes and onion rings. In a small bowl, beat together vinegar, oil, parsley, salt and pepper. Pour vinegar mixture over vegetables. Toss to mix well. Blanch frozen peas in boiling water 5 minutes. Drain; cool slightly. Cut salami in thin strips. Dice cheese. In a medium bowl, combine cooked peas, salami strips and diced cheese. In a small bowl, combine remaining mayonnaise, yogurt, paprika, salt and pepper. Stir mayonnaise mixture into salami mixture. Fill French loaf with alternate spoonfuls of ham-loaf mixture and salami mixture. Cut each egg in 8 wedges. Arrange egg wedges on salad. Garnish with parsley and dill. Makes 8 servings.

Cook's Tip

For an evening party, prepare fillings in advance. Fill loaf just before serving. Lettuce leaves should prevent the bread from becoming soggy. Once filled, loosely wrap loaf in plastic wrap. Store in a cool place until ready to serve.

Mosaic Loaf

1 small light-rye loaf
3/4 cup soft butter
2 hard-cooked eggs
1/2 carrot, cooked
2 oz. canned mushrooms, drained
4 oz. ham
1 green onion
1 tablespoon capers
10 pimiento-stuffed olives, sliced
Pinch celery salt
1/2 teaspoon salt
1/2 teaspoon pepper

Cut off 1 end of rye loaf. Using a long sharp knife, cut all around inside of loaf, 1/2 inch from crust. Using your hand, scoop out bread from inside. Beat butter in a medium bowl until light and creamy. Cut eggs in half; separate egg whites and egg yolks. Sieve egg yolks into butter; mix well. Finely dice egg whites and carrot. Finely chop mushrooms, ham, green onion and capers. Stir diced egg whites and carrot into butter mixture. Add chopped mushrooms, ham, green onion and capers. Add olives; carefully stir in. Season with celery salt, salt and pepper. Spoon mixture into hollow loaf, filling it completely. Press down, filling all air spaces. Replace end-piece originally sliced off. Wrap loaf in foil. Refrigerate several hours. To serve, cut in slices. Makes 8 servings.

Stuffed Party Rolls

6 long rolls
1 lb. farmer's cheese or ricotta cheese
4 drops Tabasco sauce
2 tablespoons white wine
1/4 teaspoon salt
1/4 teaspoon white pepper
3 tablespoons chopped fresh mixed herbs or 2 teaspoons dried mixed herbs
1 green bell pepper
2 sweet gherkins
8 oz. ham
4 oz. cooked chicken
6 button mushrooms
1/2 cup pistachio nuts, if desired
2 teaspoons grated gingerroot
1 to 2 teaspoons chopped mixed candied peel
2 tablespoons sherry

Slice off 1/3 of each roll. Scoop out bread from inside. Place half the cheese in a medium bowl. Stir in Tabasco, white wine, salt, white pepper and herbs. Finely dice green pepper, sweet gherkins and half the ham. Stir diced green pepper, gherkins and ham into cheese mixture. Place remaining cheese in a medium bowl. Finely chop remaining ham, chicken, mushrooms and pistachios; add to remaining cheese. Stir in gingerroot, candied peel and sherry. Fill 3 rolls with ham-herb mixture. Fill remaining 3 rolls with ham-chicken mixture. Set 2 sections of each roll back together again. Wrap in foil. Refrigerate before serving. Makes 6 servings.

Cheese Bonnets

1 bunch parsley
3 tablespoons farmer's cheese or ricotta cheese
1/3 cup mayonnaise
1 tablespoon wine vinegar
1 cup diced Cheddar or Emmentaler cheese
12 thin slices salami
12 slices French bread
3 tablespoons butter

Finely chop parsley, reserving 3 to 4 sprigs for garnish. In a bowl, mix farmer's cheese or ricotta cheese with mayonnaise, vinegar and chopped parsley. Add Cheddar or Emmentaler cheese. Cut a straight line to center of each salami slice. Fold cut edges over each other to make a bonnet. Toast bread; cool slightly. Spread butter on bread. Spoon cheese mixture on each slice of bread. Top each slice with a salami bonnet. Garnish with parsley sprigs. Makes 12 servings.

Cook's Tip

Make this recipe as a sandwich snack by cutting rounds from large white slices of bread using a pastry cutter. For this larger size, double quantities for cheese mixture, and make the bonnets from mortadella or garlic-sausage slices.

Savory Butter Slices

1/2 cup plus 2 tablespoons soft butter
Pinch salt
1/2 teaspoon lemon juice
1 bunch chives
3 tablespoons grated Cheddar or Emmentaler cheese
1 teaspoon paprika
2 oz. smoked ham
2 hard-cooked eggs
1 tablespoon whipping cream
2 oz. lobster or crab paste
8 slices white bread
2 radishes
4 pimiento-stuffed olives
4 chilies
4 sweet gherkins

In a small bowl, cream together butter, salt and lemon juice. Divide butter mixture in 3 equal portions, placing each in a small bowl. Finely slice chives; stir into 1 butter portion. Stir grated cheese and paprika into 1 butter portion. Finely dice ham and eggs; stir into remaining butter portion. Add cream to ham mixture. Lobster or crab paste makes the fourth filling. Spread 2 slices of bread with chive-butter mixture, dividing mixture equally between slices. Cut slices in half; trim off crust. Repeat using 2 slices of bread for each of the remaining 3 fillings. Slice radishes and olives. Cut gherkins in a fan-shape by slicing almost to bottom of each. Spread out sliced sections. Garnish chive-butter fingers with radish slices. Garnish cheese-butter fingers with chilies. Garnish ham-butter fingers with sliced gherkins. Garnish lobster- or crab-butter fingers with olives. Makes 16 servings.

Party Nests

1/2 cup soft butter
1/4 teaspoon salt
Pinch white pepper
1 teaspoon lemon juice
1 basket alfalfa sprouts
10 small rounds whole-wheat bread
3/4 cup chopped walnuts
Pinch each celery salt, garlic salt and ground ginger
2 drops Tabasco sauce
10 small rounds pumpernickel bread
3 strips canned pimiento
Parsley sprigs

In a small bowl, cream together 1/4 cup butter, salt, white pepper and lemon juice. Spread whole-wheat bread with butter mixture. Sprinkle sprouts around edges. Chop walnuts; place walnuts in center of each round. In a small bowl, combine remaining 1/4 cup butter, celery salt, garlic salt, ginger and Tabasco. Drain pimiento; chop finely. Place butter mixture in a pastry bag fitted with a small star tip. Pipe around edges of pumpernickel bread. Fill centers with diced pimiento. Garnish each round with parsley. Makes 20 servings.

Cook's Tip

If bread is not in rounds, use a pastry cutter to make bread rounds.

Smoked-Fish Canapés

1 bunch chives
1/4 cup soft butter
1 tablespoon grated fresh horseradish or prepared creamed
  horseradish
Generous pinch each salt and garlic salt
4 slices whole-wheat bread
14 oz. smoked halibut or haddock
2 tomatoes
2 lettuce leaves
Dill or parsley sprigs
Coarsely ground black pepper

Finely chop chives. In a small bowl, cream together chopped chives, butter, horseradish, salt and garlic salt. Spread chive mixture on bread. Cut each slice diagonally to form 2 triangles. Skin the fish; remove any bones. Cut fish in pieces to fit bread triangles. Place 1 piece of fish on each triangle. Slice tomatoes; place a slice on half the fish pieces. Tuck half a lettuce leaf under other fish pieces. Garnish with dill or parsley sprig. Sprinkle with black pepper. Makes 8 servings.

Cheese Sticks

1 lb. Edam or Emmentaler cheese
2 oz. thinly sliced salami
24 pimiento-stuffed olives
2 small tomatoes
Parsley sprigs

Cut cheese in 1/2-inch cubes. Roll up salami slices. Thread each salami roll onto a wooden pick with a cheese cube, an olive and a small parsley sprig. Cut each tomato in 8 wedges. Thread each tomato wedge on a wooden pick with an olive and a cheese cube. Thread remaining cheese cubes and olives alternately on wooden picks. Garnish with parsley sprigs.

Stuffed Tomatoes

3 tablespoons long-grain rice
4 tomatoes
1 tablespoon mayonnaise
1 tablespoon whipping cream
1 tablespoon chopped fresh mixed herbs or 1 teaspoon dried mixed herbs
1 tablespoon grated Cheddar cheese
Salt and white pepper
6 pimiento-stuffed olives

Cook rice following package instructions; cool. Slice off tomato tops to make lids. Scoop out seeds and discard. In a small bowl, combine rice, mayonnaise, cream, herbs and cheese. Season with salt and white pepper. Slice olives; stir into rice mixture. Stuff tomatoes with rice mixture. Replace tomato lids. Makes 4 servings.

Curried Croquettes

2 onions
Parsley sprigs
1 lb. ground beef, lamb or pork
2 eggs
3 tablespoons breadcrumbs
2 teaspoons mild curry powder
1/2 teaspoon salt
1/4 teaspoon black pepper
Oil for deep-frying

Garnishes:
Mandarin-orange segments, pineapple segments, maraschino cherries, grapes, blue and Camembert cheese, a sprinkling of chopped nuts, pimiento-stuffed olives, chilies, canned baby sweet-corn cobs, lettuce leaves and parsley

Finely chop onions and parsley. In a medium bowl, combine chopped onion and parsley, ground meat, eggs, breadcrumbs, curry powder, salt and pepper. Wet your hands; shape meat in small balls. Pour oil in a deep heavy skillet to a depth of 1-1/2 inches. Heat oil to 350F (175C). Place meat balls, a few at a time, in hot oil. Fry 5 to 8 minutes. Using tongs or a slotted spoon, remove meat balls from oil. Drain on paper towel. Thread meat balls on wooden picks. Garnish as desired with fruit pieces, cheese or vegetables. Line a serving dish with lettuce. Arrange croquettes on top. Makes about 30 servings.

Savory Tidbits

Pickles & Smoked Ham
10 thin slices smoked ham
1/2 teaspoon black pepper
10 sweet gherkins

Dates & Cream Cheese
10 pitted dates
1 hard-cooked egg, halved
3 tablespoons whipping cream
1 (3-oz.) pkg. cream cheese
1/2 teaspoon finely chopped dill
1/2 teaspoon chopped borage, if desired

Olives & Bacon
10 thin bacon slices
10 pimiento-stuffed olives

Sprinkle ham with pepper. Wrap each gherkin in a ham slice; secure with a wooden pick.

Slice dates lengthwise. Sieve egg yolk into a bowl. Stir in cream and cream cheese. Add dill and borage, if desired. Place egg mixture in a pastry bag fitted with a small star tip. Pipe into dates. Keep stuffed dates cool until ready to serve.

In a small skillet, fry bacon until cooked on both sides, but not crisp. Drain on paper towel. Wrap an olive in each bacon slice; secure with a wooden pick. Return bacon rolls to skillet. Fry until crisp, turning occasionally.

Makes 30 servings.

Game & Mushroom Croquettes

1 lb. mushrooms
4 oz. ham
1 bunch parsley
1/4 cup butter
1 cup all-purpose flour
2/3 cup milk
2 egg yolks
2 eggs
1-1/4 lbs. ground game meat
1/4 cup Madeira wine
Pinch salt
1/4 teaspoon black pepper
1 teaspoon ground allspice
4 oz. dried breadcrumbs
Oil for deep-frying

Clean mushrooms; cut off tips of stems. Finely chop ham and parsley. Melt 2 tablespoons butter in a medium saucepan over low heat. Add 1/4 cup flour. Cook, stirring until golden in color. Slowly add milk, stirring constantly 10 minutes or until slightly thickened; cool slightly. Stir in 2 egg yolks. In a small shallow bowl, beat 2 eggs; set aside. In a medium bowl, combine cooked butter mixture, ground meat, chopped ham and parsley, 1/4 cup flour, 2 tablespoons butter, Madeira, salt, pepper and allspice. Knead to form a smooth dough. Wet your hands. Surround each mushroom with a ball of ground-meat mixture, lightly pressing meat together. Roll balls in remaining 1/2 cup flour. Dip balls in beaten egg. Roll balls in breadcrumbs, pressing crumbs evenly onto balls. Pour oil in a deep heavy skillet to a 1-1/2-inch depth. Heat oil to 350F (175C). Fry croquettes, a few at a time, 6 to 8 minutes or until brown and crisp. Drain on paper towel. Allow to cool. Serve with Cumberland sauce or cranberry jelly. Makes about 36 servings.

Prawn Croquettes

8 oz. frozen prawns or medium shrimp
2 tablespoons butter
1/2 cup all-purpose flour
2/3 cup milk
2 to 3 teaspoons lemon juice
1/2 teaspoon salt
1/4 teaspoon white pepper
1 tablespoon chopped fresh parsley or 1 teaspoon dried parsley
1 egg, beaten
4 oz. dried breadcrumbs
Oil for deep-frying

Thaw and drain prawns or shrimp; finely chop. Melt butter in a medium saucepan over low heat. Add 1/4 cup flour. Cook, stirring until golden. Slowly add milk, stirring constantly, until slightly thickened. Add chopped prawns or shrimp, lemon juice, salt, white pepper and parsley. Cook 2 minutes or until mixture becomes firm, stirring constantly. Chill prawn or shrimp mixture. Wet your hands. On a lightly floured surface, shape prawn or shrimp mixture in a long roll. Cut in small pieces. Shape in croquettes. Roll croquettes in remaining 1/4 cup flour. Dip croquettes in beaten egg; drain over bowl. Roll croquettes in breadcrumbs, pressing crumbs evenly onto croquettes. Pour oil in a deep heavy skillet to a 1-1/2-inch depth. Heat oil to 350F (175C). Fry croquettes 6 to 8 minutes or until golden brown. Drain on paper towel. Let stand to cool. Makes 18 servings.

Cheese Fritters

12 oz. matured Gouda or Cheddar cheese
5 oz. thin bacon slices
2 eggs
1/4 cup all-purpose flour
4 oz. dried breadcrumbs
Oil for deep-frying

Sauce:
2 cups plain yogurt
1/4 teaspoon salt
Pinch celery salt
1/4 teaspoon ground white pepper
Generous pinch ground ginger
1/4 cup chopped fresh mixed herbs (parsley, chives, dill, a little rosemary and sage) or 2 teaspoons dried mixed herbs

Cut cheese in 1-inch cubes. Wrap each cube in a bacon slice. Secure with a wooden pick. In a small bowl, beat eggs. Spread flour in a pie plate. Spread breadcrumbs in a second pie plate. Roll cheese and bacon cubes in flour. Roll cubes in breadcrumbs. Pour oil in a deep heavy skillet to a 1-1/2-inch depth. Heat oil to 350F (175C). Fry cubes 4 to 6 minutes or until golden brown. Drain on paper towel. Let stand to cool. In a small bowl, combine yogurt, salt, celery salt, white pepper, ginger and mixed herbs. Serve sauce with cheese cubes as a dip. Makes about 12 servings.

Melon & Ham Canapés

**3 slices white bread
2 tablespoons soft butter
12 thin small slices smoked ham
1/2 honeydew melon
12 mandarin-orange segments,
    fresh or canned**

Remove crusts from bread. Cut slices in quarters, making 12 small squares. Spread butter on bread squares. Fold ham slices in half. Place 1 ham slice on each piece of bread. Using a melon-baller, scoop out melon flesh. Arrange melon balls on ham. Top each canapé with a mandarin-orange segment. Makes 12 servings.

Salmon Canapés Tartare

**2 tablespoons soft butter
6 (2-1/2-inch) rounds white bread
2 leeks
10 oz. smoked salmon
1 lime or lemon, sliced
Dill or parsley sprigs**

Spread butter on bread. Cut leeks in 2-1/2-inch-long pieces. Remove outer leaves from leeks. Blanch leek centers in boiling water 2 minutes. Drain leeks; let cool. Unroll leek leaves. Trim leaves to cover each bread round exactly. Coarsely chop salmon. Spoon salmon on leeks. Garnish with a slice of lime or lemon and dill or parsley sprigs. Makes 6 servings.

Ham Rolls with Horseradish Cream

**8 slices baked ham
3/4 cup plus 2 tablespoons whipping cream
1/4 teaspoon salt
1 tablespoon grated fresh horseradish
1 tablespoon orange juice
1/2 orange
8 pimiento-stuffed olives**

Place ham slices on work surface. In a small bowl, whip cream with salt until very stiff. Stir in horseradish and orange juice. Spread half of each ham slice with cream mixture, using all but 2 tablespoons of cream mixture. Roll up ham slices. Using a teaspoon, fill the larger opening of each ham roll with remaining horseradish cream. Arrange rolls on a platter. Cut orange in thin slices; cut slices in half. Garnish platter with orange slices and olives. Makes 8 servings.

Cook's Tip

If fresh horseradish is not available, use prepared horseradish. In this case, use more horseradish, because prepared horseradish has less taste than the fresh variety.

Party Canapés

14 oz. cream cheese
1/2 cup dairy sour cream
1/4 teaspoon salt
1/4 teaspoon curry powder
Pinch sugar
1 teaspoon ketchup
1/2 teaspoon paprika
1 teaspoon Dijon-style mustard
1/2 cup soft butter
50 to 60 crackers
2 oz. blue cheese
2 oz. Cheddar cheese
2 oz. sliced smoked tongue

Garnishes:
Prawns, baby shrimp, caviar, smoked salmon, sliced salami, hard-cooked eggs, tomatoes, cucumber, chilies, sweet gherkins, pimiento-stuffed olives, truffles, radishes, walnuts, canned baby sweet-corn cobs, capers, mushrooms, avocado cubes, alfalfa sprouts, dill, parsley, strips of lettuce and fruit of your choice

In a medium bowl, beat together cream cheese, sour cream and salt until light and fluffy. Divide cheese mixture into 3 equal portions. Mix 1 portion with curry powder and sugar. Mix 1 portion with ketchup and paprika. Leave 1 portion plain. In a small bowl, combine butter and mustard. Spread butter mixture on crackers. Cut cheeses and smoked tongue in small cubes. Top each cracker with a piece of cheese or smoked tongue. Place 3 portions of cream-cheese mixture in separate pastry bags fitted with star tips. Pipe an equal quantity of crackers with each flavor cheese mixture. Top crackers with choice of suggested garnishes. Makes 50 to 60 servings.

Dominoes

1 hard-cooked egg
6 oz. cream cheese
1/4 cup whipping cream
1/2 teaspoon salt
Pinch white pepper
1 teaspoon hot mustard
Generous pinch saffron, if desired
1/2 teaspoon tomato paste
1/4 teaspoon paprika
Few drops lemon juice
Pinch sugar
1 tablespoon chopped fresh mixed herbs or 1 teaspoon dried mixed
  herbs
1 (8-oz.) loaf pumpernickel bread

Remove yolk from egg; reserve white for another use. In a small bowl, beat together cream cheese, cream and salt until creamy. Divide in 4 equal portions. Stir white pepper and mustard into 1 portion. Press egg yolk through a sieve. Stir egg yolk and saffron, if desired, into 1 portion. Stir tomato paste and paprika into 1 portion. Stir lemon juice, sugar and mixed herbs into 1 portion. Spread pumpernickel slices alternately with 4 flavors of cheese mixture. Stack pumpernickel slices neatly, one above the other. Top with a fifth slice of pumpernickel. Place a flat plate on top of bread to prevent edges from curling. Refrigerate 1 hour or more. To serve, cut bread into squares or rectangles with a sharp knife. Makes 8 servings.

Cheese & Herb Crackers

1 large carrot
8 oz. farmer's cheese or ricotta cheese
1/4 cup whipping cream
1 teaspoon lemon juice
1/2 teaspoon salt
Generous pinch red (cayenne) pepper
Generous pinch sugar
1/2 small onion
2 tablespoons chopped fresh mixed herbs (chervil, chives, parsley,
  dill) or 1 teaspoon dried mixed herbs
24 crackers
24 mild chilies
Parsley sprigs

In a small saucepan, bring water to a boil. Add carrot; blanch 2 minutes. Drain carrot; cool slightly. In a medium bowl, beat together cheese, cream, lemon juice, salt, red pepper and sugar until smooth. Finely chop onion; stir in chopped onion and mixed herbs. Place cheese mixture in a pastry bag fitted with a star tip. Pipe on crackers. Slice carrot in 24 pieces. Using a patterned pastry cutter or a knife, cut carrot slices in flower shapes. Garnish each cracker with a carrot flower, a chili and a sprig of parsley. Makes 24 servings.

Liver-Sausage Snacks

9 oz. liver sausage
1 egg yolk
1 onion
1/2 red bell pepper
2 small dill pickles
4 pimiento-stuffed olives
1/2 garlic clove, crushed
Pinch white pepper
1/2 teaspoon paprika
1/4 cup chopped parsley
12 crackers
2 hard-cooked eggs
Few leaves fresh lemon balm, if desired
Parsley sprigs

In a small bowl, combine liver sausage and egg yolk. Finely chop onion, red pepper, dill pickles and olives; add to sausage mixture. Season mixture with garlic, white pepper, paprika and chopped parsley. Spread sausage mixture on crackers. Cut each egg in 6 wedges. Garnish each cracker with a wedge of egg, a parsley sprig and a leaf of lemon balm, if desired. Makes 12 servings.

Meat-Salad Rolls

4 slices processed meat loaf, not too thin
1 tablespoon mustard
1 tablespoon grated fresh horseradish or prepared horseradish
2 to 3 medium carrots
2 large dill pickles
1 red bell pepper
8 pickled cocktail onions

Cut meat-loaf slices in half, lengthwise. Coat 1 side of each slice with mustard. Sprinkle with horseradish. Cut carrots in long thin strips. In a small saucepan, bring a small amount of salted water to a boil. Add carrot strips; blanch 2 minutes. Drain; then plunge in cold water. Drain again; cool thoroughly. Cut 4 round slices from each pickle; set aside. Slice remainder of each pickle in long thin strips. Cut red pepper in long thin strips. Lay strips of blanched carrot, dill pickle and red pepper alternately on each slice of meat loaf. Roll up and secure with a wooden pick. Garnish each pick with a slice of dill pickle and a cocktail onion. Makes 8 servings.

Celeriac Rounds

1 celeriac
1 teaspoon salt
1 tablespoon vinegar
1 teaspoon sugar
1 leek
1 lb. roast breast of duck, skinned
1 teaspoon Dijon-style mustard
2 teaspoons vegetable oil
1 teaspoon soy sauce

Remove tough outer skin of celeriac. Place celeriac in a saucepan with water to cover. Add salt, vinegar and sugar. Cover; simmer 40 minutes. Wash leek thoroughly, cutting off tough green leaves at top and roots. Cut leek in 4 slices. Place leek in another saucepan; cover with water. Cover; simmer 15 minutes. Drain cooked vegetables; cool slightly. Slice duck diagonally. Slice celeriac crosswise in 4 equal pieces; round off edges. Thinly spread celeriac slices with mustard. Top with a slice of duck. Cut leek in thin strips. Garnish celeriac rounds with leek. In a small bowl or jar, combine oil and soy sauce. Sprinkle oil mixture over duck and celeriac. Makes 4 servings.

Cook's Tip

Instead of celeriac, use rounds of apple, sprinkled with lemon juice to prevent discoloration, as a base for duck. Jícama can also be used. Replace leek with finely chopped celery stalks.

Party Slices

1 small loaf white bread
1 dill pickle
1 small onion
1/2 green bell pepper
2 canned anchovy fillets
10 oz. ground beef sirloin or tenderloin
2 egg yolks
3 tablespoons Madeira wine
1/2 teaspoon salt
Pinch each black pepper, paprika and garlic salt
1 tablespoon chopped fresh mixed herbs or 1 teaspoon dried mixed
  herbs
1 cup crumbled Stilton cheese
1/2 cup soft butter
3 tablespoons whipping cream
Pinch dried sage
3/4 cup chopped walnuts
4 oz. cream cheese
3 oz. ground pistachio nuts or hazelnuts
Pimiento-stuffed olives

Remove crusts from bread. Cut loaf lengthwise in 6 equal slices. Finely chop dill pickle, onion, green pepper and anchovies. In a medium bowl, combine chopped pickle, onion, green pepper, anchovies, ground beef, 1 egg yolk, Madeira, salt, black pepper, paprika, garlic salt and mixed herbs. Spread 2 long slices of bread thickly with ground-beef mixture. In a medium bowl, combine cheese, butter, remaining egg yolk, cream, sage and walnuts. Season to taste. Spread 2 other slices with cheese mixture. Build slices into 2 separate stacks, starting with a layer of ground beef, followed by a cheese layer. Top with remaining slices of bread. Coat stacks with 3 ounces cream cheese. Sprinkle with pistachios or hazelnuts. Cut stacks in slices. Garnish with piped rosettes of remaining cream cheese and olives. Makes 6 servings.

Quail's-Egg Tarts

8 oz. turkey livers
Generous pinch each salt, pepper, ground allspice and grated orange
   peel
6 tablespoons butter
2 shallots
3/4 cup whipping cream
1 egg yolk
8 slices white bread
2 small oranges
8 pickled quail's eggs
Truffle slices, if desired
Lettuce leaves

In a small bowl, chop turkey livers. Add salt, pepper, allspice
and orange peel. In a small skillet, melt 3 tablespoons butter
over medium heat. Add seasoned livers; fry 3 minutes. Using a
slotted spoon, remove livers from skillet; set aside. Finely chop
shallots. Sauté shallots in skillet with butter 2 to 3 minutes; cool
slightly. In a blender or food processor fitted with a steel blade,
combine livers and shallots. Process until smooth. In a small
bowl, beat cream. Beat together whipped cream, liver mixture
and egg yolk. Using a pastry cutter, cut bread in 2-1/2-inch
rounds. Fry in remaining butter in skillet on both sides until
golden brown. Peel oranges; remove pith. Cut each orange in 4
slices. Place an orange slice on each bread round. Place liver
mixture in a pastry bag fitted with a large star tip. Pipe rosettes
on each orange slice. Place 1 quail's egg in center of each
rosette. Garnish with a sliced truffle, if desired. Serve on lettuce
leaves. Makes 8 servings.

Smoked Eel & Danish Cheese

1 lb. Havarti cheese
12 oz. smoked-eel fillet
Endive leaves
2 teaspoons vegetable oil
1 teaspoon wine vinegar
Salt and pepper
6 slices white bread
2 tablespoons butter

Slice cheese in 12 rectangles. Skin eel; cut in slices to fit cheese
rectangles. Tear endive in small pieces. In a small bowl or jar,
combine oil, vinegar, salt and pepper. Pour oil mixture over
endive. Toss lightly to coat. Cut slices of bread in half. Toast
bread halves lightly. Spread butter on bread. Cover each bread
slice with endive. Top with a piece of cheese and an eel fillet.
Makes 12 servings.

Cook's Tip

**Almost any kind of hard cheese—matured Cheddar, Edam, Em-
mentaler, Tilsit—would be suitable for this canapé. Serve with ice-
cold schnapps, if possible, for a particularly delicious snack.**

Steak-Tartare Rounds

1 bunch fresh mixed herbs (parsley, chives, a little rosemary and
   thyme) or 2 teaspoons dried mixed herbs
1/2 red bell pepper
1/2 small onion
1 small dill pickle
2 teaspoons capers
12 oz. ground beef sirloin or tenderloin
2 egg yolks
1/2 teaspoon salt
Pinch garlic salt
1 teaspoon paprika
Pinch black pepper
3 tablespoons brandy
8 slices white bread
2 tablespoons butter
1 hard-cooked egg
4 pitted black olives
8 parsley sprigs

Finely chop herbs, red pepper, onion, dill pickle and capers. In a
medium bowl, combine red pepper, dill pickle, onion, capers
and ground beef. Add herbs, egg yolks, salt, garlic salt, paprika,
black pepper and brandy. Mix together thoroughly. Cover and
refrigerate 20 to 30 minutes. Cut bread in 8 (3-inch) rounds
with a pastry cutter. Toast bread rounds on both sides. Spread
butter on bread. Arrange ground-meat mixture on toast rounds.
Cut egg in 8 wedges. Slice olives in half. Garnish each round
with a wedge of egg, half an olive and a parsley sprig. Makes 8
servings.

Prawn-Tartare Slices

8 oz. frozen or canned prawns or medium shrimp
2 shallots
1 bunch fresh dill or 1 teaspoon dried dill
1 to 2 tablespoons olive oil
1 to 2 teaspoons lemon juice
Generous pinch each salt and white pepper
4 slices pumpernickel bread
1 tablespoon butter
1 lemon

Thaw and drain prawns or shrimp. Chop dill, reserving 8 small
sprigs. Finely chop shallots and prawns or shrimp. In a medium
bowl, combine prawns or shrimp, shallots, dill, oil, lemon juice,
salt and pepper. Cut pumpernickel slices in half lengthwise.
Spread butter on each slice. Spread prawn or shrimp mixture on
bread. Cut 8 thin slices from center of lemon. Garnish with a
lemon slice and dill sprig, if desired. Makes 8 servings.

Cook's Tip

You can also spread prawn or shrimp mixture on toasted white-bread
rounds. Garnish with lumpfish caviar.

Liver-Sausage Swirls

1 medium celeriac
5 leaves fresh sage or a pinch dried sage
8 oz. liver sausage
2/3 cup whipping cream
1 hard-cooked egg
Pinch each freshly ground white pepper and salt
1 tablespoon pistachio nuts, if desired
4 pitted black olives

Scrub celeriac thoroughly in cold water. In a small saucepan, bring 2 to 3 cups salted water to a boil. Add celeriac; simmer 45 minutes. Remove from heat; let stand in water to cool. Finely chop sage leaves. In a medium bowl, combine liver sausage, cream and sage. Cut egg in half; remove yolk. Press yolk through a sieve; add to liver mixture. Sieve egg white; add to liver mixture. Beat liver mixture until creamy. Season with salt and pepper. Chop pistachios, if desired. Cut cooled celeriac in 4 equal slices. Cut slices in 2-inch rounds, using a fluted pastry cutter. Place liver mixture in a pastry bag fitted with a star tip. Pipe on celeriac slices. Sprinkle with chopped pistachios, if desired. Garnish with olives. Makes 4 servings.

Veal Tournedos Elysée

4 slices white bread
2 tablespoons butter
4 (2-oz.) tournedos of veal
Pinch each salt and white pepper
3 tablespoons vegetable oil
1/2 head lettuce
3 tablespoons mayonnaise
1/4 cup whipping cream
Pinch each paprika and sugar
Few drops lemon juice
2/3 cup Madeira Aspic, page 18
2 maraschino cherries, halved
4 canned mandarin-orange segments

Using a pastry cutter, cut bread in 4 (2-inch) rounds. Melt butter in a medium skillet over medium heat. Add bread rounds; fry until golden brown on both sides. Rub veal with salt and white pepper. Heat oil in skillet. Add veal; fry 6 minutes, turning once. Remove veal; drain on paper towel. Cool slightly. Cut lettuce in strips; place in a bowl. In a medium bowl, beat together mayonnaise, cream, paprika, sugar and lemon juice. Season with salt. Stir together mayonnaise mixture and lettuce strips. Arrange lettuce mixture on fried bread rounds. Top with fried veal pieces. Coat veal with Madeira Aspic. Let stand to set. Garnish each round with half a cherry and a mandarin-orange segment. Makes 4 servings.

Royal Sole with Curried Cream

8 small frozen sole fillets
2 oz. young green beans
2 tablespoons chopped parsley
Generous pinch white pepper
1/2 teaspoon dried tarragon
Juice of 1/2 lemon
2/3 cup White-Wine Aspic, page 18
8 slices white bread
1 small tomato
2/3 cup whipping cream
Pinch each salt and sugar
Few drops lemon juice
1/4 teaspoon curry powder

Thaw and drain sole fillets. In a medium saucepan, bring 2/3 cup salted water to a boil. Add green beans; simmer 10 minutes. Drain and cool. Sprinkle sole fillets with parsley, white pepper, tarragon and juice of 1/2 lemon. Place a few cooked beans on each fillet. Roll fillet up; secure with a wooden pick. In a medium saucepan, bring 3-1/2 cups salted water to a boil over medium heat. Add rolled fillets. Reduce heat; simmer 15 minutes. Remove fish from water. Cool slightly. Coat fish with White-Wine Aspic. Using a pastry cutter, cut bread slices in 8 (3-inch) rounds. Toast on both sides. Place a cooked fillet roll on each piece. Peel tomato; cut in quarters. Remove seeds; dice tomato. In a small bowl, beat cream until stiff. Fold in salt, sugar, lemon juice and curry powder. Place in a pastry bag fitted with a star tip. Pipe a rosette on each toast round. Top with diced tomato. Makes 8 servings.

Roquefort Boats

4 oz. ham
1/2 onion
8 pimiento-stuffed olives
1 tablespoon vegetable oil
8 homemade pie-crust pastry boats, as in Chicken Tartlets, page 57
8 oz. Roquefort cheese or other blue cheese
1/2 cup soft butter
2 egg yolks
8 walnut halves

Finely chop ham, onion and olives. Heat oil in a skillet. Sauté chopped ham and onion 2 to 3 minutes; cool slightly. Combine sautéed ham and onion with olives. Spoon ham mixture in pastry boats. In a medium bowl, crumble cheese with a fork. Add butter and egg yolks to cheese; stir until creamy. Place cheese mixture in a pastry bag fitted with a star tip. Pipe cheese mixture on ham mixture in pastry boats. Garnish each boat with a walnut half. Makes 8 servings.

Cook's Tip

This dish can be made in advance. Prepare ham and cheese mixtures. Store in refrigerator. To serve, bring cheese mixture to room temperature ahead of time so it will pipe easily.

Ham Mousse

1 cup White-Wine Aspic, page 18
1 tablespoon butter
2 tablespoons all-purpose flour
1-1/4 cups veal or chicken stock
12 oz. ham, minced
1/2 cup hot beef stock
1/4 oz. gelatin
Salt and white pepper
2/3 cup whipping cream
1/4 tomato
6 slices hard-cooked egg
6 individual herb stems (dill, parsley, chervil or tarragon)

Line 6 dariole molds with a thin coating of wine aspic. Refrigerate until set. Melt butter in a skillet over medium heat. Add flour; stir until blended. Add veal or chicken stock; bring to a boil. Simmer 1-1/2 hours. Strain; stir until completely cool. In a blender, combine minced ham and stock mixture. Pour beef stock in a bowl. Stand bowl in a pan of hot water. Sprinkle gelatin over beef stock. Stir until dissolved. Stir hot gelatin liquid into ham mixture. Season with salt and pepper. Let stand until it begins to set. In a small bowl, beat cream until stiff. Fold whipped cream into ham mixture. Peel tomato; remove seeds. Cut into 6 small squares. Cut egg slices into flower shapes. Use egg, tomato and herb stems to make a decoration on top of each aspic in molds. Pour ham mousse into molds. Refrigerate until nearly set. Top with remaining wine aspic. Refrigerate 30 to 60 minutes or until firmly set. Before serving, dip molds in hot water for a few seconds to loosen sides. Turn mousse out onto a plate. Makes 6 servings.

Tomato Mousse

1 cup White-Wine Aspic, page 18
4 medium tomatoes
1/4 cup ketchup
3 tablespoons tomato juice
1/4 cup tomato paste
Pinch each salt, sugar and red (cayenne) pepper
1/4 cup hot beef stock
1/4 oz. gelatin
2/3 cup whipping cream

Line 6 dariole molds with a thin coating of wine aspic. Refrigerate until set. Place tomatoes in a heatproof bowl. Pour boiling water over tomatoes. Let stand 10 to 15 seconds. Remove tomatoes from water. Carefully remove tomato skin. Cut tomatoes in half. Remove seeds; dice tomatoes. Divide into 2 portions. Press 1 portion of tomatoes through a fine sieve. In a small bowl, combine sieved tomato, ketchup, tomato juice, tomato paste, salt, sugar and red pepper. Pour beef stock in a small bowl. Stand bowl in a pan of hot water. Sprinkle gelatin over beef stock. Stir until dissolved. Whisk hot stock mixture into tomato mixture. In a small bowl, beat cream until stiff. Fold into tomato mixture. Mix remaining diced tomato into tomato mixture. Pour tomato mixture into molds. Refrigerate until nearly set. Top with remaining aspic. Refrigerate 30 to 60 minutes or until firmly set. Before serving, dip molds in hot water for a few seconds to loosen sides. Turn mousse out onto a plate. Makes 6 servings.

Stuffed Eggs with Endive Salad

1 tomato
6 hard-cooked eggs
3/4 cup plus 2 tablespoons soft butter
Salt and pepper
1/2 cup whipping cream
2 teaspoons lumpfish caviar
1 medium head Belgian endive
1 tablespoon herb vinegar
3 tablespoons vegetable oil
1/2 teaspoon sugar
1/4 teaspoon salt
1/2 teaspoon finely chopped onion
1/2 teaspoon each chopped fresh parsley and dill or a pinch of dried
    parsley and dill

Place tomato in a heatproof bowl. Pour boiling water over tomato to cover. Let stand 10 to 15 seconds. Remove from water. Carefully remove skin. Finely dice tomato. Cut eggs in half crosswise. Remove egg yolks. Press yolks through a sieve into a small bowl. Add butter; blend well. Season to taste; set aside. In a small bowl, beat cream until stiff. Fold in lumpfish caviar. Spoon whipped-cream mixture into egg whites. Place egg-yolk mixture in a pastry bag fitted with a small star tip. Pipe a rosette onto each stuffed egg. Garnish each rosette with a tomato cube. Slice off endive root. Remove hard core at endive base. In a small bowl or jar, combine vinegar, oil, sugar, salt, onion, parsley and dill. Cut endive in thin strips. Toss endive with dressing. Divide salad between 4 individual plates. Serve 3 stuffed eggs with each salad. Makes 4 servings.

Oyster Salad

8 oz. young green beans
1 celery stalk
1 small tomato
8 canned artichoke hearts, drained
4 oz. Stilton cheese
2 oz. young spinach or watercress
3 tablespoons wine vinegar
Salt and pepper
1/3 cup walnut oil
8 oysters
Few drops of lemon juice

Trim beans, cutting larger ones in half. Cut celery in very thin strips. In a medium saucepan, bring salted water to a boil. Blanch beans in water 2 minutes. Immediately plunge beans into cold water. Drain well. Blanch celery 2 minutes. Immediately plunge celery into cold water. Drain well. Cut tomato in half. Remove seeds. Slice tomato in fine strips. Cut artichoke hearts in quarters. Cut Stilton into 4 thin slices. Arrange beans, celery, tomato, artichokes, young spinach or watercress and Stilton on 4 individual plates. In a small bowl or jar, combine vinegar, salt, pepper and oil. Sprinkle dressing over salad. Open oysters. Sprinkle with lemon juice. Arrange 2 oysters on each plate. Makes 4 servings.

Sicilian Seafood Salad

1-1/2 onions
1/2 garlic clove
1/2 teaspoon salt
3/4 cup white wine
1 cup water
1 lb. squid
1 small carrot
2 peppercorns
4 oz. mussels
1 small romaine lettuce
4 oz. fresh or thawed frozen scampi, drained
Lemon slices

Dressing:
1 shallot
3 garlic cloves
1 small bunch parsley
1/2 cup olive oil
Juice of 1 lemon
1/2 teaspoon salt
Generous pinch of white pepper

Dice whole onion coarsely. Crush garlic with half the salt. Place diced onion, garlic and 1/2 cup wine in a large saucepan. Add 1/2 cup water. Prepare each squid by removing *backbone* which runs the length of the sack. Separate backbone from flesh at opening of sack. Carefully draw out and discard. Slice tentacles off squid, leaving head exposed. Cut away head; discard. Carefully clean inner sack of squid. Thoroughly wash squid, including tentacles. Cut in narrow strips. Bring prepared wine stock to a boil. Add squid. Cover and simmer over low heat 30 minutes.

Finely dice carrot. Cut remaining onion half into 8 wedges. Place carrot, onion wedges, remaining 1/4 cup wine, peppercorns and remaining salt in a saucepan. Add 1/2 cup water. Bring to a boil. Scrub mussels under cold running water. Remove *beards.* Drop mussels in boiling liquid. **Do not use any mussels which have opened.** Cover and simmer 10 minutes. Mussels are cooked when all shells have opened. Set aside to cool in liquid. Drain squid. Cool slightly. Arrange lettuce on a large platter. To make the dressing, finely chop shallot, garlic and parsley. In a small bowl, beat together oil, lemon juice, salt, pepper, shallot, garlic and parsley. Mix together scampi and squid. Arrange scampi mixture on lettuce. Drain mussels. Arrange in their opened shells on platter. Sprinkle dressing over seafood. Cover with plastic wrap and marinate 10 minutes. Serve garnished with lemon slices. Makes 6 servings.

Cook's Tip

When using fresh mussels, never cook any whose shells have opened slightly. Also, discard any mussels which remain firmly closed after ample cooking time.

Beccafico Sardines (Stuffed Sardines)

36 fresh sardines
3 garlic cloves
1/2 cup finely chopped parsley
3 eggs
1-1/2 cups shredded mozzarella cheese
1/2 teaspoon salt
3 cups fresh breadcrumbs
18 bay leaves
3 tablespoons butter

Preheat oven to 425F (220C). Butter a long baking pan. Cut each sardine open along stomach, but do not cut right through the back. Remove head and tail. Rinse fish both inside and out; pat dry. Crush garlic. In a small bowl, combine parsley, garlic, eggs, cheese, salt and 6 tablespoons breadcrumbs. Stuff sardines with egg mixture, pressing it in firmly. Place stuffed sardines, side by side, in buttered baking pan. Between every 2 sardines, insert a bay leaf. Sprinkle remaining breadcrumbs over sardines. Dot with butter. Bake 15 to 20 minutes. Serve hot or cold with toast. Makes 6 servings.

Antipasto Platter

2 zucchini
2 eggplant
Sprig each fresh thyme, organo and basil or 1/2 teaspoon each dried
**   thyme, oregano and basil**
1 teaspoon lemon juice
1/2 teaspoon salt
2 cups olive oil
3 large canned pimientos
1 (7-1/2-oz.) can mushrooms
Lettuce leaves
12 pitted black olives
Sprig each parsley, thyme, oregano and basil, if desired

Thinly slice zucchini and eggplant. Place zucchini and eggplant in a medium bowl. Finely chop fresh herbs, if used. In a small bowl, combine herbs, lemon juice, salt and oil. Pour herb mixture over sliced vegetables. Cover and marinate 4 hours at room temperature. Heat a large skillet over medium heat. Drain zucchini and eggplant. Place drained vegetables in skillet. Fry 1 to 2 minutes on each side, adding a little extra oil if necessary. Drain on paper towel. Drain pimientos and mushrooms. Cut pimientos in half. Arrange lettuce, mushrooms, zucchini, eggplant, pimientos and olives on a platter. Garnish with parsley, thyme, oregano and basil sprigs, if desired. Makes 4 servings.

Artichokes with Vegetable Julienne

6 canned artichoke bottoms
6 oz. young carrots
4 oz. green beans
1 egg yolk
Generous pinch white pepper
Pinch sugar
6 tablespoons olive oil
Few sprigs chervil and basil or 1/2 teaspoon each dried chervil and basil
1 tablespoon farmer's cheese or ricotta cheese
1 teaspoon mustard
1 teaspoon lemon juice
6 tarragon leaves, chopped, if desired

Drain artichoke bottoms. Cut carrots and beans in very fine strips. Place 1 cup salted water in each of 2 small saucepans. Bring to a boil. Add carrots to one, beans to the other. Simmer each 8 minutes. Drain vegetables. Cool slightly. Arrange cooled vegetables inside artichoke bottoms. In a small bowl, beat together egg yolk, pepper and sugar. Add oil, a few drops at a time, beating continously. Finely chop fresh chervil and basil, if used. Stir herbs, farmer's or ricotta cheese, mustard and lemon juice into egg mixture. Spoon 1 tablespoon dressing over each artichoke bottom. Sprinkle with chopped fresh tarragon, if desired. Makes 6 servings.

Chanterelle Tartlets

Pie-Crust Pastry, page 14, using half the recipe
Pinch caraway seeds
1 lb. chanterelle mushrooms
3 tablespoons butter
1/4 teaspoon salt
1 to 2 shallots
1/4 cup vegetable oil
3 tablespoons wine vinegar
1 tablespoon chopped parsley
1/4 teaspoon salt
Pinch pepper
3 tablespoons whipping cream
3 tablespoons mayonnaise
1/2 cup Sherry Aspic, page 18

Preheat oven to 425F (220C). Roll out pastry and use to line 4 (3-inch) tartlet pans. Bake 10 to 12 minutes or until golden brown. Cool pastry slightly. Then turn out onto a rack. Crush caraway seeds to a powder. Trim, wash and drain chanterelles. Melt butter in a medium saucepan over medium heat. Add chanterelles, salt and caraway. Cook 10 to 15 minutes, stirring often. Cool slightly. Finely chop shallots. In a small bowl, beat together oil, vinegar, chopped shallots, parsley, salt and pepper. Stir dressing into chanterelles. Spoon chanterelle salad into tartlets. In a small bowl, combine cream and mayonnaise. Pour 1 tablespoon cream mixture onto each tartlet. Garnish with diced Sherry Aspic. Makes 4 servings.

Cook's Tip

If you cannot obtain chanterelles, ordinary field mushrooms will also make delicious tartlets.

Chicken Tartlets

Pie-Crust Pastry, page 14, using half the recipe
8 oz. cooked chicken breast
8 oz. canned asparagus tips
1/4 cup olive oil
1 teaspoon lemon juice
Generous pinch ground ginger
1 bunch dill or parsley
5 pickled green peppercorns or freshly ground black pepper
1 tablespoon whipping cream
1 tablespoon mayonnaise
Generous pinch salt
Dash Worcestershire sauce
Dill or parsley sprigs
Fresh chopped tarragon, if desired

Preheat oven to 425F (220C). Roll out pastry and use to line 4 (3-inch) tartlet pans. Bake 10 to 12 minutes or until golden brown. Cool pastry slightly. Then turn out onto a rack. Chop chicken breast into small pieces. Drain asparagus tips. In a medium bowl, combine chicken and asparagus. In a small bowl, beat together oil, lemon juice and ginger. Pour oil mixture over chicken mixture. Cover; marinate 30 minutes. Drain well. Finely chop dill or parsley. Chop peppercorns, if used. In a small bowl, beat together cream, mayonnaise, dill or parsley, salt and Worcestershire sauce. Add chopped peppercorns or black pepper. Spoon chicken salad into tartlets. Top each portion with mayonnaise dressing. Garnish each tartlet with dill or parsley and a sprinkling of chopped tarragon, if desired. Makes 4 servings.

Hearts of Palm in Ham

1 (15-oz.) can hearts of palm
1 tablespoon vinegar
1 teaspoon lemon juice
1/4 cup olive oil
Generous pinch each salt and white pepper
Few sprigs fresh basil or 1/2 teaspoon dried basil
2 canned anchovy fillets
8 slices smoked ham
1 tablespoon pickled green peppercorns or freshly ground black pepper
1/4 cup whipping cream
1/3 cup mayonnaise

Drain hearts of palm. In a small bowl, beat together vinegar, lemon juice, oil, salt and pepper. Finely chop fresh basil, if used, reserving a little. Finely chop anchovy fillets. Stir basil and anchovy into oil and vinegar mixture. Pour over hearts of palm. Cover and marinate 1 hour at room temperature, occasionally turning hearts of palm. Lay ham slices individually on a board. Drain hearts of palm. Roll each heart in a slice of ham. Arrange rolls on a flat dish. Sprinkle with reserved basil. Finely chop green peppercorns, if used. Stir together cream and mayonnaise. Add chopped peppercorns or freshly ground black pepper. Serve mayonnaise separately with hearts-of-palm rolls. Makes 4 servings.

Lobster Cocktail

2 to 3 celery stalks
1 (1-3/4-lb.) boiled fresh lobster or 1-1/2 (8-oz.) cans lobster
8 canned artichoke hearts
2 oranges
2 tablespoons brandy
1 tablespoon lemon juice
Salt and pepper
Small bunch fresh dill or 1/2 teaspoon dried dill
4 fresh mint leaves or a pinch dried mint
8 lettuce leaves
1/4 cup mayonnaise
1/4 cup whipping cream
Generous pinch each celery salt and red (cayenne) pepper
4 slices truffle, if desired

Cut celery in fine strips. Blanch in boiling salted water 5 minutes. Drain and cool. Cut boiled fresh lobster in half lengthwise. Take out flesh. Or, drain canned lobster. Break flesh into small pieces. Drain artichoke hearts. Slice into quarters. Peel 1 orange; remove pith. Chop orange flesh. In a medium bowl, combine orange, celery, lobster and artichoke. In a small bowl, combine brandy and lemon juice. Season to taste. Pour brandy mixture over lobster. Cover and marinate 30 minutes. Finely chop fresh herbs, if used. Remove lobster mixture from marinade; drain well. Line 4 individual glass dishes with lettuce leaves. Spoon lobster cocktail over lettuce. In a small bowl, beat together mayonnaise, cream, celery salt, red pepper and herbs. Pour mayonnaise mixture over lobster. Cut 4 slices from center of remaining orange. Garnish cocktails with orange and truffle slices, if desired. Makes 4 servings.

Prawn Cocktail

2 tomatoes
2 slices canned pineapple
8 pimiento-stuffed olives
1 lb. thawed frozen prawns or medium shrimp, drained
1/4 cup vegetable oil
1 tablespoon wine vinegar
1 tablespoon lemon juice
Generous pinch each salt, white pepper and sugar
Few lettuce leaves
1 lemon
4 dill or parsley sprigs

Skin and quarter tomatoes. Remove seeds; cut tomatoes into thin strips. Drain and chop pineapple. Cut olives in half. In a medium bowl, combine prawns or shrimp, tomatoes, pineapple and olives. In a small bowl, beat together oil, vinegar, lemon juice, salt, pepper and sugar. Pour over seafood mixture. Cover and refrigerate 1 to 2 hours. Tear lettuce in small pieces. Carefully stir lettuce into cocktail just before serving. Adjust seasoning as needed. Spoon cocktail into 4 individual glass dishes. Cut 4 thin slices from center of lemon. Garnish cocktails with lemon slices and dill or parsley sprigs. Makes 4 servings.

Chicken Cocktail

1 lb. cooked chicken
1 small sweet melon
2 tomatoes
4 oz. mushrooms
2 teaspoons lemon juice
1 tablespoon chopped fresh mixed herbs or 1 teaspoon dried mixed
   herbs
Pinch each salt, celery salt and white pepper
1/2 teaspoon paprika
1-1/4 cups plain yogurt
1 hard-cooked egg

Cut chicken into small pieces. Cut melon in half. Remove seeds and scoop out flesh with a melon-baller or teaspoon. Peel tomatoes; cut each into 8 wedges. Remove seeds. Thinly slice mushrooms; sprinkle with half the lemon juice. In a medium bowl, combine chicken, melon balls, tomatoes and mushrooms. In a medium bowl, combine herbs, salt, celery salt, pepper, remaining lemon juice, paprika and yogurt. Pour dressing over chicken mixture. Cover and refrigerate 1 hour. To serve, season chicken mixture to taste. Arrange in 4 individual glass dishes. Cut egg into 8 wedges. Garnish each cocktail with 2 wedges of egg. Makes 4 servings.

Mushroom Cocktail

1 lb. fresh mushrooms or 8 oz. canned mushrooms
1 garlic clove
1 fresh sage leaf or a sprinkling of dried sage
1 sprig fresh thyme or 1/2 teaspoon dried thyme
Small bunch fresh parsley or 1 teaspoon dried parsley
2 green onions
1/4 cup vegetable oil
1 tablespoon lemon juice
Generous pinch salt
Pinch sugar
4 lettuce leaves
1 lime or lemon

If using fresh mushrooms, place in a saucepan with 1 cup salted water. Simmer over low heat 15 to 20 minutes. Drain and let cool. Drain canned mushrooms. Crush garlic. Finely chop fresh sage, thyme and parsley, if used. Finely chop green onions. In a small bowl, beat together oil, lemon juice, salt, sugar, garlic and herbs. Add chopped green onion. Chop mushrooms and toss in dressing. Cover and let stand 20 minutes. Line 4 individual glass dishes with lettuce leaves. Arrange mushroom mixture over lettuce. Cut 4 thin slices from center of lime or lemon. Garnish each cocktail with lime or lemon slices. Makes 4 servings.

Avocado Cocktail

1 lime
2 avocados
1/3 cup mayonnaise
1 teaspoon Dijon-style mustard
1 teaspoon grated fresh horseradish or 1-1/2 teaspoons prepared
    creamed horseradish
6 tablespoons plain yogurt
Dash Tabasco sauce

Place 4 individual glass dishes in refrigerator to chill. Cut 4 thin slices from center of lime. Cut avocados in half lengthwise. Remove pits. Peel avocados. Dice flesh evenly. Sprinkle avocado cubes with lime juice. In a small bowl, beat together mayonnaise, mustard, horseradish, yogurt and Tabasco. Place avocado cubes in chilled dishes. Pour mayonnaise mixture over avocados. Cut to the centers of lime slices and twist. Garnish each dish with a lime twist. Makes 4 servings.

Cook's Tip

Avocados and shrimp go well together, so for special occasions garnish the cocktail with a few shrimp.

Hearts-of-Palm Cocktail

1 (15-oz.) can hearts of palm
1/3 cup olive oil
3 tablespoons wine vinegar
Generous pinch salt
4 oz. smoked ham
1/2 teaspoon mustard
3 tablespoons mayonnaise
Small bunch fresh chervil and tarragon or 1 teaspoon each dried
    chervil and tarragon
16 pickled quail's eggs

Drain hearts of palm. Cut into 1/4-inch slices; place in a medium bowl. In a small bowl, beat together oil, vinegar and salt. Pour oil mixture over hearts of palm. Cover and marinate at room temperature 40 minutes. Place 4 individual glass dishes in refrigerator to chill. Trim fat from ham; dice ham. In a small bowl, combine mustard and mayonnaise. Finely chop fresh herbs. Drain quail's eggs. Finely dice 4 eggs. Stir herbs and diced eggs into mayonnaise mixture. Drain hearts of palm. Place in chilled dishes. Sprinkle with diced ham. Pour mayonnaise mixture over ham. Garnish each serving with 3 quail's eggs. Makes 4 servings.

Cook's Tip

For variety, make this cocktail with canned artichoke hearts instead of hearts of palm.

Mussel Cocktail

14 oz. canned mussels
1/2 (14-oz.) can artichoke hearts
1 small head lettuce
1/3 cup mayonnaise
3 tablespoons lemon juice
Pinch sugar
3 tablespoons brandy
Dash Tabasco sauce
Pinch salt
5 pimiento-stuffed olives
1 lemon

Drain mussels and artichoke hearts. Separate lettuce into leaves; cut in thin strips. Line 4 individual glass dishes with strips of lettuce. Arrange mussels and artichoke hearts over lettuce. In a small bowl, beat together mayonnaise, lemon juice, sugar, brandy, Tabasco sauce and salt. Spoon over mussels and artichokes. Slice olives. Sprinkle over mussels. Cut 4 thin slices from center of lemon. Garnish each cocktail with a lemon slice. Makes 4 servings.

Spicy Melon Cocktail

1 medium honeydew melon
1/4 cup ketchup
1 teaspoon grated fresh horseradish or 1-1/2 teaspoons prepared creamed horseradish
Few drops Worcestershire sauce
Few drops Tabasco sauce
Juice of 1/2 lemon
1/2 cup dairy sour cream
Pinch each salt and white pepper

Place 4 individual fruit dishes in refrigerator to chill. Cut melon in half; remove seeds. Scoop out melon flesh with a melon-baller. Place melon balls in a bowl. In a small bowl, combine ketchup, horseradish, Worcestershire sauce, Tabasco, lemon juice, sour cream, salt and pepper. Adjust seasoning. Pour ketchup mixture over melon balls. Cover and refrigerate 30 minutes. Transfer melon mixture to chilled fruit dishes. Makes 4 servings.

Cook's Tip

Taste a melon ball before adding dressing. If the melon doesn't have much flavor, add a little sugar to the dressing and increase quantities of seasonings.

Pork Fillet en Croûte

Pastry:
2-1/2 cups all-purpose flour
1/2 teaspoon salt
3/4 cup butter or margarine
1 egg yolk
1/2 cup water

Filling:
1 lb. roast pork fillet
2 tablespoons butter
1/4 cup all-purpose flour
1/2 cup broth
1 egg
Salt and pepper
Pinch ground nutmeg
Beaten egg to glaze

Sift flour and salt into a bowl. Cut butter or margarine into flour until mixture resembles fine breadcrumbs. Form a well in center of flour mixture. Add egg yolk and water. Quickly knead together to form a dough. Wrap in foil or waxed paper. Refrigerate 30 minutes. To make the filling, chop pork fillet. Using a grinder fitted with a fine blade or a food processor fitted with a steel blade, finely grind pork. Melt butter in a large saucepan over medium heat. Sprinkle flour over melted butter. Cook, stirring constantly, until lightly browned. Slowly add broth. Reduce heat and simmer 5 to 7 minutes, stirring constantly. Separate egg. In a small bowl, beat yolk. Add yolk to broth mixture. Season with salt, pepper and nutmeg. Add pork. Whisk egg white until stiff. Fold into mixture. Preheat oven to 425F (220C). Divide chilled pastry into 3 equal portions. Return 2 portions to refrigerator. Roll out third portion on a lightly floured surface to a 10-inch round. Grease a 10-inch spring-form pan. Place pastry round in pan, trimming around edges to fit. Keep pastry trimmings. Prick base several times with a fork. Roll out second piece of dough into a long, even strip. Use to line side of pan. Press joint between base and side firmly together. Spoon filling into pan. Smooth the surface. Roll out remaining dough to a 10-inch round. Place over filling, trimming any excess pastry from edges. Press top firmly to pastry side. Prick several times with a fork. Use half the beaten egg to brush over top of pie. Roll out any leftover pastry until quite thin. Cut out leaves and half-moon shapes. Make a thin roll to decorate center of pie. Brush shapes with beaten egg. Arrange on pie. Brush top of pie again with beaten egg. Bake 30 minutes or until golden brown. Cool in pan 15 minutes. Turn out onto a rack. Makes 10 servings.

Meat Pasty

Pastry:
1-1/2 cups all-purpose flour
Pinch salt
1/2 cup butter or margarine
1 egg yolk
1 tablespoon cold water

Filling:
1 onion
2 oz. mushrooms
2 tablespoons butter
8 oz. ground beef
2 tablespoons chopped parsley or 2 teaspoons dried parsley
4 oz. ham
3 tablespoons fresh white breadcrumbs
2 tablespoons brandy
Salt and pepper
Pinch each ground nutmeg and dried marjoram
1/2 teaspoon grated lemon peel
Beaten egg to glaze

Make pastry following method for Pork Fillet en Croûte, opposite. Cover and refrigerate 30 minutes. To make the filling, finely chop onion and mushrooms. Melt butter in a large skillet. Add onion; sauté until soft. Add ground beef. Cook until browned. Stir in mushrooms and parsley. Finely dice ham. Mix breadcrumbs into cooked beef mixture. Add diced ham, brandy, salt, pepper, nutmeg, marjoram and lemon peel. Preheat oven to 375F (190C). Roll out pastry into 2 oval shapes about 12 inches long. Spread one with meat filling. Place second pastry oval on top. Trim any excess pastry off edges, pressing edges firmly together. Prick the top several times. Roll out pastry trimmings and cut into shapes for decoration. Brush top with beaten egg. Add trimmings and brush again with egg. Bake 30 to 40 minutes or until golden brown. Makes 6 servings.

Liver Pasties

Pastry:
Brioche Pastry, page 14

Filling:
4 oz. chicken livers
3 oz. pig's liver
6 oz. pork fillet
6 oz. bacon
Grated peel of 1/2 orange
2 teaspoons paprika
Pinch each ground ginger, allspice and basil
1/2 teaspoon rosemary
1 bay leaf
2 tablespoons brandy
2 oz. shallots
1 garlic clove
1/3 cup whipping cream
1 egg white
3/4 cup fresh white breadcrumbs

Make dough. Line 12 brioche molds or deep patty pans with two-thirds of dough. To make the filling, chop livers, pork and bacon and place in a medium bowl. Add orange peel, spices, herbs and brandy. Dice shallots. Crush garlic. Add shallots and garlic to liver mixture. Cover with foil or plastic wrap. Marinate 1 hour. Preheat oven to 400F (205C). In a blender or food processor, combine liver mixture, cream, egg white and breadcrumbs. Process until smooth. Spoon liver mixture into lined molds or patty pans. Roll out lids from remaining dough. Moisten pastry edges. Cover pasties with dough. Press edges firmly together. Use leftover pastry to make decorations, if desired. Place on top of pasties. Bake 20 to 25 minutes or until golden brown. Turn out on a wire rack. Cool slightly. Makes 12 servings.

Pâté d'Escargots

3 tablespoons butter
4 oz. shallots, diced
1 small egg white
1 cup fresh white breadcrumbs
1 tablespoon whipping cream
4 oz. lean veal
Pinch salt and pepper
1/2 cup whipping cream
1 (7-oz.) can snails (escargots)
1 tablespoon Pernod
1 tablespoon brandy
1/2 cup broth
2 garlic cloves, crushed
1 teaspoon chopped fresh thyme or pinch dried thyme
8 oz. pastry (as for Meat Pasty, page 63)

Melt 2 tablespoons butter in a small skillet over medium heat. Add half the shallots; sauté until soft. In a small bowl, beat egg white. Add breadcrumbs and 1 tablespoon whipping cream. Cut veal into strips. In a blender, combine veal, breadcrumb mixture, sautéed shallots, salt and pepper. Process well. Place veal mixture in a medium bowl. In a small bowl, beat 1/2 cup whipping cream. Fold into veal mixture. Preheat oven to 400F (205C). Drain snails, reserving liquid. Cut snails in half. Melt remaining 1 tablespoon butter in a skillet. Add remaining shallots; sauté until soft. Add Pernod, brandy, broth, juice from canned snails, garlic and thyme. Season to taste. Bring to a boil. Simmer until liquid evaporates. Add snails. Cool mixture slightly. Stir snail mixture into veal mixture. Roll out two-thirds of pastry and use to line a 9'' x 5'' loaf pan. Spoon filling into pan. Roll out remaining one-third of pastry and cover filling with a pastry lid. Bake 15 minutes. Reduce oven temperature to 350F (175C). Bake 30 to 40 minutes longer. Makes 4 servings.

Haddock & Salmon Pasty

1 (1-lb.) haddock fillet
1 lb. sole fillets
1 teaspoon salt
Generous pinch ground nutmeg
1/2 teaspoon white pepper
1 egg
5 oz. thawed frozen prawns or medium shrimp, drained
1 teaspoon chopped fresh parsley or pinch dried parsley
1 teaspoon chopped fresh dill or pinch dried dill weed
2 (10-oz.) pkgs. thawed frozen patty shells
8 oz. fresh salmon
Beaten egg yolk to glaze

Preheat oven to 400F (205C). Cut haddock into 2 pieces. Grind sole fillets twice. Season with salt, nutmeg and pepper. In a small bowl, beat whole egg. Stir beaten egg into ground sole. Chop prawns or shrimp. Add to sole mixture with parsley and dill. On a lightly floured surface, arrange 6 patty shells, overlapping, in an oval. Roll out dough to form 1 long oval shape. Repeat with remaining 6 patty shells. Place 1 haddock fillet on 1 piece of dough. Cover with half the sole mixture. Lay salmon on top. Spread remaining sole mixture over salmon. Top with second haddock fillet. Cover fish with second piece of dough. Press edges firmly together, trimming off excess dough. Make decorations from trimmings. Brush pasty with egg yolk. Arrange decorations on top. Brush with egg yolk. Bake 20 minutes. Reduce oven temperature to 350F (175C). Bake 40 minutes longer or until golden brown. Makes 4 servings.

Country Terrine

2 rabbit legs
1 lb. lean pork
7 oz. bacon
Salt and freshly ground black pepper
Generous pinch grated nutmeg
12 juniper berries
4 bay leaves
1 tablespoon dried mixed herbs (marjoram, thyme, sage, savory)
2 tablespoons brandy
2 eggs
8 oz. slab bacon
12 oz. thinly sliced bacon fat or bacon
1/2 cup pork drippings

Trim and bone rabbit legs; remove any skin. Finely dice rabbit, pork and bacon. Mix diced meat in a medium bowl. Add salt, pepper, nutmeg, 6 juniper berries, 1 bay leaf, mixed herbs and brandy. Cover with foil or plastic wrap. Refrigerate 12 hours or overnight. Process marinated meat, a little at a time, in a blender or food processor. Refrigerate 2 to 3 hours longer. In a small bowl, beat eggs. Add beaten eggs to meat puree. Beat vigorously 10 minutes. Remove rind from slab bacon; finely dice bacon. Stir diced bacon into meat puree. Season to taste. Line a 1-quart ovenproof dish with a lid with overlapping slices of bacon fat or bacon, page 16. Fill with meat mixture. Smooth top and decorate with remaining bay leaves and juniper berries. Cover with buttered waxed paper. Preheat oven to 350F (175C). Cover dish. Stand dish in a pan containing enough boiling water to come up to within 1 inch of edge of terrine. Bake 2 hours. Water should not boil and should reach a maximum of 175F (80C). During cooking, meat will shrink away from sides slightly. After cooking, remove dish from water-bath. Cool. Melt pork drippings. Pour around edge of terrine. Let drippings set. Store in refrigerator up to 2 weeks. Makes 8 servings.

Cook's Tip

Before starting to make a pâté, terrine or galantine, refer to pages 14 to 17 for methods of preparation.

Mushroom Terrine

8 oz. veal or pork fillet
1 cup fresh white breadcrumbs
1/4 cup butter
4 oz. shallots, chopped
1 egg white
1/2 cup whipping cream
Generous pinch each salt, pepper, ginger and allspice
2 lbs. mushrooms or 1-3/4 lbs. mushrooms and 4 oz. diced truffles
1/4 cup vegetable oil
1 small garlic clove
1 cup chicken broth
1/2 teaspoon each dried basil, thyme, sage and caraway
1/2 cup White-Wine Aspic, page 18

Dice veal or pork. In a medium bowl, combine veal or pork and breadcrumbs. Melt 2 tablespoons butter in a skillet. Add half the shallots; sauté until soft. Add sautéed shallots to veal or pork. In a small bowl, beat egg white with 1/4 cup cream, salt, pepper, ginger and allspice. Pour cream mixture over meat. Cover with foil. Let stand 1 hour. Preheat oven to 350F (175C). Slice mushrooms. Heat oil in a small skillet over medium heat. Sauté mushrooms in hot oil; reserve liquid. Place mushrooms in a bowl. Chop garlic. Melt remaining butter. Sauté remaining shallots and garlic in hot butter over medium heat. Add mushroom juice, broth, herbs and caraway seeds. Bring to a boil. Simmer until reduced by half. Strain over mushrooms. Cover and marinate 1 hour. Blend meat mixture until smooth. Add remaining cream. Fold in mushroom mixture and truffles, if desired. Place in a greased terrine. Cover; place in a water-bath, page 14. Bake 1-1/4 hours. Pour White-Wine Aspic over terrine when cooled. Allow to set. Makes 8 servings.

Rabbit Terrine

3 lbs. boned rabbit
8 oz. fresh ham
1 onion, diced
2 shallots, diced
1 garlic clove, diced
2 celery stalks, chopped
2 carrots, chopped
Rabbit, beef or chicken bones
Few peppercorns
6-1/2 cups water
2 tablespoons butter
4 oz. diced chicken livers
2 tablespoons brandy
8 oz. ham, diced
4 oz. mushrooms, diced
2 eggs, beaten
1 teaspoon dried thyme
1 teaspoon dried sage
1/2 teaspoon ground allspice
Pinch ground cardamom
12 oz. thinly sliced bacon fat or bacon
Few sprigs fresh sage, bay leaf

Grind half the rabbit and fresh ham. Chop remaining rabbit into large pieces. Place all vegetables in a saucepan with bones, peppercorns and water. Bring to a boil. Simmer, uncovered, 2 hours, skimming surface until clear. Simmer until reduced to about 1 cup liquid; strain. Return liquid to heat. Simmer until reduced by half; strain. Melt butter. Add chicken livers; sauté until no longer pink. Add brandy. Stir liver, ham, mushrooms, eggs, ground rabbit and fresh ham, rabbit chunks, herbs and spices into stock. Line a large terrine with overlapping slices of bacon fat or bacon. Fill terrine with mixture. Decorate with sage sprigs and a bay leaf. Cover; place in a water-bath. Bake 2 hours. Makes 8 servings.

Veal Terrine

12 oz. veal fillet, diced
8 oz. lean pork, diced
8 oz. bacon, diced
Salt and pepper
1/2 teaspoon each dried basil, sage and thyme
1 cup fresh white breadrumbs
1 egg white
1/2 cup whipping cream
8 oz. calf's liver
2 tablespoons butter
2 shallots, chopped
1 garlic clove, chopped
2 tablespoons brandy
2 tablespoons Cointreau
8 oz. mushrooms, sliced
4 oz. ham, sliced
3 tablespoons chopped parsley
Generous pinch each ground ginger and cardamom
12 oz. thinly sliced bacon fat or bacon

Place diced meat in a bowl. Season with salt, pepper and dried herbs. Add breadcrumbs. Beat egg white and cream. Pour egg-white mixture over meat mixture. Cover and refrigerate 12 hours. Place meat mixture in blender or food processor. Process well. Refrigerate. Preheat oven to 350F (175C). Dice liver. Melt butter in a skillet. Sauté shallots, garlic and liver. Add brandy and Cointreau. In a medium bowl, combine liver, shallots, mushroom, ham, parsley, spices and salt. Stir into chilled meat puree. Line a 1-quart earthenware dish with overlapping slices of bacon fat or bacon, page 16. Fill lined dish with meat mixture. Cover; place dish in a water-bath, page 14. Bake 2 hours. Makes 8 servings.

Italian Veal Galantine

2-1/4 lbs. boned breast of veal
Salt and pepper
12 oz. veal fillet
12 oz. pork loin
8 oz. bacon
1 bay leaf
1 teaspoon each chopped fresh thyme and basil or pinch each dried thyme and basil
1 onion
2 tablespoons butter
1 garlic clove, crushed
2 tablespoons grappa or brandy
1 cup fresh white breadcrumbs
1/4 cup whipping cream
1 egg
4 oz. ham, diced
1/4 cup chopped pistachio nuts
7-1/2 cups veal or chicken stock
6 oz. candied fruits

Rub breast of veal with salt and pepper. Cut veal fillet, pork and bacon into strips. Place in a bowl. Sprinkle with bay leaf, thyme and basil. Cut onion into rings. Melt butter in a skillet. Sauté onion and garlic. Add sautéed onion, garlic, grappa or brandy and breadcrumbs to meat mixture. Beat together cream and egg; pour over meat mixture. Cover meat mixture with foil. Refrigerate 1 hour. Puree chilled meat mixture in a blender or food processor. Add ham and pistachios to blender or processor. Puree mixture. Spread puree over veal. Roll veal and tie, using thin string, at 1-inch intervals. Pour stock into a large saucepan; bring to a boil. Add veal. Simmer 60 to 70 minutes or until tender. Remove from heat. Allow veal to cool in stock. Drain and serve with candied fruits. Makes 10 servings.

Crudités

1 small celeriac
1/2 cauliflower
2 small heads red endive
4 small tomatoes
1/2 cucumber
4 small carrots
1 red bell pepper
2 medium onions
12 pimiento-stuffed olives
4 oz. young spinach or watercress
Freshly ground black pepper
Juice of 1 lemon
1 tablespoons chopped fresh
    mixed herbs (chives, parsley,
    tarragon, dill)
1/2 cup vegetable oil
1/4 cup wine vinegar
1/2 teaspoon salt
Generous 1/2 cup plain yogurt
1 hard-cooked egg, if desired
Parsley sprig

Peel celeriac, if necessary. Boil celeriac in salted water in a covered pan 20 minutes. Break cauliflower into flowerets. Blanch flowerets in boiling salted water 5 minutes; drain well. Separate red-endive leaves. Cut tomatoes in quarters. Thinly slice cucumber. Shred carrots. Slice red pepper into strips. Cut onions in rings. Carefully mix half the onions with tomatoes. Mix remaining onions with red pepper. Cut olives in half crosswise. Drain celeriac; cool slightly. Slice thinly. Arrange all ingredients, except olives, in portions on a large platter or serving dish. Sprinkle with black pepper, lemon juice and 1 tablespoon chopped herbs. Scatter olives over vegetables. In a small bowl or jar, combine oil, vinegar, salt, remaining herbs and yogurt. Spoon dressing over salad, or serve dressing on the side. Cut hard-cooked egg into 8 wedges, if desired. Place egg wedges in salad center as garnish. Top with a parsley sprig. Makes 4 servings.

Carrot & Apple Salad

4 medium carrots
2 apples, peeled
2 oz. shelled walnut halves
2 teaspoons lime juice
2 teaspoons sugar
Generous 1/2 cup plain yogurt

Coarsely shred carrots and apples. In a small bowl, combine shredded carrots and apples. Reserve 1 walnut half; chop remaining walnuts. In a small bowl, beat together lime juice, chopped walnuts, sugar and yogurt. Pour half the yogurt dressing over carrot mixture. Let stand 15 minutes. Spoon remaining dressing over carrot mixture just before serving. Top with reserved walnut half. Makes 4 servings.

Cook's Tip

Make this salad richer by substituting dairy sour cream or whipping cream for yogurt, or use half yogurt and half cream.

Celery & Avocado Salad

1 celery stalk
1 green bell pepper
2 medium onions
3 medium carrots
2 avocados
1 teaspoon orange juice
1 teaspoon lemon juice
1/3 cup vegetable oil
1 tablespoon wine vinegar
Salt and pepper
1/4 teaspoon hot mustard
1 firm tomato
Parsley sprig

Thinly slice celery. Slice green pepper in strips. Cut onions into rings. Coarsely shred carrots. In a medium bowl, combine celery, green pepper, onions and carrots. Arrange on a platter. Cut avocados in half; remove pits. Peel and slice avocados. In a small bowl, combine orange juice and lemon juice. Pour juice mixture over avocado slices. In a small bowl, beat together oil, vinegar, salt, pepper and mustard. Sprinkle oil mixture over vegetables. Arrange avocado slices over salad. Cut tomato into 8 wedges. Garnish platter with tomato wedges and parsley. Makes 4 servings.

Chinese-Cabbage Salad

1 lb. Chinese cabbage
1 large head red endive
2 oz. fresh young spinach
1 bunch chives
1/4 cup vegetable oil
3 tablespoons wine vinegar
Salt and white pepper
1/4 teaspoon soy sauce

Cut cabbage in half lengthwise. Wash thoroughly under cold running water. Drain well. Remove stalk from cabbage. Slice leaves into 1/2-inch strips. Separate endive into leaves. Tear larger leaves in half. Gently mix cabbage, endive and spinach together in a large bowl. Finely chop chives. In a small bowl, beat together oil, vinegar, salt, pepper and soy sauce. Pour oil mixture over salad. Sprinkle chives over salad. Makes 4 servings.

Fennel Salad

2 heads fennel
1/2 cucumber
2 tomatoes
1 bunch radishes
1 small bunch chives
1 onion
1/3 cup olive oil
3 tablespoons wine vinegar
1/2 teaspoon salt
Pinch sugar
Coarsely ground black pepper

Trim fennel and cut into thin strips. Cut cucumber in thick slices; then cut slices into strips. Cut each tomato in 8 wedges. Slice radishes. In a medium bowl, combine fennel, cucumber, tomatoes and radishes. Finely chop chives. Finely dice onion. In a small bowl, beat together oil, vinegar, salt, sugar and onion. Pour oil mixture over salad. To serve, sprinkle with chives and black pepper. Makes 4 servings.

Celery & Carrot Salad

4 medium carrots
2 celery stalks
Juice of 1/2 lemon
Pinch sugar
1/4 cup whipping cream
1/2 teaspoon pickled green peppercorns, crushed, or 1/4 teaspoon
freshly ground black pepper
1/2 teaspoon salt

Coarsely shred carrots in long strips. Thinly slice celery. Combine carrots and celery in a salad bowl. Sprinkle lemon juice and sugar over vegetables. Lightly toss salad. In a small bowl, beat together cream, peppercorns or black pepper and salt. Pour cream mixture over salad. Mix together at table. Makes 4 servings.

Cook's Tip

Many recipes do not use celery leaves, but these need not be wasted. They can go into a stockpot, or be chopped and used to sprinkle on soup just before serving.

Mixed-Pepper Salad

4 medium bell peppers, green, yellow or red
1 onion
1 garlic clove
1/2 teaspoon salt
1/4 cup wine vinegar
1/2 cup vegetable oil
2 teaspoons chopped fresh mixed herbs (parsley, basil, marjoram,
burnet) or 1 teaspoon dried mixed herbs
1/2 teaspoon coarsely ground white pepper

Slice peppers in very thin rings. Discard seeds and core. Cut onion into thin rings. Cut garlic clove in half. Using the cut side, rub garlic around the inside of a salad bowl. Arrange pepper and onion rings in bowl. In a small bowl, beat together salt, vinegar and oil. Pour oil mixture over salad. Cover and let stand 30 minutes. To serve, sprinkle salad with herbs and freshly ground white pepper. Makes 4 servings.

Balkan Tomato Salad

1-1/2 lbs. firm tomatoes
4 oz. mozzarella or feta cheese
1 small onion
2 leaves each fresh lemon balm and mint, if desired
1 garlic clove
20 pitted black olives
1 tablespoon lemon juice
3 tablespoons wine vinegar
Salt and freshly ground black pepper
1/2 cup olive oil
1 hard-cooked egg

Slice tomatoes. Break up cheese with a fork. Finely dice onion. Coarsely chop fresh herbs, if desired. Cut garlic clove in half. Using cut side, rub garlic inside a large salad bowl. Place tomatoes, cheese, onion and olives in salad bowl. Sprinkle with chopped herbs, if desired. In a small bowl, beat together lemon juice, vinegar and salt, until salt has dissolved. Add pepper and oil; blend. Sprinkle lemon-juice mixture over salad. Cover and let stand 30 minutes. Cut hard-cooked egg in 8 wedges. To serve, toss salad lightly. Garnish with egg wedges. Makes 4 servings.

Red-Endive Salad with Piquant Dressing

1/2 head lettuce
3 small heads red endive
1 yellow bell pepper
1 red onion
4 fresh basil leaves or pinch dried basil
1/4 cup plain yogurt
1/4 cup whipping cream
1/2 teaspoon each salt and celery salt
1 tablespoon pickled green peppercorns or 1 teaspoon freshly ground white pepper

Separate lettuce and endive leaves. Line a salad bowl with lettuce. Slice bell pepper in rings. Discard seeds and core. Slice onion into rings. In a medium bowl, combine bell pepper, onion and endive. Finely chop fresh basil. In a small bowl, beat together yogurt, cream, salt, celery salt, basil and green peppercorns or white pepper. Pour yogurt mixture over pepper mixture. Let stand a few minutes. Toss lightly and transfer to lettuce-lined bowl. Makes 4 servings.

Cook's Tip

To give the salad extra zest, shred ends of 1 or 2 red-endive stems and add to salad dressing.

Mussel & Bean-Sprout Salad

8 oz. fresh bean sprouts
1 large cooked carrot
1 (8-3/4-oz.) can mussels or smoked oysters
8 to 10 strips canned pimiento
3 tablespoons canned baby sweet-corn cobs, if desired
2 pickled cucumbers or dill pickles
3 tablespoons pickled cocktail onions
3 tablespoons vegetable oil
1 tablespoon soy sauce
1 tablespoon lemon juice
1/4 teaspoon each white pepper and sugar

Wash bean sprouts; drain well. Thinly slice carrot. Drain mussels or oysters, pimiento, baby sweet-corn cobs, if desired, and pickles. Cut pimiento and sweet-corn cobs into pieces. Cut pickles in thin slices. In a medium bowl, combine bean sprouts, carrot slices, mussels or oysters, pimiento, sweet-corn cobs, pickle slices and cocktail onions. In a small bowl, beat together oil, soy sauce, lemon juice, white pepper and sugar. Pour oil mixture over salad. Makes 4 servings.

Cook's Tip

As a variation, make this salad with shrimp instead of mussels or oysters. Omit carrot, baby sweet-corn cobs and cocktail onions; substitute 1 or 2 freshly shredded crisp apples.

Endive & Fruit Salad

4 small heads Belgian endive
2 grapefruit
2 fresh mandarin oranges or 1/2 (11-oz.) can mandarin-orange segments
1/4 cup vegetable oil
2 to 3 tablespoons fresh lime juice
1 teaspoon sugar
Generous pinch ground ginger
1/2 teaspoon coarsely ground black pepper
1/2 teaspoon hot mustard
1 lime

Separate endive leaves. Line 4 individual bowls with endive. Peel grapefruit, removing all pith. Separate grapefruit segments, carefully removing skin. Cut each segment into quarters; discard any seeds. Peel oranges; cut segments in half, discarding any seeds. Drain canned mandarin oranges and cut in half. In a small bowl, beat together oil, lime juice, sugar, ginger, pepper and mustard. Pour oil mixture over fruit segments. Mix thoroughly. Cover and let stand a few minutes. Cut lime into thin slices. Spoon fruit mixture into individual endive-lined bowls. Garnish with lime slices. Makes 4 servings.

Iceberg Salad with Port Dressing

1 small head iceberg lettuce
1/2 cucumber
4 oz. mushrooms
4 tomatoes
2 hard-cooked eggs
1/2 cup vegetable oil
1/4 cup wine vinegar
1/2 cup port
Salt and white pepper
1 small bunch fresh tarragon or 1 teaspoon dried tarragon
1 basket alfalfa sprouts

Tear lettuce in large pieces. Slice cucumber. Cut smaller mushrooms in quarters, larger mushrooms in eighths. Cut tomatoes in quarters. Cut hard-cooked eggs in eighths. Combine lettuce, cucumber, mushrooms, tomatoes and egg in a large salad bowl. In a small bowl, beat together oil, vinegar, port, salt and pepper. Pour oil mixture over salad; toss carefully. Chop fresh tarragon. Snip sprouts with kitchen scissors. Rinse in cold water; drain well. Sprinkle tarragon and sprouts over salad. Makes 4 servings.

Bamboo-Shoot Salad

1 (1-lb. 3-oz.) can bamboo shoots
1 garlic clove
1 teaspoon salt
3 tablespoons vegetable oil
2 teaspoons fresh lime or lemon juice
Generous pinch red (cayenne) pepper

Drain bamboo shoots. Cut into thin slices and place in a bowl. Finely slice garlic; sprinkle garlic with salt. Crush garlic with the blade of a knife. In a small bowl, beat together oil, lime or lemon juice, garlic and red pepper. Pour oil mixture over bamboo shoots. Cover and let stand a few minutes. Makes 4 servings.

Cook's Tip

Although traditionally part of a Chinese meal, Bamboo-Shoot Salad makes a delicious accompaniment to any meat or poultry dish. It goes particularly well with cold chicken for a summer buffet.

Red-Endive & Spinach Salad

1 medium head red endive
8 oz. young spinach
1/2 (14-oz.) can artichoke hearts
2 onions
1 garlic clove
1 hard-cooked egg
6 tablespoons olive oil
1/4 cup wine vinegar
Salt and white pepper

Remove outer endive leaves; discard. Slice off endive stem; shred stem. Separate remaining endive leaves. Remove long stems from spinach. Drain artichoke hearts; cut each in half. Slice onions into thin rings. Cut garlic clove in half. Using the cut side, rub garlic around the inside of a salad bowl. Combine endive, spinach and artichoke hearts in salad bowl. Scatter onion rings over greens. Chop hard-cooked egg. In a small bowl, beat together oil, vinegar, salt, pepper and shredded endive stem. Pour oil mixture over salad. To serve, sprinkle with chopped egg. Makes 4 servings.

Spring Salad

1 head lettuce
4 oz. young spinach
3 to 4 radishes
1 small bunch each fresh tarragon, dill and parsley or 1 teaspoon each
    dried tarragon, dill and parsley
1 apple
1 onion
2 hard-cooked eggs
1/4 cup dry sherry
3 tablespoons vegetable oil
2 teaspoons wine vinegar
1 teaspoon lemon juice
1/2 teaspoon sugar
Salt and white pepper

Separate lettuce leaves and tear into pieces. Place in a large salad bowl. Remove heavy stalks from spinach. Thinly slice radishes. Finely chop fresh herbs. Thinly slice apple. Slice onion into thin rings. Add spinach, radishes, apple and onion to salad bowl. Cut hard-cooked eggs into wedges. In a small bowl, beat together sherry, oil, vinegar, lemon juice, sugar, salt and pepper. Pour sherry mixture over vegetables; toss lightly. Sprinkle herbs over salad. To serve, garnish with egg wedges. Makes 4 servings.

Mushroom Salad

12 oz. mushrooms
1/2 (5-oz.) can prawns or shrimp
1/4 cup vegetable oil
2 teaspoons wine vinegar
2 teaspoons lemon juice
Salt and pepper
Pinch sugar
3 tablespoons sherry
Small bunch each parsley and chives

Thinly slice mushrooms. Drain prawns or shrimp. Rinse in cold water; drain thoroughly. In a salad bowl, combine prawns or shrimp and mushrooms. In a small bowl, beat together oil, vinegar, lemon juice, salt, pepper, sugar and sherry. Pour oil mixture over salad. Cover and refrigerate 30 minutes. Finely chop parsley and chives. To serve, gently stir in chopped parsley and chives. Makes 4 servings.

Cook's Tip

For a milder dressing, use apple juice instead of vinegar. Seafood can be replaced with thin strips of ham.

Asparagus Salad

12 oz. fresh or canned asparagus
1/2 teaspoon each salt and sugar
3 tomatoes
4 hard-cooked eggs
6 tablespoons vegetable oil
1/4 cup wine vinegar
Salt and pepper
1 small bunch parsley

Lightly peel lower part of fresh asparagus stems. Bring a small amount of salted and lightly sugared water to a boil in a large shallow saucepan. Add fresh asparagus. Cover and simmer over low heat 20 minutes or until tender. Make a cross-cut in base of each tomato. Place each tomato briefly in boiling water. Drain and peel. Cut tomatoes into quarters. Remove and discard seeds. Finely dice tomatoes. Drain fresh asparagus. Rinse in cold water; cool slightly. Or, drain canned asparagus. Cut asparagus spears into 1-inch pieces. Cut hard-cooked eggs into 8 wedges. Arrange asparagus, tomatoes and eggs on a flat dish. In a small bowl, beat together oil and vinegar. Season to taste. Pour oil mixture over salad. Cover and refrigerate 20 minutes. Finely chop parsley. To serve, sprinkle chopped parsley over salad. Makes 4 servings.

Cucumber & Dill Salad

1 cucumber
1 garlic clove
1/3 cup plain yogurt
2 teaspoons lemon juice
1 small onion
1 small bunch fresh dill or 1 teaspoon dried dill
Salt and freshly ground black pepper

Cut cucumber into thick slices; cut each slice in thin strips. Place cucumber strips in a large salad bowl. Crush garlic. In a small bowl, beat together yogurt, lemon juice and garlic. Grate onion into yogurt mixture. Chop fresh dill, reserving 1 sprig. Stir salt, pepper and dill into yogurt mixture. Pour yogurt mixture over cucumber. Garnish with sprig of fresh dill. Makes 4 servings.

Cook's Tip

If fresh or dried dill is hard to find, you can still make a delicious and refreshing cucumber salad by using fresh mint in the yogurt dressing.

Celeriac Salad

1 lb. celeriac
Juice of 1 lemon
1/4 cup olive oil
1 tablespoon wine vinegar
1/4 teaspoon each salt and sugar
1/2 basket alfalfa sprouts

Peel celeriac; cut in large pieces. Shred celeriac in long thin strips. Sprinkle with lemon juice to prevent discoloration. In a small bowl, beat together oil, vinegar, salt and sugar. Pour oil mixture over celeriac. Toss lightly. Cover and let stand 20 minutes. Snip sprouts with kitchen scissors; wash and drain. To serve, sprinkle sprouts over celeriac. Makes 4 servings.

Cook's Tip

You can make this salad with cooked celeriac. Place whole celeriac root in a pan containing boiling salted water. Cover and simmer over low heat 20 to 30 minutes. Cool slightly before cutting in thin strips.

Mushroom Salad in Tomato Rings

6 tomatoes
1/4 cup lemon juice
1 teaspoon salt
1/2 cup vegetable oil
12 oz. mushrooms
2 oz. canned morel mushrooms, if desired
1 small onion
1 garlic clove
8 fresh basil leaves, if desired
1/4 teaspoon white pepper

Slice tomatoes thinly; place in a flat dish. In a small bowl, beat together 1 tablespoon lemon juice, 1/2 teaspoon salt and 3 tablespoons oil. Sprinkle lemon-juice mixture over tomatoes. Cover and let stand 20 minutes. Thinly slice mushrooms. Drain morels; cut in half lengthwise, if desired. In a small bowl, combine mushrooms and morels. Cut onion in pieces. Squeeze out onion juice, either with a juicer or by squeezing small pieces of onion at a time through a garlic press. Crush garlic. Add to onion juice. Beat together remaining lemon juice, 1/2 teaspoon salt, remaining oil and white pepper. Add garlic and onion juice. Arrange tomato slices in rings on 4 individual plates. Place mushrooms in center of each plate. Pour dressing over salad. Garnish with basil leaves, if desired. Makes 4 servings.

Apple & Quail's-Egg Salad

1/2 head lettuce
1/4 garlic clove
2 teaspoons lemon juice
1/4 teaspoon salt
3 tablespoons brandy
1 tablespoon vegetable oil
2 apples
1 bunch radishes
1 small bunch parsley
8 fresh tarragon leaves or 1/4 teaspoon dried tarragon
3 tablespoons tarragon vinegar
12 pickled quail's eggs

Cut lettuce in strips. Crush garlic. In a small bowl, beat together lemon juice, salt, garlic, brandy and oil. Pour dressing over lettuce. Cover and let stand 15 minutes. Peel apples. Cut apples and radishes in long thin strips. Finely chop parsley and fresh tarragon. In a small bowl, beat together parsley, tarragon and tarragon vinegar. Season to taste. Pour parsley mixture over apple and radish strips. Arrange lettuce in a ring on 4 individual plates. Place salad in centers. Top each serving with 3 quail's eggs. Makes 4 servings.

Shrimp & Green-Bean Salad

5 oz. thawed frozen or canned small shrimp
8 oz. young green beans
2 limes
2 shallots
1 small bunch parsley
3 leaves each fresh mint and basil or a pinch each dried mint and basil
3 tablespoons wine vinegar
1/2 teaspoon salt
1/4 cup dry sherry
1/3 cup olive oil
Generous pinch red (cayenne) pepper

Drain shrimp; dry well. Blanch green beans in salted boiling water 8 minutes. Immediately plunge beans in cold water. Drain well; cool. Cut limes in thin slices. Finely chop shallots. Chop parsley, fresh mint and basil. In a small bowl, beat together vinegar, salt, sherry, oil, red pepper, chopped shallot, parsley, mint and basil. Arrange lime slices in a ring on 4 individual plates. Top with green beans and shrimp. Sprinkle with herb dressing. Makes 4 servings.

Chicken & Red-Endive Salad

1 qt. chicken broth
2 chicken breasts
3 medium carrots
1 cup fresh or frozen peas
2 heads red endive
1/3 cup whipping cream
1 teaspoon lemon juice
1 tablespoon brandy
Salt and white pepper

Bring broth to a boil in a large saucepan. Add chicken breasts. Cover and cook over low heat 15 minutes. Drain chicken; cool slightly. Cut carrots in thin strips. In a small saucepan, bring 2 cups salted water to a boil. Add carrots and peas; blanch 4 minutes. Plunge carrots and peas into cold water. Drain well, cool slightly. Separate endive leaves. Arrange smaller leaves in a ring on each of 4 individual plates. Slice chicken; arrange slices in center of endive. Top with carrots and peas. Sprinkle with salt and pepper. In a small bowl, beat together cream, lemon juice and brandy. Add salt and pepper. Spoon cream mixture over chicken and vegetables. Makes 4 servings.

Seasonal Sausage Salad

2 hard-cooked eggs
1/2 head Boston lettuce
1/2 head romaine lettuce
1 bunch radishes
1 bunch green onions
4 oz. ham loaf or meat loaf, thinly sliced
4 oz. mortadella sausage
1 bunch fresh mixed herbs (parsley, chives, dill, lovage, tarragon)
1/4 cup wine vinegar
1/2 cup vegetable oil
Salt and white pepper
Generous pinch sugar
1/3 cup mayonnaise

Cut each egg in 8 wedges. Separate lettuce leaves. Thinly slice radishes. Finely chop green onions. Cut ham loaf or meat-loaf slices in half. Cut mortadella in thin strips. Line a flat serving dish with lettuce leaves. Arrange eggs, radishes, onions and meats on top. Finely chop mixed herbs, reserving a few sprigs. In a small bowl, beat together vinegar, oil, salt, pepper and sugar. Stir mixed herbs into dressing. Pour dressing over salad. Spoon mayonnaise into center of salad platter. Garnish with remaining sprigs of herbs. Makes 4 servings.

Cook's Tip

If green onions are not obtainable, replace them with 1 large Spanish onion, cut in thin rings. You can add 2 tomatoes, peeled and quartered, and 4 ounces young green beans that have been blanched in boiling salted water for 10 minutes.

Iceberg Lettuce with Garnished Eggs

1 head iceberg lettuce
1/2 red bell pepper
8 pimiento-stuffed olives
Generous 1/2 cup plain yogurt
3 tablespoons mayonnaise
1 teaspoon Dijon-style mustard
1/2 teaspoon lemon juice
Salt and white pepper
4 hard-cooked eggs
1 (2-oz.) jar lumpfish caviar

Cut lettuce in quarters. Arrange on 4 individual plates. Dice red pepper. Cut olives in half. In a small bowl, beat together yogurt, mayonnaise, mustard, lemon juice, salt and pepper. Pour over lettuce quarters and sprinkle with diced red pepper. Cut eggs in half lengthwise. Garnish with lumpfish caviar and olives. Makes 4 servings.

Cook's Tip

Instead of garnished eggs, you could serve stuffed eggs with the salad.

Tuna Salad

2 (7-oz.) cans tuna
18 pimiento-stuffed olives
6 oz. pickled cocktail onions
6 oz. cooked beets
1/4 cup mayonnaise
Generous 1/2 cup plain yogurt or generous 1/2 cup dairy sour cream
1/4 teaspoon salt
1/2 teaspoon paprika
1 tablespoon tomato paste
1 hard-cooked egg
4 sprigs dill, if desired

Drain tuna well. Place tuna in a medium bowl. Flake tuna, using a fork. Thinly slice 10 olives; cut remaining 8 olives in half. Rinse onions in cold water; drain well. Cut beets in thin strips. Add thinly sliced olives, onions and beets to tuna; mix well. In a small bowl, beat together mayonnaise, yogurt or sour cream, salt, paprika and tomato paste. Pour mayonnaise mixture over tuna mixture. Gently stir in. Arrange salad on 4 individual plates. Cut hard-cooked egg in 8 wedges. Garnish each salad with 2 egg wedges, 4 olive halves and a sprig of dill, if desired. Makes 4 servings.

Cook's Tip

For a milder salad, substitute diced banana and strips of Belgian endive for cocktail onions and olives.

Cucumber & Prawn Salad

8 oz. thawed frozen or canned prawns or shrimp
1 cucumber
1 tablespoon wine vinegar
Salt and white pepper
1/2 teaspoon grated lemon peel
1/2 teaspoon sugar
1/4 cup vegetable oil
1/2 basket alfalfa spouts

Rinse prawns or shrimp in cold water; drain well. Cut cucumber in half lengthwise. Scrape or scoop out seeds using a grapefruit spoon or teaspoon. Slice cucumber halves very thinly. In a medium bowl, combine prawns or shrimp and cucumber. In a small bowl, beat together vinegar, salt, pepper, lemon peel and sugar. Add oil. Stir dressing into cucumber mixture. Cover and let stand 1 hour. Snip sprouts with kitchen scissors. Rinse and drain well. To serve, sprinkle sprouts over salad. Makes 4 servings.

Exotic Chicken Salad

1-1/4 cups frozen peas
1-1/4 lbs. cooked chicken
4 oz. canned asparagus tips
4 oz. mushrooms
4 oz. canned or fresh pineapple
1/3 cup mayonnaise
1/2 cup plain yogurt
3 tablespoons brandy
1 teaspoon lemon juice
Salt and pepper
Pinch each sugar and curry powder
1 lime
4 sprigs dill, if desired

Cook peas according to package directions. Drain; cool. Remove skin or bones from chicken. Cut chicken in 1-inch pieces. Drain asparagus tips. Cut in half. Thinly slice mushrooms. Drain canned pineapple. Cut pineapple in small pieces. Place peas, chicken, asparagus, mushrooms and pineapple in a medium bowl. In a small bowl, beat together mayonnaise, yogurt, brandy, lemon juice, salt, pepper, sugar and curry powder. Pour dressing over chicken mixture; stir gently. Cover and let stand 1 hour. Cut 4 thin slices from center of lime. Arrange salad on 4 individual plates. Garnish each salad with a lime slice and a dill sprig, if desired. Makes 4 servings.

Potato & Sausage Salad

1 lb. potatoes
8 oz. frozen green beans
8 oz. ham loaf, unsliced
1 bunch radishes
2 small onions
1 bunch each parsley and chives
1/2 cup mayonnaise
1 tablespoon Dijon-style mustard
2 to 3 teaspoons lemon juice
Salt and pepper

Peel potatoes. Boil in salted water 20 to 25 minutes. Drain well; cool slightly. Cook beans according to package directions. Drain; cool. Thickly slice ham loaf. Cut slices in thin strips. Slice radishes. Cut onions in rings. Finely chop parsley and chives. Slice potatoes. In a medium bowl, combine potato slices, cooked green beans, ham-loaf strips, radish slices, onion rings and chopped parsley and chives. In a small bowl, beat together mayonnaise and mustard. Add lemon juice. Season to taste. Serve mustard dressing separately. Makes 4 servings.

Corn & Cheese Salad

8 oz. ham loaf, unsliced
8 oz. Edam or Gouda cheese
2 small onions
1 red bell pepper
1 green bell pepper
4 tomatoes
1 pickled cucumber or dill pickle
1 (10-oz.) can whole-kernel corn
1 tablespoon wine vinegar
1/4 cup vegetable oil
1/2 teaspoon Dijon-style mustard
Salt and black pepper
Pinch each sugar, paprika, pepper and red (cayenne) pepper

Cut ham loaf and cheese in narrow strips. Cut onions in rings. Cut red and green peppers in narrow strips. Slice tomatoes and pickle. Drain corn. In a medium bowl, combine ham-loaf strips, cheese strips, onion rings, pepper strips, sliced tomatoes, sliced cucumber and corn; mix well. In a small bowl, beat together vinegar, oil, mustard, salt, pepper, sugar, paprika and red pepper. Pour dressing over salad. Cover and let stand 30 minutes. Season to taste. Arrange salad on 4 individual plates. Makes 4 servings.

Swiss Salad

8 oz. Emmentaler cheese
8 oz. ham
2 celery stalks
8 oz. cooked macaroni
1 tablespoon wine vinegar
1 egg yolk
Pinch each salt, pepper, paprika,
  sugar and garlic salt
1/4 cup vegetable oil
2 oz. shelled walnuts
8 oz. canned morello or tart
  cherries, drained

Dice cheese, ham and celery. In a medium bowl, combine cheese, ham, celery and macaroni. In a small bowl, beat together vinegar, egg yolk, salt, pepper, paprika, sugar and garlic salt. Gradually add oil. Pour dressing over salad. To serve, sprinkle with walnuts and cherries. Makes 4 servings.

Huntsman's Salad

8 Game & Mushroom Croquettes,
  page 41
French Dressing, opposite
1 head lettuce
1 cucumber
1 small bunch radishes
4 tomatoes
2 hard-cooked eggs

Prepare Game & Mushroom Croquettes and French Dressing. Tear lettuce in bite-size pieces. Slice cucumber, radishes, tomatoes and hard-cooked eggs. In a large bowl, combine croquettes, lettuce, cucumber, radishes, tomatoes and eggs. Pour French Dressing over salad. Toss lightly. Makes 4 servings.

Rice Salad

1 lb. frozen mixed vegetables
8 oz. rice
8 oz. salami, unsliced
1 apple
1/4 celeriac, peeled
Generous 1/2 cup plain yogurt
1 tablespoon lemon juice
1/4 cup vegetable oil
Salt and pepper
3 tablespoons chopped parsley

Cook mixed vegetables and rice, separately, according to package directions. Drain; cool slightly. Dice salami, apple and celeriac. In a medium bowl, combine cooked vegetables and rice, salami, apple and celeriac. In a small bowl, beat together yogurt, lemon juice, oil, salt, pepper and parsley. Pour dressing over vegetable mixture. Makes 4 servings.

Balkan Salad

1 green bell pepper
1 red bell pepper
1 yellow bell pepper
1 large red onion
8 oz. feta or mozzarella cheese

French Dressing:
3 tablespoons wine vinegar
1/3 cup olive oil
Salt and white pepper
Pinch sugar
Generous pinch dried oregano

Slice bell peppers; discard pith and seeds. Cut onion into rings. Break up cheese with a fork. In a medium bowl, combine bell-pepper rings, onion rings and cheese. To make French Dressing, in a small bowl, beat together vinegar, oil, salt, pepper and sugar. Stir in oregano. Sprinkle French Dressing over salad. Cover and let stand a few minutes. Makes 4 servings.

Cook's Tip

Pepper rings can be blanched in boiling water 3 minutes then plunged into cold water. Drain well before using.

Chicken Salad with Ham & Cheese

1 small head lettuce
2 tomatoes
2 cooked chicken breasts
4 oz. ham
4 oz. Gruyère or Emmentaler cheese
1 garlic clove
Parsley sprig
1 egg yolk, room temperature
Salt and freshly ground white pepper
Generous pinch sugar
1/2 cup vegetable oil, room temperature
1 tablespoon lemon juice
Generous pinch hot mustard powder

Tear lettuce in bite-size pieces. Slice tomatoes. Remove skin and bones from chicken. Cut chicken, ham and cheese into thin strips. Cut garlic in half. Rub cut side of garlic around inside of salad bowl. Line salad bowl with lettuce. Arrange tomatoes, ham, chicken and cheese on lettuce. Garnish with parsley. In a small bowl, beat together egg yolk, salt, pepper and sugar until mixture begins to thicken. Slowly add oil, a few drops at a time. As soon as mayonnaise begins to thicken, stir in lemon juice and mustard. Season to taste. Serve mayonnaise separate from salad. Makes 4 servings.

Rice & Tuna Salad

8 oz. rice
1 red bell pepper
1 (7-oz.) can tuna
4 oz. pickled cocktail onions
3 tablespoons capers
1 tablespoon lemon juice
Salt and white pepper
Grated peel of 1/2 lemon
1/2 cup mayonnaise
Parsley sprig

Cook rice according to package directions. Drain; rinse with cold water. Drain again; cool slightly. Dice red pepper. Drain tuna; flake tuna with a fork. Drain onions. In a medium bowl, combine rice, red pepper, tuna and onions. In a small bowl, beat together capers, lemon juice, salt, pepper, grated lemon peel and mayonnaise. Stir dressing into salad. Cover and let stand a few minutes. To serve, garnish with a parsley sprig. Makes 4 servings.

Cook's Tip

Cook the rice while preparing another rice dish. If covered, rice will keep in the refrigerator for 3 to 4 days.

Piquant Beef Salad

1 lb. cooked lean beef
2 small onions
2 pickled cucumbers or dill pickles
2 cooked medium carrots
1 red bell pepper
4 oz. mushrooms
1 large apple
1 small bunch parsley
1/4 cup vinegar
1/2 cup vegetable oil
1 teaspoon Worcestershire sauce
Pinch garlic salt
1/2 teaspoon black pepper

Cut beef into 1-inch cubes. Cut onions into rings. Thinly slice pickles and carrots. Cut bell pepper into strips. Cut small mushrooms in quarters, larger mushrooms in eighths. Peel apple; cut in thin slices. Finely chop parsley. Place beef cubes, onion rings, cucumber and carrot slices, pepper strips, mushrooms, apple slices and parsley in a medium bowl. In a small bowl, beat together vinegar, oil, Worcestershire sauce, garlic salt, pepper and parsley. Pour dressing over salad. Toss to coat lightly. Cover and let stand 1 hour. Makes 4 servings.

Lima-Bean Salad

8 oz. large lima beans
1/2 teaspoon dried thyme
1 celery stalk
1/4 small celeriac
1 medium carrot
2 small onions
20 pimiento-stuffed olives
1/2 cup vegetable oil
1/4 cup wine vinegar
Salt and pepper
2 strips canned pimiento
Parsley sprig

Soak beans in twice their volume of cold water at least 12 hours or overnight. Drain beans; place in a saucepan with fresh water and thyme. Do not add salt at this stage as it tends to toughen the bean skins. Cover; bring to a boil. Simmer over low heat 1 hour. Cut celery in thick slices. Dice celeriac and carrot. Cut onions in rings. Place celery, celeriac, carrot and onions in a medium saucepan with a small amount of boiling salted water. Cover; simmer 15 to 20 minutes or until cooked. Drain beans and vegetables separately. Allow to cool. Cut stuffed olives in half. In a small bowl, beat together oil, vinegar, salt and pepper. In a large bowl, combine beans and vegetables. Pour dressing over beans. Mix well. Sprinkle salad with olives. Cover; let stand 30 minutes. To serve, thinly slice pimiento. Garnish salad with pimiento and parsley sprig. Makes 4 servings.

Potato Salad with Cream Dressing

2-1/4 lbs. new potatoes
4 oz. ham
2 pickled cucumbers or dill pickles
1 apple
2 shallots
1 egg yolk
Salt and pepper
1 tablespoon wine vinegar
1/2 cup vegetable oil
Generous 1/2 cup whipping cream
1 small bunch parsley

Place unpeeled potatoes in a large saucepan of boiling salted water. Simmer over medium heat 20 to 25 minutes. Drain, cool slightly. Cut ham in strips. Slice pickles. Peel apple; cut in thin strips. Finely chop shallots. Peel and slice potatoes. In a large bowl, combine potatoes, ham, pickles and apple. In a small bowl, beat together egg yolk, salt, pepper and vinegar. Gradually add oil. Stir in shallots and cream. Pour cream dressing over salad. Cover and let stand 30 minutes. Finely chop parsley. To serve, sprinkle parsley over salad. Makes 4 servings.

Sauerkraut Salads

Sauerkraut & Smoked Fish

1 lb. canned or bottled sauerkraut
3 celery stalks
1 small red bell pepper
1 large apple
1 (7-oz.) can tuna
10 pimiento-stuffed olives
8 oz. smoked fish
1/4 cup vegetable oil
Juice of 1 lemon
Salt and pepper
Generous pinch sugar

Place sauerkraut in a large bowl; toss with 2 forks. Chop celery. Slice red pepper in thin strips. Dice apple. Drain tuna, reserving oil. Flake tuna. Add celery, red pepper, apple and tuna to sauerkraut. Cut olives in half. Slice smoked fish. Add olives and smoked fish to sauerkraut. In a small bowl, beat together tuna oil, vegetable oil, lemon juice, salt, pepper and sugar. Stir dressing into salad. Cover and let stand at room temperature 30 minutes. Makes 4 servings.

Sauerkraut & Ham

1 lb. canned or bottled sauerkraut
12 oz. ham
4 slices canned pineapple
6 tablespoons canned pineapple juice
1 tablespoon honey
3 tablespoons vegetable oil
3 tablespoons lemon juice
Pinch salt

Place sauerkraut in a large bowl; toss lightly. Finely dice ham. Drain and chop pineapple slices. Mix pineapple and ham with sauerkraut. In a small saucepan, heat pineapple juice over low heat. Add honey, stirring until dissolved. Stir in oil, lemon juice and salt. Pour dressing over salad. Cover and let stand 30 minutes. Makes 4 servings.

Sauerkraut & Fruit

1 lb. canned or bottled sauerkraut
6 oz. grapes
2 small apples
1 large pear
1 small onion
Juice of 1 lemon
1/4 teaspoon each salt and sugar
3 tablespoons cranberry sauce

Place sauerkraut in a bowl; toss lightly. Cut grapes in half; remove seeds. Quarter apples and pear; remove cores. Thinly slice friut. Dice onion. Stir onion and fruit into sauerkraut. In a small bowl, beat together lemon juice, salt and sugar. Pour mixture over salad. Cover and let stand 30 minutes. Stir in cranberry sauce just before serving. Makes 4 servings.

Cook's Tip

Any of these salad combinations goes well with a blanched red cabbage. Add 3 tablespoons vinegar to the water when blanching red cabbage to preserve the color.

Cervelat Salad

12 oz. cervelat sausage or other dry, smoked sausage, unsliced
1 red bell pepper
1 green bell pepper
3 medium tomatoes
2 apples
2 dill pickles
1 tablespoon lemon juice
1 teaspoon paprika
1/4 teaspoon white pepper
Generous pinch mustard powder
1/3 cup mayonnaise

Remove skin from sausage; thickly slice sausage. Cut each sausage slice into narrow strips. Cut bell peppers in thin strips. Dip tomatoes briefly in boiling water. Plunge in cold water. Peel and quarter tomatoes; remove seeds. Peel and dice apples. In a medium bowl, combine sausage and pepper strips, tomatoes and diced apple. Spoon salad onto 4 individual plates. Peel and finely dice pickles. In a small bowl, combine lemon juice, paprika, white pepper, mustard, diced pickles and mayonnaise. Spoon dressing over salads. Makes 4 servings.

Seville Meat Salad

4 oz. cold roast pork
4 oz. cold roast beef
4 oz. ham
2 green bell peppers
4 medium tomatoes
10 pitted black olives
10 pimiento-stuffed olives
1 onion
4 oz. pickled cocktail onions
1/3 cup vegetable oil
3 tablespoons wine vinegar
Salt and white pepper
1 small bunch parsley

Cut pork, beef and ham into narrow strips. Cut bell peppers in thin strips. Dip tomatoes in boiling water; then plunge in cold water. Peel and quarter tomatoes; remove seeds. Cut olives in half, if desired. Cut onion in rings. Drain cocktail onions. In a large bowl, combine meat strips, pepper strips, tomatoes, olives, onion rings and cocktail onions. In a small bowl, beat together oil, vinegar, salt and pepper. Pour dressing over salad. Arrange salad on 4 individual plates. Finely chop parsley. To serve, sprinkle parsley over salads. Makes 4 servings.

Pea Salad

12 oz. frozen baby peas
4 tomatoes
8 oz. mushrooms
8 oz. green grapes
8 oz. ham
1/4 cup wine vinegar
1/3 cup vegetable oil
Salt and pepper
4 hard-cooked eggs
1 tablespoon chopped fresh parsley
1/3 cup mayonnaise
1/3 cup tomato paste
1/3 cup whipping cream
Dash Worcestershire sauce

Cook peas according to package directions. Rinse in cold water; drain well. Peel tomatoes; cut each in 8 wedges and remove seeds. Finely slice mushrooms. Peel grapes; cut in half. Remove seeds. Cut ham in strips. In a medium bowl, combine peas, tomatoes, mushrooms, grapes and ham. In a small bowl, beat together 3 tablespoons vinegar, oil, salt and pepper. Pour dressing over salad. Cover and let stand 15 minutes. Cut each hard-cooked egg in 8 wedges. Arrange on salad. Sprinkle salad with chopped parsley. In a small bowl, beat together mayonnaise, remaining vinegar, tomato paste, cream and Worcestershire sauce. Season to taste. Serve separately with salad. Makes 4 servings.

Broccoli Salad

1-1/4 lbs. young broccoli
1 tablespoon wine vinegar
1/4 cup dry sherry
Salt and pepper
2/3 cup vegetable oil
1 egg yolk
1 teaspoon mild tarragon mustard or whole-grain mustard
1/2 teaspoon mustard powder
2 tablespoons lemon juice
Dash Worcestershire sauce
4 oz. mushrooms

Remove any tough stalks from broccoli. Blanch broccoli in boiling salted water 3 minutes. Drain; cool slightly. In a small bowl, beat together vinegar, sherry, salt, pepper and 1/4 cup oil. Separate broccoli in small flowerets; place in a bowl. Pour dressing over broccoli. Cover and let stand 1 hour. In a small bowl, beat together egg yolk, tarragon mustard or whole-grain mustard, mustard powder, 1 tablespoon lemon juice and Worcestershire sauce. Season to taste. Gradually whisk in remaining oil, a little at a time. Mixture should become creamy. Finely slice mushrooms; sprinkle with remaining lemon juice. Arrange broccoli mixture and mushrooms on a flat dish. Serve dressing separately. Makes 4 servings.

Smoked-Salmon Platter

12 oz. frozen green beans
4 tomatoes
1 small head lettuce
1 head red endive
1 onion
4 oz. baby pickles
1 (6-oz.) can crabmeat
4 oz. thinly sliced smoked salmon
1 garlic clove
1/4 cup wine vinegar
1/2 cup olive oil
1/2 teaspoon hot mustard
1/2 teaspoon dried oregano
1 tablespoon chopped fresh parsley
Salt and black pepper

Cook beans according to package directions. Drain; cool slightly. Peel tomatoes; cut each in 8 wedges and remove seeds. Separate lettuce and endive leaves. Cut onion in thin strips. Drain pickles and cut into strips. Drain crabmeat; break up with a fork. Remove any bones from crabmeat. Roll up slices of smoked salmon. Line a flat dish with lettuce and endive leaves. Arrange other salad ingredients in spoonfuls on top of lettuce. Crush garlic. In a small bowl, beat together vinegar, oil, mustard, garlic, oregano, parsley, salt and pepper. Sprinkle dressing over salad. Makes 4 servings.

Fish & Pea Salad

12 oz. frozen baby peas
1 tablespoon lemon juice
1/4 cup water
1/4 cup white wine
1/4 teaspoon salt
1 lb. frozen white-fish fillets
3 celery stalks
2 medium dill pickles
1 lettuce
3 tablespoons mayonnaise
1/4 cup plain yogurt
Generous 1/2 cup dairy sour cream
2 drops Tabasco sauce
Salt and pepper
2 hard-cooked eggs
1 tablespoon chopped fresh parsley

Cook peas according to package directions. Drain; sprinkle with lemon juice. In a large shallow skillet, bring water, white wine and salt to a boil. Add frozen fish. Cover and simmer 20 minutes. Remove from heat and cool fish in cooking liquid. Cut celery and pickles in thin strips. Line a salad bowl with lettuce leaves. Strain fish, reserving stock. Separate fish into pieces. Arrange fish on lettuce with peas, celery and pickles. In a small bowl, beat together mayonnaise, yogurt, sour cream, 3 tablespoons fish stock and Tabasco. Season to taste. Pour dressing over salad. Toss lightly. Slice eggs; arrange slices on salad. To serve, sprinkle with parsley. Makes 4 servings.

Vegetable-Salad Platter

1 small cauliflower
2 medium carrots
6 oz. frozen peas
6 oz. frozen beans
4 small boiled potatoes
4 oz. mushrooms
1 bunch radishes
1 hard-cooked egg
1 small bunch parsley
1 onion
2/3 cup vegetable oil
1/4 cup wine vinegar
1 tablespoon Dijon-style mustard
Salt and white pepper
Pinch sugar
6 pimiento-stuffed olives
4 canned anchovy fillets
Garlic Bread, page 11, if desired

Break cauliflower in flowerets. Slice carrots. In a medium saucepan, bring a small amount of salted water to a boil. Add cauliflower and carrots; blanch 5 minutes. Drain well. Cook peas and beans according to package directions. Rinse all cooked vegetables in cold water. Drain; cool slightly. Peel and slice cold potatoes. Finely slice mushrooms and radishes. Slice hard-cooked egg. Arrange all vegetables in spoonfuls on a flat serving dish. Top with egg slices. Finely chop parsley. Dice onion. In a small bowl, beat together oil, vinegar, mustard, salt, pepper, sugar, diced onion and parsley. Pour dressing over salad. Slice olives. Roll anchovy fillets. Sprinkle olives and anchovies over salad. Serve with Garlic Bread, if desired. Makes 4 servings.

Chanterelle Salad

2 sprigs thyme
1 lb. chanterelle mushrooms
4 basil leaves
4 canned anchovy fillets
1 garlic clove
Juice of 1 lime or lemon
1 egg yolk
Generous 1/2 cup olive oil
1 bunch parsley

In a small saucepan, bring 1-1/2 cups salted water and thyme to a boil. Continue to boil 5 minutes. Add mushrooms. Cover and simmer over medium heat 5 minutes. Drain; cool. Finely chop basil and anchovy fillets. Crush garlic. In a small bowl, combine garlic, basil, anchovy and lime or lemon juice. Whisk egg yolk in a small bowl. Gradually beat in oil, a few drops at a time, until creamy. Stir in anchovy mixture. Place mushrooms in a large bowl. Pour oil mixture over mushrooms. Cover and let stand 30 minutes. Chop parsley. Sprinkle salad with parsley. Serve with freshly toasted white bread and butter. Makes 4 servings.

Cook's Tip

You can also make this salad using field mushrooms. If you do so, fry mushrooms in 3 tablespoons olive oil for 5 minutes instead of simmering them. Sprinkle with thyme while cooking.

Rice & Mackerel Salad

8 oz. rice
4 tomatoes
2 (4.4-oz.) cans mackerel fillets
1 small bunch each chives and parsley
1 tablespoon wine vinegar
1 teaspoon Dijon-style mustard
Salt and black pepper
1/4 cup vegetable oil
1 (1-3/4-oz.) can anchovy fillets

Cook rice according to package directions. Rinse with cold water; drain well. Dip 3 tomatoes in boiling water. Peel tomatoes; dice flesh, discarding seeds. Drain mackerel; break into pieces. In a medium bowl, combine rice, tomatoes and mackerel. Finely chop chives and parsley. In a small bowl, beat together vinegar, mustard, salt, pepper, herbs and oil. Pour dressing over rice mixture. Cover and let stand 30 minutes. Cut remaining tomato in half. Drain anchovies; roll anchovies. To serve, top salad with tomato halves and anchovies. Makes 4 servings.

Riviera Salad Platter

8 oz. thawed frozen or canned prawns or shrimp
1 head lettuce
1/2 basket alfalfa sprouts
2 avocados
Juice of 1/2 lemon
1/2 to 2/3 cup Thousand Island Dressing
4 slices white bread

Rinse prawns or shrimp in cold water; drain well. Separate lettuce leaves and use to line a salad platter. Snip sprouts with kitchen scissors. Rinse under cold water; drain. Cut avocados in half; remove pits. Peel and slice avocados. Arrange slices in a ring on lettuce. Sprinkle with lemon juice to prevent discoloration. Place prawns or shrimp on top. Spoon Thousand Island Dressing over salad. Garnish with sprouts. Lightly toast bread; cut in half diagonally. Serve toast with salad. Makes 4 servings.

Asparagus & Sprout Salad

1 lb. asparagus
1/2 teaspoon salt
1 sugar cube
1/4 cup vegetable oil
1 tablespoon wine vinegar
Few lettuce leaves
2 hard-cooked eggs
1 basket alfalfa sprouts
1/3 cup plain yogurt
1/2 cup mayonnaise
1 hard-cooked egg yolk, chopped
1 tablespoon chopped fresh mixed herbs

Lightly peel lower part of asparagus stalks. Tie into 2 or 3 bundles with thread. Place salt and sugar cube in a tall pot. Add 8 cups water and bring to a boil. Place asparagus bundles upright in pot. Simmer over low heat 20 to 30 minutes or until tender. Drain asparagus bundles; cool. Remove thread. In a small bowl, beat together oil and vinegar. Sprinkle dressing over asparagus. Cover and marinate 15 minutes. Line a large flat dish with lettuce leaves. Remove asparagus from marinade and arrange on lettuce. Cut 2 eggs into quarters. Snip sprouts with kitchen scissors. Rinse in cold water; drain. Arrange sprouts and egg wedges around asparagus. In a small bowl, beat yogurt and mayonnaise. Spoon over asparagus. Garnish with chopped egg yolk and fresh herbs. Makes 4 servings.

Summerhouse Salad

1/2 head endive
4 oz. young spinach or watercress
1 head lettuce
1 cucumber
1 avocado
2 tomatoes
4 oz. blue cheese (Stilton, dolcelatte, Roquefort)
1 tablespoon whipping cream
1 tablespoon lemon juice
6 tablespoons mayonnaise
Pinch each salt and sugar
5 drops Tabasco sauce
3 tablespoons chopped fresh chives

Cut endive into thin strips. Trim young spinach or watercress. Remove dark green outer leaves of lettuce and use in another salad. Separate inner leaves of lettuce. Cut cucumber in half lengthwise and remove seeds. Thinly slice cucumber halves. Cut avocado in half; remove pit. Peel and slice avocado. Halve tomatoes. Arrange endive, spinach or watercress, lettuce, cucumber, avocado and tomatoes on a salad platter. Press cheese through a sieve into a small bowl. Add cream, lemon juice and mayonnaise; beat together. Stir in salt, sugar and Tabasco sauce. Spoon dressing into center of salad. Sprinkle chives over the top. Makes 4 servings.

Chef's Salad Platter

3 tomatoes
1 cucumber
2 hard-cooked eggs
4 oz. Emmentaler or Edam cheese, sliced
8 oz. ham
2 small red onions
1 small head endive or 1 head iceberg lettuce
Few round lettuce leaves
Coarsely ground black pepper
6 tablespoons vegetable oil
1/4 cup wine vinegar
1 tablespoon chopped fresh mixed herbs or 1 tablespoon dried mixed
  herbs
Salt and white pepper

Thinly slice tomatoes and cucumber. Finely chop eggs. Cut cheese and ham into fine strips. Slice onions into rings. Cut endive or iceberg lettuce into strips. Mix together tomatoes and cucumber. Arrange on one side of a salad dish. Sprinkle chopped eggs over the top. Place round lettuce leaves on another part of the dish. Top with ham and onion. Sprinkle with black pepper. Cover the rest of the dish with endive or iceberg lettuce. Sprinkle with cheese. In a small bowl, beat together oil, vinegar, herbs, salt and white pepper. To serve, pour dressing over salad. Makes 4 servings.

Chicken & Vegetable Salad

1/2 cauliflower
1 roast chicken
1 leek
1/2 celeriac
1/2 red bell pepper
1/2 green bell pepper
1 carrot
Generous 1/2 cup dairy sour cream
Generous 1/2 cup plain yogurt
Juice of 1 lemon
Salt and pepper
3 tablespoons chopped fresh mixed herbs, if desired

Break cauliflower into flowerets. Blanch in boiling salted water 4 to 5 minutes. Plunge into ice-cold water; drain and cool. Remove skin and bones from chicken. Cut meat into small slices. Trim and thoroughly wash leek. Slice into thin strips. Peel and wash celeriac. Cut into thin strips. Blanch leek and celeriac in a little boiling salted water 4 minutes. Rinse in cold water; drain and cool. Quarter peppers. Remove and discard seeds and pith. Cut peppers into strips. Finely shred carrot. In a small bowl, beat together sour cream, yogurt, lemon juice, salt and pepper. Stir in herbs. Arrange cauliflower, chicken, leek, celeriac, peppers and carrot in a large bowl. Spoon dressing on top. Makes 4 servings.

Chicken & Asparagus Salad

1 lb. asparagus
12 oz. frozen peas
1 roast chicken
4 hard-cooked eggs
1 bunch parsley
4 slices canned pineapple
6 tablespoons mayonnaise
3 tablespoons whipping cream
1/4 cup canned pineapple juice
1 teaspoon lemon juice
Generous pinch salt and sugar

Lightly peel lower part of asparagus stalks. Tie into 2 or 3 bundles with thread. Bring 8 cups salted water to a boil in a tall pot. Place asparagus bundles upright in pot. Simmer over low heat 20 to 30 minutes or until tender. Drain asparagus bundles; cool. Remove thread. Cook peas following package instructions. Drain and cool. Remove skin and bones from chicken. Cut meat into pieces. Cut asparagus into equal lengths. Finely chop eggs. Chop parsley. Drain sliced pineapple and cut into chunks. In a small bowl, beat together mayonnaise, cream, pineapple juice, lemon juice, salt and sugar. Place chicken, asparagus, peas and pineapple in a salad bowl. Pour dressing over salad and sprinkle with chopped egg and parsley. Makes 4 servings.

Italian Salad

1 red bell pepper
1 green bell pepper
1 medium onion
1/4 head lettuce
2 small oranges
8 oz. cooked chicken
12 pimiento-stuffed olives
1 (5-oz.) can prawns or shrimp
1 (4-oz.) can mussels or smoked oysters
1/4 cup Rémoulade Sauce, page 13
3 tablespoons whipping cream
Salt and white pepper
1 to 2 tablespoons lemon juice
2 hard-cooked eggs

Halve peppers. Remove and discard seeds and pith. Slice peppers into strips. Dice onion. Separate lettuce into leaves. Tear into pieces. Peel oranges. Remove skin from segments. Dice orange flesh. Cut chicken into strips. Slice olives. Drain prawns or shrimp. Rinse in cold water; drain well. Drain mussels or smoked oysters. Mix prawns or shrimp, mussels or oysters, peppers, lettuce, onion, oranges, chicken and olives in a salad bowl. In a small bowl, beat together Rémoulade Sauce, cream, salt, white pepper and lemon juice. Stir dressing into salad. Let stand a few minutes. Cut eggs into 8 wedges and use to garnish salad. Makes 4 servings.

Feta-Cheese Salad

12 oz. feta cheese
6 tablespoons olive oil
3 tablespoons wine vinegar
1/2 teaspoon coarsely ground black pepper
2 stalks celery
1/2 head endive
1/4 teaspoon salt
1 oz. shelled pecans

Dice cheese and place in a bowl. In a small bowl, beat together 1/4 cup oil, 1 tablespoon vinegar and pepper. Sprinkle dressing over cheese. Cover and let stand at room temperature 40 minutes. Slice celery. Cut endive into strips. Place celery and endive in a salad bowl. Mix together remaining oil and vinegar; add salt. Pour dressing over salad. Carefully add cheese. Top with pecans. Makes 4 servings.

Cook's Tip

For a variation, substitute pitted black olives for the pecans and sprinkle the salad with a few freshly chopped mint leaves. Walnuts can also be substituted for pecans.

Danish Macaroni Salad

8 oz. frozen peas
8 oz. frozen carrots
8 oz. macaroni
1 lb. ham loaf, unsliced
1 pickled cucumber or dill pickle
1 large onion
1 cup mayonnaise
Generous 1/2 cup plain yogurt
1 tablespoon lemon juice
Salt and pepper
1/2 teaspoon sugar
3 tablespoons chopped fresh mixed herbs (dill, parsley, chives)
2 hard-cooked eggs
2 tomatoes

Bring a little salted water to a boil in a saucepan. Add frozen peas and carrots. Simmer over low heat 6 minutes. Drain and cool. Cook macaroni in plenty of salted water, following package instructions. Cook until tender but firm to the bite. Rinse through with cold water; drain. Cut ham loaf into 1/2-inch cubes. Slice pickle into strips. Cut onion into rings. Place peas, carrots, macaroni, ham loaf, pickle and onion in a salad bowl. In a small bowl, beat together mayonnaise, yogurt, lemon juice, salt, peppper, sugar and chopped herbs. Stir dressing into salad. Cover and let stand at room temperature 30 minutes. Slice eggs. Cut tomatoes into eighths. Garnish salad with tomatoes and eggs. Makes 4 servings.

Meat & Vegetable Salad

12 oz. frozen mixed vegetables
8 oz. cold roast pork
1 red onion
4 strips canned pimiento
3 tablespoons wine vinegar
1 teaspoon hot mustard
5 drops Tabasco sauce
1/4 teaspoon salt
Pinch sugar
1/3 cup vegetable oil
4 oz. Wensleydale or Stilton cheese
3 tablespoons chopped mixed fresh herbs, if desired

Cook frozen vegetables following package instructions. Drain and cool. Slice roast pork into strips. Cut onion into rings. Drain and dice pimiento. Combine mixed vegetables, pork, onion and pimiento in a salad bowl. In a small bowl, beat together vinegar, mustard, Tabasco, salt, sugar and oil. Stir dressing into salad. Cover and let stand at room temperature 15 minutes. To serve, crumble cheese and sprinkle over salad. Sprinkle with chopped herbs, if desired. Makes 4 servings.

Cheese & Salami Salad

1 garlic clove
6 tablespoons vegetable oil
1/4 cup wine vinegar
Salt and black pepper
1/4 teaspoon sugar
Pinch dried rosemary
1 bay leaf
4 oz. green noodles
4 oz. thinly sliced salami
8 oz. Emmentaler cheese
2 onions

Finely chop garlic. In a small bowl, beat together oil, vinegar, garlic, salt, pepper and sugar. Crush rosemary and bay leaf between your finger and thumb; add to dressing. Cover and let stand at room temperature 2 hours. Cook noodles in plenty of salted water, following package instructions. Cook until tender but firm to the bite. Rinse through with cold water, drain and cool. Cut salami and cheese into thin strips. Cut onions into rings. Mix noodles, salami, cheese and onions in a salad bowl. Cover and let stand in a cool place. Strain dressing and sprinkle over salad just before serving. Makes 4 servings.

Pepper & Herring Salad

1 cup milk
1/2 cup water
8 pickled-herring fillets
1 green bell pepper
1 red bell pepper
2 tomatoes
1 small onion
1/3 cup vegetable oil
3 tablespoons wine vinegar
Lettuce leaves
2 hard-cooked eggs
1 bunch dill or parsley

In a small bowl, combine milk and water. Rinse herring fillets in cold water. Place in milk mixture and let soak 1 hour. Cut peppers in half. Remove and discard seeds and pith. Slice peppers into rings. Dip tomatoes into boiling water, then plunge into cold water. Remove skins. Cut each tomato into 8 wedges. Remove herring from milk mixture; drain. Cut herring into strips. Cut onion into rings. In a small bowl, beat together oil and vinegar. Place herring, peppers, tomatoes and onion in a bowl. Pour dressing over salad. Cover and let stand 10 minutes. Line a salad dish with lettuce leaves. Arrange herring mixture on lettuce. Chop eggs. Chop parsley or dill. Sprinkle eggs and parsley or dill over salad before serving. Makes 4 servings.

Salad Supreme

2 heads Belgian endive
4 oz. young spinach or watercress
1 yellow bell pepper
2 tomatoes
1 small honeydew melon
1 onion
4 oz. Edam cheese
4 oz. smoked or boiled ham
2 oz. canned tuna
2 smoked-trout fillets
2 oz. canned prawns or shrimp
1 to 2 green onions
1 bunch fresh mixed herbs, if
**   desired**
1/3 cup vegetable oil
1 tablespoon wine vinegar
1 tablespoon fresh lime juice
1/2 teaspoon sugar
Salt and coarsely ground black
**   pepper**
Generous pinch ground ginger
10 pitted black olives

Separate endive leaves. Trim
young spinach or watercress.
Cut pepper in half. Remove
and discard seeds and pith.
Slice pepper into rings. Cut
tomatoes into 8 wedges. Slice
melon in half. Remove seeds.
Scoop out melon flesh with a
melon-baller or teaspoon. Cut
onion into rings. Cut cheese
and ham into strips. Drain
tuna; flake with a fork. Skin and
flake trout fillets. Drain prawns
or shrimp. Rinse through with
cold water; drain well. Finely
chop green onions and herbs, if
used. In a small bowl, beat
together oil, vinegar, lime
juice, sugar, salt, pepper and
ginger. Arrange endive, spinach
or watercress, pepper, tomatoes, melon, onion, cheese,
ham, tuna, trout, prawns or
shrimp, green onions and herbs
in 4 individual cocktail glasses
or dishes. Sprinkle with dressing
and garnish with olives. Makes
4 servings.

Camembert Cocktail

2 medium carrots
1 (9-1/2-oz.) jar mixed pickled vegetables
4 strips canned pimiento
2 small onions
1/2 (14-oz.) can artichoke hearts
12 oz. Camembert cheese
4 oz. mushrooms
3 tablespoons tarragon vinegar
1 teaspoon lemon juice
1/2 teaspoon sugar
1/2 teaspoon salt
6 tablespoons vegetable oil
1 small bunch parsley

Blanch carrots in a little boiling salted water 2 minutes. Drain and cut into slices. Drain mixed pickled vegetables and canned pimiento; cut into pieces. Slice onions into very thin rings. Drain and halve artichoke hearts. Cut Camembert into thick slices. Finely chop mushrooms. Mix carrots, pickled vegetables, pimiento, onions, artichoke hearts, Camembert and mushrooms in a large bowl. In a small bowl, beat together vinegar, lemon juice, sugar, salt and oil. Sprinkle dressing over salad. Cover and let stand at room temperature 30 minutes. Finely chop parsley. Arrange salad in 4 individual glasses. Sprinkle parsley over each serving. Serve with buttered whole-wheat or pumpernickel bread. Makes 4 servings.

Corned-Beef & Cheese Salad

6 oz. frozen peas
2 (7-oz.) cans corned beef
4 oz. Cheddar or Emmentaler cheese
2 green bell peppers
2 hard-cooked eggs
4 tomatoes
4 oz. canned whole-kernel corn
20 pimiento-stuffed olives
1 small bunch parsley
1 garlic clove
6 tablespoons vegetable oil
1/4 cup vinegar
Salt and pepper

Cook frozen peas following package instructions. Rinse under cold water; drain. Cut corned beef and cheese into strips. Cut peppers in quarters. Remove and discard seeds and pith. Slice peppers. Cut eggs into eighths. Cut tomatoes into 8 wedges. Drain corn. Slice olives. Finely chop parsley. Crush garlic. In a small bowl, beat together garlic, oil, vinegar, salt and pepper. Place peas, corned beef, cheese, peppers, eggs, tomatoes, corn and olives in a salad bowl. Mix dressing into salad. Cover and let stand 15 minutes. Sprinkle with parsley before serving. Makes 4 servings.

Apple & Celery Salad

1 bunch celery
3 small red apples
1 teaspoon lemon juice
1/2 cup chopped hazelnuts
4 oz. feta or cottage cheese
1 cup whipping cream
Salt and white pepper

Break celery into stalks and cut off leaves. Chop celery very finely. Cut apples into quarters; remove cores. Thinly slice apples and sprinkle with lemon juice. Mix celery and apples with half the nuts. Arrange on a flat serving dish. Break up feta or cottage cheese in a bowl with a fork. Beat in cream, salt and pepper. Stir remaining nuts into dressing. Serve dressing separately with salad. Makes 4 servings.

Cook's Tip

Blue-cheese dressing also goes very well with this salad. Substitute 3 to 4 ounces Gorgonzola or Danish blue for the feta or cottage cheese and proceed as above.

Potato & Apple Salad

1 lb. new potatoes
1 head lettuce
1 small cucumber
2 apples
2 onions
1 (12-oz.) can whole-kernel corn
1 bunch dill, if desired
3 tablespoons wine vinegar
1 tablespoon lemon juice
3 tablespoons apple juice
1 teaspoon Dijon-style mustard
Salt and pepper
1/4 teaspoon sugar
6 tablespoons vegetable oil

Simmer potatoes in boiling salted water 20 to 25 minutes. Drain potatoes and peel; cool. Slice and place in a large bowl. Tear lettuce leaves into strips. Cut cucumber in half lengthwise and scoop out seeds. Thinly slice cucumber halves. Cut apples into quarters; remove cores. Thinly slice apples. Cut onions into rings. Drain corn. Add lettuce, cucumber, apples, onions and corn to potatoes. Chop dill, if used. In a small bowl, beat together vinegar, lemon juice, apple juice, mustard, salt, pepper, sugar and oil. Pour dressing over salad and mix well. Before serving, sprinkle with dill, if used. Makes 4 servings.

For Fall

White-Cabbage Salad
1 small white cabbage
4 oz. thick bacon slices
1 large onion
6 tablespoons wine vinegar
5 tablespoons vegetable oil
1 teaspoon sugar
1 teaspoon caraway seeds

Trim cabbage and cut into quarters. Remove stalk. Shred cabbage. Blanch in boiling salted water 5 to 8 minutes. Drain well; cool. Cut bacon into small pieces. Fry in a skillet until crisp. Finely chop onion. In a small bowl, beat together vinegar, oil and sugar. Place cabbage, bacon and onion in a bowl. Pour dressing over salad. Sprinkle with caraway seeds. Cover and let stand in a cool place 20 minutes before serving. Makes 4 servings.

Red-Cabbage Salad
1 small red cabbage
1 large or 2 small apples
1 onion
6 tablespoons vegetable oil
1/4 cup wine vinegar
1 tablespoon lemon juice
1 tablespoon sugar
1/4 cup orange juice
Grated peel of 1/2 orange
Generous 1/2 cup dairy sour cream

Trim cabbage and cut into quarters. Remove stalk. Shred cabbage. Blanch in boiling salted water 5 to 8 minutes. Drain well; cool. Peel and quarter apple; remove core. Thinly slice apple. Finely dice onion. In a small bowl, beat together oil, vinegar, lemon juice, sugar, orange juice, orange peel and diced onion. Place red cabbage and sliced apple in a large bowl. Pour dressing over salad; mix well. Let stand in a cool place 20 minutes. Top with sour cream before serving. Makes 4 servings.

Savoy-Cabbage Salad
1 small Savoy cabbage
1 onion
6 tablespoons wine vinegar
1/3 cup vegetable oil
1 teaspoon sugar
1/4 teaspoon salt
Pinch white pepper
Generous pinch curry powder
1 oz. each shelled almonds, hazelnuts and cashews

Trim cabbage and cut into quarters. Remove stalk. Shred cabbage. Blanch in boiling salted water 5 to 8 minutes. Drain well; cool. Place in a medium bowl. Finely dice onion. In a small bowl, beat together vinegar, oil, sugar, salt, pepper, curry powder and onion. Mix dressing thoroughly into cabbage. Cover and let stand in a cool place 20 minutes. Stir in nuts before serving. Makes 4 servings.

Strawberry & Radish Salad

1 bunch large radishes
1 apple
4 oz. strawberries
1 tablespoon lemon juice
1/2 teaspoon salt
1/2 teaspoon sugar
Generous pinch red (cayenne) pepper
3 tablespoons vegetable oil

Trim radishes; shred. Peel and quarter apple; remove core. Slice apple thinly. Hull strawberries. Cut into halves or quarters. In a small bowl, beat together lemon juice, salt, sugar, red pepper and oil. Combine radishes, apple and strawberries in a large bowl. Sprinkle with dressing. Makes 4 servings.

Cook's Tip

You may prefer to shred the apple as well as the radishes. If so, peel the apple first as it is difficult to shred with the peel.

Endive Boats

1 large head Belgian endive
1 (5-oz.) can prawns or shrimp
6 pimiento-stuffed olives
8 pitted black olives
1 tablespoon wine vinegar
1/4 cup vegetable oil
1 teaspoon Dijon-style mustard
Salt and pepper
2 hard-cooked eggs, if desired
1 small bunch dill or parsley

Break off 4 large endive leaves; reserve. Separate remaining endive into leaves. Cut into thin strips. Drain prawns or shrimp. Rinse through with cold water; drain well. Cut stuffed olives in half. Place endive strips, prawns or shrimp and olives in a bowl. In a small bowl, beat together vinegar, oil, mustard, salt and pepper. Mix dressing into salad. If used, cut each egg into 8 wedges. Break dill or parsley into sprigs. Arrange reserved 4 endive leaves on a platter. Fill each with salad. Garnish with dill or parsley sprigs. Garnish platter with egg wedges. Makes 4 servings.

Avocado & Ham Salad

4 avocados
Juice of 1 lemon
4 oz. smoked or boiled ham, thinly sliced
1 (11-oz.) can mandarin-orange segments
1/4 cup vegetable oil
1 tablespoon brandy
Generous pinch salt
3 to 4 lemon-balm leaves, if desired

Cut avocados in half and remove pits. Scoop out flesh with a melon-baller. Place avocado balls in a bowl; sprinkle with a little lemon juice. Slice ham into very fine strips. Drain mandarin-orange segments, reserving juice. Add orange segments and ham to avocado. In a small bowl, beat together remaining lemon juice, 1 tablespoon reserved mandarin-orange juice, oil, brandy and salt. Stir dressing into salad. Cover and let stand a few minutes. Cut lemon balm into strips, if used. Arrange salad on a serving dish. Sprinkle with lemon balm. Makes 4 servings.

Angelo's Chicken Salad

3 cooked chicken breasts
1/2 cucumber
4 tomatoes
1 apple
Juice of 1/2 lemon
1 tablespoon mild or whole-grain mustard
6 tablespoons mayonnaise
1 bunch dill or parsley
1 tablespoon sugar
3 tablespoons wine vinegar
1/4 cup orange juice
Grated peel of 1/2 orange

Remove skin and bones from chicken breasts. Cut meat into thin slices. Cut cucumber in half lengthwise. Scoop out seeds with a spoon. Slice cucumber very finely. Peel and quarter tomatoes. Remove seeds. Dice tomato flesh. Peel and quarter apple; remove core. Thinly slice apple. Sprinkle with lemon juice. Combine chicken, cucumber, tomatoes and apple in a bowl. In a small bowl, beat together mustard and mayonnaise. Finely chop dill or parsley. In a small bowl, blend sugar, vinegar and orange juice. Stir into mayonnaise with dill or parsley and grated orange peel. Arrange salad in 4 individual glasses. Top each serving with 1 tablespoon dressing. Makes 4 servings.

Grapefruit Salad

2 grapefruit
1/4 cup sugar
1/4 cup Grand Marnier
1 tablespoon honey
8 fresh or maraschino cherries

Peel grapefruit, removing all pith. Thinly slice grapefruit. Discard seeds. Place fruit in a shallow bowl. Sprinkle sugar and Grand Marnier over grapefruit. Cover and refrigerate 2 hours. Strain grapefruit, reserving juice in a bowl. Stir honey into juice. Divide grapefruit between 4 individual plates. Pour honey mixture over fruit. Decorate each serving with 2 fresh or maraschino cherries. Makes 4 servings.

Orange Salad

4 oranges
1/3 cup sugar
1/3 cup water
1/2 cup grenadine syrup
1 tablespoon Cointreau
1 tablespoon fresh mint leaves, if
**   desired**

Wash and dry oranges. Remove a thin layer of peel, taking care not to include any pith. Place peel in a small saucepan with sugar and water. Bring to a boil; simmer over low heat 5 minutes. Strain syrup. Add grenadine and bring to a boil again. Remove from heat. Stir in Cointreau and mint, if used. Reserve a few mint leaves. Let syrup cool. Remove all pith from oranges. Thinly slice orange flesh and place in a shallow bowl. Pour syrup over oranges. Refrigerate 2 hours. If mint leaves are used, strain oranges before serving, reserving syrup. Discard marinated mint leaves. Pour syrup over orange salad. Decorate with reserved fresh mint leaves. Makes 4 servings.

Jamaican Fruit Salad

1 pineapple
2 limes
1 coconut
2 to 3 tablespoons sugar
1 tablespoon white rum
3 tablespoons lime juice
4 sprigs mint, if desired

Slice pineapple and cut tough outer peel off each slice. Cut flesh into strips, discarding any hard parts of the core. Wash and dry limes. Cut into thin slices. Puncture 3 holes in the 3 indentations at the top of the coconut. Pour out milk into a jug. Break open coconut with a cleaver or hammer. Remove flesh with a sharp knife; shred. Arrange lime slices in a semi-circle on 4 individual plates. Place pineapple in the center. Top with shredded coconut. In a small bowl, beat together sugar, 3 tablespoons coconut milk, rum and lime juice. Sprinkle dressing over salad. Garnish each serving with a mint sprig, if desired. Makes 4 servings.

Kiwi Salad with Orange Cream

6 kiwi
1/2 cup orange juice
2 to 3 tablespoons sugar
1 tablespoon curaçao liqueur
1/2 cup whipping cream
Grated peel of 1 orange
Generous pinch ground ginger
1 teaspoon pickled pink or green peppercorns, if desired

Thinly peel and slice kiwi. Place in a shallow bowl. In a small bowl, beat together 2 tablespoons orange juice, sugar and curaçao until sugar has dissolved. Sprinkle dressing over kiwi. Cover and refrigerate 2 hours. Arrange kiwi on 4 individual plates. In a small bowl, beat together cream, remaining orange juice, half the grated orange peel and ground ginger. Spoon orange cream onto fruit. Sprinkle remaining orange peel over the top. Sprinkle with pickled pink or green peppercorns, if desired. Makes 4 servings.

Cook's Tip

For a variation, use chopped pistachio nuts instead of peppercorns to garnish the kiwi.

Melon Salad

1 small honeydew melon
1 large Spanish onion
1/4 cup vegetable oil
1 tablespoon wine vinegar
1/4 teaspoon each salt, paprika and white pepper
1/2 cup port

Slice melon into 8 wedges. Remove and discard seeds; cut flesh into cubes. Cut onion in half. Slice or shred as thinly as possible. Place melon and onion in a bowl. In a small bowl, beat together oil, vinegar, salt, paprika and pepper. Pour dressing over melon mixture. Cover and refrigerate 20 minutes. To serve, pour port over salad.

Cook's Tip

For a variation, replace the onion with 1/2 head fennel, cut into fine strips.

Banana & Tomato Salad

4 medium tomatoes
2 bananas
Juice of 1 lemon
1/4 cup vegetable oil
Salt and black pepper
1/4 teaspoon curry powder
1/2 teaspoon pink peppercorns, if desired

Cut tomatoes into thin slices. Arrange tomatoes in a circle on a salad dish or 4 individual plates. Slice bananas. Arrange over tomato slices and sprinkle immediately with 1 teaspoon lemon juice to prevent discoloration. In a small bowl, beat together oil, remaining lemon juice, salt, pepper and curry powder. Pour dressing over salad. Crush pink peppercorns, if used. Sprinkle over salad. Makes 4 servings.

Cook's Tip

This salad tastes equally delicious if you replace one of the bananas with 4 ounces canned bamboo shoots. If you do this, the tomatoes and bananas should be peeled and diced, then combined with the bamboo shoots in a bowl. Stir in the dressing.

Spicy Fruit Salad

2 apples
2 tablespoons lemon juice
3 to 4 celery stalks
8 oz. canned mandarin-orange segments
4 oz. black grapes
1/4 chopped walnuts
1/4 chopped almonds
Generous 1/2 cup dairy sour cream
3 tablespoons mayonnaise
1 tablespoon chili sauce
Pinch each salt and sugar
1 small lettuce

Peel and quarter apples; remove cores. Thinly slice apples. Sprinkle with 1/2 tablespoon lemon juice to prevent discoloration. Dice celery. Drain mandarin-orange segments and cut in half. Halve grapes and remove seeds. Combine apples, celery, mandarin-orange segments and chopped nuts in a bowl. In a small bowl, beat together, sour cream, mayonnaise, chili sauce, remaining lemon juice, salt and sugar. Pour dressing over salad. Cover and refrigerate 15 minutes. Separate lettuce leaves. Line a salad bowl with lettuce. Arrange fruit salad over lettuce. Makes 4 servings.

Apple Salad with Rum Dressing

1 lb. apples
8 oz. green grapes
Juice of 1 lemon
1/2 cup white wine
1/4 cup sugar
1 tablespoon honey
Generous pinch each ground cinnamon and ginger
3 tablespoons white rum
1/3 cup fresh or packaged shredded coconut
4 dates

Peel and quarter apples; remove cores. Finely dice apples. Peel and halve grapes; remove seeds. Combine apples, grapes, lemon juice, white wine and sugar. Cover and let stand at room temperature 2 hours. Strain salad marinade into a small saucepan. Bring marinade to a boil. Simmer over low heat until liquid is reduced by half. Stir in honey; cool. Add cinnamon, ginger and rum. Pour dressing over fruit salad. Arrange salad in 4 individual salad bowls or empty coconut shells. Sprinkle coconut over the top. Garnish each serving with a date. Makes 4 servings.

Apple & Orange Salad

3 medium apples
Juice of 1 lemon
1 lb. oranges
2 oz. almond paste or marzipan
1 tablespoon honey
3 tablespoons Bénédictine liqueur
1/2 cup whipping cream
1/2 cup chopped walnuts

Peel and quarter apples; remove cores. Thinly slice apples. Sprinkle with lemon juice to prevent discoloration. Peel and slice oranges, taking care to remove all pith. Cut each slice into 8 pieces. Remove seeds. Combine apples and oranges in a large bowl. In a medium bowl, beat together almond paste or marzipan, honey, Bénédictine and cream. Stir mixture into fruit. Cover and let stand 15 minutes. Arrange salad in a serving bowl. Sprinkle walnuts over salad. Makes 4 servings.

Plum & Ginger Salad

1 lb. ripe plums
4 pieces preserved ginger in syrup or crystallized ginger
1/2 cup whipping cream
2 to 3 tablespoons brandy
2 tablespoons powdered sugar
Generous pinch ground ginger

Scald plums briefly in boiling water; plunge into cold water. Drain and remove skins. Halve and pit plums. Place in a bowl. Drain preserved ginger, if used. Cut ginger into thin strips. Stir into plums. In a medium bowl, beat together cream, brandy, powdered sugar and ground ginger. Pour dressing into the center of the plums. Cover and refrigerate 30 minutes. To serve, stir dressing into plums. Makes 4 servings.

Cook's Tip

You can add extra spice to the dressing by beating 1 tablespoon preserved-ginger syrup into the cream and brandy. Syrup will sweeten the dressing so powdered sugar can be omitted, or stirred in, according to taste.

Fall Fruit Salad

2 apples
2 pears
2 teaspoons lemon juice
8 oz. plums
4 oz. green grapes
4 oz. black grapes
2 cups walnuts
3 tablespoons sugar
Juice of 2 oranges
2 to 3 tablespoons kirsch

Quarter apples and pears; remove cores. Slice quarters into thin wedges. Sprinkle with lemon juice. Cut plums into quarters; remove pits. Combine apples, pears, plums, grapes and walnuts in a bowl. Mix sugar and orange juice in a small saucepan. Bring to a boil. Simmer over low heat, stirring constantly, until syrup begins to form. Cool. Add kirsch. Pour dressing over salad. Makes 4 servings.

Cook's Tip

This makes an excellent fruit salad for a children's party if you leave out the alcohol.

Grape & Walnut Salad

1 lb. green grapes
1/3 cup sweet sherry
1 small lettuce
1/2 cup chopped walnuts
1/4 cup fresh lime juice
Generous pinch salt
1/3 cup walnut or sunflower oil
2 to 3 tablespoons sugar
1/2 teaspoon pickled pink or green peppercorns, if desired

Peel grapes. Place in a large bowl. Pour sherry over grapes. Cover and refrigerate 2 hours. Remove outer leaves from lettuce, reserving them for use in another salad. Cut inner lettuce leaves into fine strips. Stir lettuce and walnuts into grape mixture. In a small bowl, beat together lime juice, salt and walnut or sunflower oil. Add sugar to taste. Pour dressing over salad. Crush peppercorns, if used. Sprinkle over salad before serving. Makes 4 servings.

Raspberry & Kiwi Salad

8 oz. raspberries
3 tablespoons sugar
1 pear
Juice of 1/2 lemon
1 tablespoon Poire William or kirsch liqueur
2 canned peach halves
4 canned apricot halves
4 kumquats or 1/4 cup drained canned mandarin-orange segments
2 kiwi
Generous 1/2 cup whipping cream
1 tablespoon powdered sugar
Few drops vanilla extract

Place raspberries in a large bowl. Sprinkle with sugar. Peel and quarter pear; remove core. Cut pear into thin wedges. Place in a shallow bowl. Sprinkle with lemon juice and Poire William or kirsch. Let stand 10 minutes. Drain peach and apricot halves. Cut into slices. Slice kumquats, if used. Mix pear, peach, apricots and kumquats or mandarins with raspberries. Thinly peel and slice kiwi. Arrange in a ring on each of 4 individual plates. Top with fruit salad. In a medium bowl, beat cream and powdered sugar. Add vanilla to taste. To serve, spoon dressing over salads. Makes 4 servings.

Chinese Fruit Salad

8 oz. strawberries
3 tablespoons sugar
8 oz. canned lychees
8 oz. canned mandarin-orange segments
1 tablespoon lemon juice
3 tablespoons arrack or Cointreau
1/4 cup whipping cream
1 teaspoon powdered sugar
1 tablespoon chopped pistachio nuts, if desired

Place strawberries in a bowl. Sprinkle with sugar. Drain lychees and mandarin-orange segments. Mix with strawberries. Sprinkle lemon juice and 1 tablespoon arrack or Cointreau over fruit. Cover and let stand 15 minutes. Arrange fruit in a serving dish or on individual plates. In a medium bowl, beat cream and powdered sugar. Stir in remaining arrack or Cointreau. To serve, spoon dressing over fruit salad. Top with chopped pistachio nuts, if desired. Makes 4 servings.

Sicilian Salad

1 small honeydew melon
2 persimmons
2 prickly pears
2 oranges
Juice of 1 lemon
1/2 cup white Corvo or other dry
    white wine
1/3 cup sugar

Cut melon in wedges; remove seeds and rind. Cut melon flesh in long thin slices. Peel and slice persimmons, prickly pears and oranges. Place fruit pieces in a medium bowl. Sprinkle with lemon juice. Cover and refrigerate 1 hour. In a small saucepan, combine Corvo or white wine and sugar. Cook over medium heat until reduced by half. Cool slightly. Pour over fruit. Makes 4 servings.

Caribbean Salad

1 small pineapple
1 papaya
2 fresh guavas or 4 canned guava
    halves
2 limes
1/2 cup sugar
Juice of 1 orange
1/2 cinnamon stick or 1/2
    teaspoon ground cinnamon
1 vanilla pod or few drops vanilla
    extract
Pinch grated nutmeg
Generous pinch ground ginger
1 tablespoon white rum

Slice pineapple. With a sharp knife, cut around each slice just inside the skin. Remove skin; discard. Cut papaya and fresh guavas in pieces. Drain and slice canned guavas. Thinly slice limes. Combine fruit in a medium bowl. In a small saucepan, combine sugar, orange juice, cinnamon and vanilla. Simmer over low heat, stirring constantly, until sugar dissolves. Strain sugar mixture; cool slightly. Season sugar mixture with nutmeg and ginger. Stir in rum. Pour sugar mixture over fruit. Refrigerate. Serve salad very cold. Makes 4 servings.

Summer Fruit Salad

1 honeydew melon
1 banana
Juice of 1 lemon
1 apple
1 peach
2 apricots
4 oz. cherries
4 oz. strawberries
4 oz. raspberries
8 oz. green grapes
1/3 cup sugar
2/3 cup Malaga or Madeira wine, or port

Slice off 1 end of melon. Scoop flesh out of the slice; discard rind. Carefully scoop flesh out of the rest of the melon. Dice melon flesh. Cut a zig-zag pattern around top edge of melon shell. Slice banana; sprinkle immediately with a little lemon juice. Peel and slice apple; sprinkle with remaining lemon juice. Peel peach. Finely dice peach and apricots. Remove pits from cherries and hulls from strawberries. In a medium bowl, combine all fruits. In a small bowl, beat together sugar and Malaga or Madeira, or port. Pour mixture over fruits. Refrigerate 1 hour. Spoon fruit salad into melon shell. Place on crushed ice cubes to serve. Serve with hot Sweet-Wine Sauce, page 19, if desired. Makes 4 servings.

Fruit Salad in Pineapple

1 pineapple
3 kiwi
4 oz. strawberries
4 oz. cherries
4 oz. grapes
8 oz. canned mandarin-orange segments
Juice of 1 lemon
6 tablespoons sugar
1 tablespoon maraschino or kirsch liqueur
2/3 cup whipping cream
Few drops vanilla extract
1 maraschino cherry

Cut a lengthwise wedge from pineapple, leaving an opening measuring about one-third of the pineapple. Peel this wedge; discard rind and firm core. Dice pineapple flesh. Scoop remaining flesh from pineapple. Dice flesh, removing core if tough. Peel and thinly slice kiwi. Remove hulls from strawberries and pits from cherries. Cut strawberries, grapes and cherries in half. Drain mandarin-orange segments. In a large bowl, gently combine all fruits. In a small saucepan, bring lemon juice and 1/4 cup sugar to a boil. Simmer, stirring constantly, until sugar dissolves. Cool slightly. Add maraschino or kirsch liqueur; stir to blend. Sprinkle sugar mixture over salad. Cover and refrigerate 1 hour. In a medium bowl, whip cream with remaining sugar and vanilla until stiff. Spoon fruit salad into pineapple shell. Spoon or pipe whipped-cream mixture over top. Decorate with a maraschino cherry. Makes 4 servings.

Stuffed Watermelon

1 small watermelon
3 oranges
Juice of 1/2 lemon
1/4 cup sugar
1 tablespoon white rum
1 tablespoon honey
4 scoops vanilla ice cream
1 teaspoon chopped pistachio nuts, if desired

Slice one-third off watermelon. Using a spoon, scoop flesh out of slice and remaining melon. Cut melon flesh in small strips. Peel 2 oranges; pull into sections. Remove thin membrane from orange sections; cut sections in small pieces. In a medium bowl, stir together melon and orange pieces. Cut a decorative scallop edge around top of melon shell. Fill melon with melon mixture. Squeeze juice from remaining orange. In a small saucepan, combine orange juice, lemon juice and sugar. Bring to a boil, stirring constantly; then simmer until sugar has dissolved. Cool slightly. Stir in rum and honey. Pour orange-juice mixture over fruit mixture. Top fruit with scoops of ice cream. Sprinkle with nuts, if desired. Makes 4 servings.

Avocado Fruit Salad

2 avocados
Juice of 1/2 lemon
4 small yellow tomatoes
3 peaches
4 oz. strawberries
1/4 cup sugar
2 teaspoons fresh lime juice
1 tablespoon port
1 teaspoon pickled green peppercorns, if desired

Cut avocados in half lengthwise; remove pits. With a melon-baller or small spoon, scoop out avocado flesh to within 1/2 inch of shell. Brush each avocado half with lemon juice. Place avocado flesh in a large bowl; sprinkle with remaining lemon juice. Cut tomatoes in thin wedges. Peel peaches; cut in thin wedges. Add tomato and peach wedges to avocado pieces. Gently mix together. Remove hulls from strawberries. In a small bowl, crush strawberries using a fork. Add sugar, lime juice and port. Beat well. Stir in pickled green peppercorns, if desired. Spoon fruit salad into avocado shells. Top with strawberry dressing. Makes 4 servings.

Salad Buffet with Assorted Dressings

For a large buffet, you will need between 6 and 8 different salad ingredients. Choose any of the following, depending on what is in season. Keep texture and color in mind: round and romaine lettuce, iceberg lettuce, Belgian endive, red endive, curly endive, dandelion leaves, watercress, sliced tomatoes and cucumber, radishes, onion rings, green and black olives, hard-cooked eggs, canned corn, green, red and yellow bell peppers cut in rings, celery, chopped fresh herbs, cooked peas and diced fruit. Wash and thoroughly drain all salad ingredients. Arrange separately in bowls or on platters as preferred. Serve with a choice of dressings.

Blue-Cheese Dressing
4 oz. blue cheese (Stilton, Roquefort, dolcelatte)
1 tablespoon whipping cream or dairy sour cream
1 tablespoon white-wine vinegar
3 tablespoons mayonnaise
Salt and white pepper

In a small bowl, crumble cheese with a fork. Stir in whipping cream or sour cream, vinegar, mayonnaise, salt and white pepper. Blue-Cheese Dressing goes especially well with all varieties of lettuce.

Egg & Herb Dressing
4 hard-cooked eggs
1/4 cup vegetable oil
1 tablespoon wine vinegar
Salt and pepper
3 tablespoons chopped fresh
   mixed herbs

Finely dice eggs. In a small bowl, beat together oil, vinegar, salt and pepper. Stir in eggs and herbs. Serve with tomato or cucumber salad.

French Dressing
1/4 cup lemon juice
Salt and pepper
1/4 teaspoon sugar
1/4 teaspoon dry mustard
2/3 cup olive oil

In a small bowl or jar, combine lemon juice, salt, pepper, sugar and dry mustard. Gradually mix in oil, beating constantly. French Dressing goes well with Belgian endive, red endive and all kinds of lettuce.

Yogurt Dressing

Generous 1/2 cup plain yogurt
3 tablespoons lemon juice
1 tablespoon vegetable oil
Salt and pepper
3 tablespoons chopped fresh
   mixed herbs

In a small bowl, combine yogurt, lemon juice and oil. Beat until creamy. Stir in salt, pepper and herbs. Yogurt Dressing goes well with Belgian endive, lettuce and hard-cooked eggs.

Thousand Island Dressing

2 strips canned pimiento
1 cup mayonnaise
1/4 cup ketchup
1 teaspoon minced green bell
   pepper
1 teaspoon grated onion
1/4 teaspoon salt
Generous pinch paprika

Drain and dice pimiento. In a small bowl, combine all ingredients. Stir to mix well. Serve with lettuce and Belgian endive, tomato or dandelion.

Sherry Dressing

1 egg
3 tablespoons sugar
3 tablespoons dry sherry
1/4 teaspoon salt
1 tablespoon melted butter
1/3 cup orange juice
3 tablespoons lemon juice
1/3 cup whipping cream

In a small bowl, beat egg. Gradually beat in sugar, sherry, salt, butter, orange juice and lemon juice. Transfer mixture to a small saucepan. Heat very gently, stirring constantly, until it begins to thicken. Do not allow mixture to boil. Remove from heat; cool slightly. In another small bowl, beat whipping cream until firm peaks form. Fold whipped cream into juice mixture. Sherry Dressing goes well with celery, red endive, canned corn and any kind of fruit salad.

Cook's Tip

Make your salad buffet more substantial by serving diced Cheddar, Edam, Emmentaler or other cheeses; cold ham, beef, chicken or pork; rolled anchovies; rollmop herring; shrimp or any kind of smoked fish. Serve with a selection of different breads.

Shrimp in Aspic

12 oz. thawed frozen or canned shrimp
1 cup clarified Fish Stock, page 17
2/3 cup dry white wine
Salt and pepper
1/4 oz. gelatin
1 large bunch dill or parsley
2/3 cup mayonnaise
1 teaspoon lemon juice
1 teaspoon curry paste
1 teaspoon chopped fresh dill or parsley
Generous pinch white pepper
3 tablespoons whipping cream

Drain shrimp. In a medium saucepan, combine stock, wine, salt and pepper. Heat stock mixture over medium heat. Pour 1/4 cup hot stock mixture into a small bowl. Set bowl in a pan of hot water. Sprinkle gelatin in 1/4 cup hot stock mixture. Stir until gelatin dissolves. Return gelatin mixture to stock. Pour a thin layer of gelatin mixture into a 1-quart mold; refrigerate until set. Finely chop dill or parsley. Layer dill or parsley and shrimp in mold, pouring gelatin mixture between layers. Allow each layer to set in refrigerator or freezer before adding another layer. When layers are completed, refrigerate mold 2 to 4 hours or until completely set. To serve, dip mold in hot water for a few seconds. Unmold aspic on a plate. In a small bowl, beat together mayonnaise, lemon juice, curry paste, chopped dill or parsley, white pepper and cream. Serve with aspic. Makes 4 servings.

Tomato & Fish Mold

1-3/4 cups water
1 small onion, peeled
3 tablespoons lemon juice
1/2 teaspoon salt
4 white peppercorns
1 small bay leaf
8 oz. white-fish fillets
3/4 cup tomato juice
6 tablespoons white wine
2 teaspoons vinegar
1/4 teaspoon each celery salt and dried tarragon
1/2 teaspoon paprika
3 tablespoons warm water
1/4 oz. gelatin
2 oz. cooked peas
Lettuce, lemon slices, dill

In a medium saucepan, combine 1-3/4 cups water, onion, lemon juice, salt, peppercorns and bay leaf. Add fish; poach gently 10 minutes. Remove from heat; cool slightly in poaching liquid. Cut fish in large pieces, trimming away any skin and bones. Strain poaching liquid, reserving 3/4 cup. In medium saucepan, combine 3/4 cup reserved poaching liquid, tomato juice, wine, vinegar, celery salt, tarragon and paprika. Heat over medium heat, but do not boil. Pour 3 tablespoons warm water in a bowl. Set in a pan of hot water. Sprinkle gelatin over 3 tablespoons warm water. Stir until gelatin dissolves. Add gelatin mixture to hot stock mixture. Pour a thin layer of gelatin mixture in a 2-cup mold; refrigerate until set. Fill mold with alternate layers of fish and peas, pouring gelatin liquid between layers and allowing each layer to set firmly before adding another. Refrigerate mold until completely set. To serve, dip mold in hot water for a few seconds. Unmold aspic on a plate. Garnish with lettuce, lemon slices and dill. Makes 4 servings.

Salmon in Riesling

3 cups salted water
10 peppercorns
Juice of 1 lemon
4 (5-oz.) fresh salmon steaks
1 lb. fresh or canned asparagus
1/2 oz. gelatin
3/4 oz. truffles, if desired
6 small tomatoes
1 egg white, beaten
2 cups Riesling or other dry white wine

Bring salted water, peppercorns and lemon juice to a boil in a medium saucepan over medium heat. Add salmon; poach gently 10 minutes. Remove salmon; drain well and dry. Wrap salmon in foil. Lightly scrape lower stems of fresh asparagus; cut in 1-inch lengths. Simmer in salmon stock until asparagus is tender. Lift out asparagus; drain and cool slightly. Drain canned asparagus. Unwrap salmon steaks; place each steak on a soup plate. Sprinkle with asparagus and truffles, if desired. Cut tomatoes in half. Place 3 tomato halves on each plate. Clarify salmon stock by bringing stock to a boil. Add egg white; simmer 2 minutes. Remove from heat; let stand until egg white gathers on top of stock. Strain stock through a piece of cheesecloth or a sieve lined with a triple thickness of paper towel. Measure 1 cup clarified stock; place in a bowl. Stand bowl in a pan of hot water. Sprinkle with gelatin; stir until dissolved. Add wine. Pour gelatin liquid into individual soup plates. Refrigerate until firmly set. Makes 4 servings.

Haddock Mold

1 lb. white-fish trimmings
2 qts. water
1/2 teaspoon salt
Juice of 1-1/2 lemons
Selection of fresh vegetables, chopped
1-3/4 lbs. haddock fillets
1 (6-1/4-oz.) can shrimp
3 hard-cooked eggs
7 oz. carrots
1 cup cooked peas
1 egg white, beaten
1/2 cup dry white wine
1/4 cup warm water
1/2 oz. gelatin
Few dill or parsley sprigs

For the stock, place fish trimmings in a large saucepan. Cover with 2 quarts water. Add salt, half the lemon juice and chopped vegetables. Simmer 20 to 30 minutes. Sprinkle haddock with remaining lemon juice. Poach haddock in 1 quart salted water 10 minutes. Drain haddock; cool slightly. Remove haddock skin; cut fish in large pieces. Rinse shrimp; drain well. Cut each egg in 6 wedges. Cut carrots in thin strips. Blanch carrots in a small amount of boiling water 2 minutes; drain well. In a large bowl, combine haddock, shrimp, eggs, peas and carrots. Divide haddock mixture between 4 soup plates. Strain fish stock. Clarify stock with egg white, see opposite in Salmon in Riesling. Strain stock again. Boil until reduced to about 1 quart. Remove from heat. Add wine. Pour about 1/4 cup warm water into a bowl. Set bowl in a pan of hot water. Sprinkle gelatin over warm water. Stir until dissolved. Add to stock. Pour liquid into 4 soup plates. Refrigerate until firm. Garnish with dill or parsley. Makes 4 servings.

Chicken & Vegetable Mold

1 onion
2 large carrots
1 (2-1/2-lb.) stewing chicken
1 teaspoon salt
Water
3/4 oz. gelatin
3 tablespoons vinegar
1/4 teaspoon Worcestershire sauce
Pinch pepper
4 oz. canned asparagus tips
2 oz. canned sliced mushrooms
2 hard-cooked eggs
2 tomatoes
1 large cooked carrot
1 large dill pickle
1 cup cooked peas
Salad seasoning or coarsely
    ground pepper and celery seed

Cut onion in half. Trim carrots. Place onion, carrots, chicken and salt in a large saucepan. Cover with water. Bring to a boil; reduce heat and simmer 1 hour. Remove chicken. Strain stock; cool slightly. Reheat 1 quart stock, but do not boil. Pour 3 tablespoons hot stock in a bowl. Place bowl in a pan of hot water. Sprinkle gelatin over hot stock. Stir until dissolved. Return gelatin mixture to stock. Add vinegar, Worcestershire sauce and pepper. Coat a 1-quart soufflé or au gratin dish with a little gelatin mixture. Refrigerate until firm. Remove skin and bones from cooled chicken. Cut meat in small pieces. Drain asparagus and sliced mushrooms. Slice eggs. Slice tomatoes, cooked carrot and pickle. Combine chicken, asparagus, mushrooms, eggs, tomatoes, carrot, pickle and peas. Place chicken mixture in gelatin-coated soufflé dish. Pour remaining gelatin mixture over chicken mixture. Sprinkle mold with mixed salad seasoning or coarsely ground pepper and celery seed. Refrigerate until firm. Serve with choice of flavored mayonnaise, pages 12 and 13. Makes 4 to 6 servings.

Ham & Vegetable Mold

1 qt. salted water
1 (10-oz.) pkg. frozen mixed
   vegetables
3 to 4 large carrots
1 tablespoon bone-marrow jelly
Generous pinch each salt and
   grated nutmeg
3/4 oz. gelatin
1 cup fat-free stock
1 cup white wine
1/4 cup vinegar
1 hard-cooked egg, sliced
Few chives and celery leaves
8 oz. sliced ham

Bring 1 quart salted water to a boil in a small saucepan. Add mixed vegetables; cook 12 minutes. Drain vegetables reserving liquid; cool slightly. In a small saucepan, combine reserved vegetable liquid, carrots and bone-marrow jelly. Simmer 20 minutes. Drain carrots. Puree carrots in a blender or food processor. Season with salt and nutmeg. Heat carrot puree over low heat. Sprinkle a fourth of gelatin over carrot puree, stirring until gelatin has dissolved. In a medium saucepan, heat stock, wine and vinegar. Pour 3 tablespoons hot stock mixture in a bowl. Place bowl in a pan of hot water. Sprinkle remaining gelatin over hot stock. Stir until dissolved. Return stock mixture to remaining stock. Line a 1-quart mold with a thin layer of stock mixture. Refrigerate until firm. Arrange egg slices, chives and celery leaves on top. Pour in another layer of stock mixture. Refrigerate until firm. Spread carrot puree over aspic; refrigerate until firm. Build the rest of the mold in layers of mixed vegetables and slices of ham. Pour aspic between layers. Allow each layer to become firm before adding the next. Refrigerate completed mold until very firm. Makes 6 to 8 servings.

Prawns in Aspic

12 oz. frozen or canned prawns or medium shrimp
1 tablespoon lemon juice
1 small cauliflower
6 oz. frozen peas
6 oz. frozen carrots
2-1/4 cups fat-free stock
1/2 oz. gelatin
2 cups white wine
Generous pinch each salt, white pepper, sugar and red (cayenne
 pepper
1 (11-oz.) can whole-kernel corn
7 oz. canned asparagus tips
Lettuce leaves

Place frozen prawns or shrimp in a bowl. Sprinkle with lemon juice. Cover and thaw 1 hour at room temperature. Or, drain canned prawns or shrimp. Rinse in cold water; drain well. Cut cauliflower in flowerets; trim off any excess stems. Place cauliflowerets in a steamer in a medium saucepan. Steam over unsalted water 10 to 15 minutes. Plunge cauliflower in cold water; drain well. Cool slightly. Bring 1 cup salted water to a boil in a small saucepan. Add peas and carrots. Cover and simmer 8 minutes; drain well. Plunge into cold water. Drain and cool. Heat 1/3 cup stock. Pour heated stock in a medium bowl. Place bowl of stock in a pan of boiling water. Sprinkle gelatin over heated stock. Stir until gelatin dissolves. Add remaining stock, white wine, salt, white pepper, sugar and red pepper. Season to taste, adding a few drops of lemon juice, if desired. Rinse a 1-1/2- to 2-quart mold with cold water. Pour 1/2 inch gelatin mixture in mold. Refrigerate until firm. Drain corn and aspar-agus tips; mix with cauliflowerets, peas and carrots. Fill mold with alternate spoonfuls of prawns or shrimp and vegetables. Pour some gelatin mixture in mold between each spoonful of meat or vegetables. Refrigerate each time until firm. Continue this process until mold is full. Refrigerate a few hours until firmly set. To serve, arrange lettuce leaves on a platter. Dip mold in hot water for a few seconds. Unmold aspic on lettuce-lined platter. Makes 10 servings.

Cook's Tip

For full instructions on making and using an aspic, see page 17.

Summer Salad Mold

2 cups salted water
8 white peppercorns
Large bunch fresh mixed herbs (parsley, sage, chervil, tarragon, thyme)
1 bunch parsley
1 small cauliflower
8 oz. frozen peas
1/2 oz. gelatin
About 2 cups dry white wine
Generous pinch each salt, white pepper and sugar
Few drops lemon juice
2 hard-cooked eggs
1/2 red or yellow bell pepper
Small bunch dill or chives
Few mint sprigs

Bring 2 cups salted water to a boil in a medium saucepan. Add peppercorns and mixed herbs. Cover and simmer 10 minutes. Strain liquid; reserving in another pan. Cut cauliflower in flowerets; trim off any excess stem. Place flowerets in herb stock. Cover and simmer 15 minutes. Lift flowerets from stock and plunge in cold water; reserve stock. Drain flowerets and cool slightly. Place peas in reserved stock. Cover and cook 3 minutes. Lift peas from stock; plunge in cold water. Drain peas and cool. Sprinkle gelatin over stock. Stir until dissolved. Add enough white wine to make 4-1/2 cups liquid, adding water, if necessary. Season with salt, pepper, sugar and lemon juice. Cool slightly. Rinse a 1-1/2- to 2-quart mold with cold water. Pour gelatin mixture in mold to a depth of 1/4 inch. Refrigerate until firm. Slice eggs. Cut red or yellow pepper in thin strips. Finely chop all but a few chives, if desired. Arrange egg, pepper strips, dill sprigs or chopped chives on top of mold. Reserve a few dill sprigs or chives for garnish. Pour a small amount of gelatin mixture over egg slices. Refrigerate until firm. Add half the peas followed by cauliflower. Cover with gelatin mixture. Refrigerate until firm. Remove parsley sprigs from stems, keeping a few sprigs on 1 side for garnish. Place parsley on top of cauliflower layer. Top with remaining gelatin mixture. Refrigerate 3 to 4 hours or until firm. To serve, loosen edges with a sharp knife. Dip mold in hot water for a few seconds. Turn out on a plate. Garnish with remaining parsley, dill or chives and mint sprigs. Makes 10 servings.

Party Eggs

10 hard-cooked eggs

Fillings for 4 egg halves at a time:
3 tablespoons cream cheese
1 tablespoon chopped fresh mixed herbs
3 tablespoons milk
Pinch salt

3 tablespoons cottage cheese
1 tablespoon finely grated carrot
1 teaspoon ground hazelnuts
Pinch each salt and pepper

3 tablespoons cream cheese
1 teaspoon mild curry powder
1 teaspoon mashed avocado
1 teaspoon lemon juice
1 tablespoon milk
Pinch salt

3 tablespoons farmer's cheese or ricotta cheese
1 teaspoon chopped fresh dill or parsley
Grated lemon peel
Pinch salt

3 tablespoons farmer's cheese or ricotta cheese
1 tablespoon tomato paste
1/2 teaspoon paprika
Pinch salt

Garnishes:
Canned baby sweet-corn cobs and pickled green peppercorns
Chilies and parsley
Black olives and parsley
Rolled anchovies, diced tomato and capers
Sliced kiwi and maraschino cherries
Sliced lemon, prawns or shrimp, and dill or parsley
Smoked-salmon rolls and dill or parsley
Lumpfish caviar and alfalfa sprouts
Pickles and sliced mild chilies
Pimiento-stuffed olives and alfalfa sprouts

Cut each egg in half lengthwise. Remove yolks. In a small bowl, combine yolks from 4 egg halves with choice of filling ingredients. Spoon or pipe filling into egg halves. Garnish as shown. A choice of 2 garnishes is shown for each of the 4 basic fillings.

Piquant Eggs with Bean Salad

Eggs:
3 hard-cooked eggs
3 tablespoons mayonnaise
1/4 cup soft butter
Salt and freshly ground black pepper
1 tablespoon brandy
1 teaspoon pickled green peppercorns, if desired

Salad:
8 oz. green beans
1/4 cup vegetable oil
8 oz. calf's liver
2 shallots
Small bunch parsley
1 tablespoon tarragon vinegar
Sprig watercress or other greens

Cut eggs in half crosswise. Remove yolks. Press yolks through a sieve into a small bowl. Beat in mayonnaise, butter, salt, pepper and brandy. Place yolk mixture in a pastry bag fitted with a star tip. Pipe yolk filling into egg whites. Garnish eggs with pickled green peppercorns, if desired. For the salad, cook beans in a medium saucepan of boiling salted water 10 minutes. Drain; cool slightly. Heat 1 tablespoon oil in a small skillet. Slice liver in thin strips. Fry liver strips in hot oil 2 to 3 minutes. Finely chop shallots and parsley. In a small bowl, beat together remaining oil, vinegar, chopped shallots and parsley. Season to taste. Place beans and liver together in center of a platter. Sprinkle with dressing. Arrange stuffed eggs around salad. Garnish with watercress or other greens. Makes 6 servings.

Party Egg Platter

10 hard-cooked eggs
1/2 cup mayonnaise
Salt and pepper
1 tablespoon chopped parsley
Juice of 1/2 lemon
3 tablespoons vegetable oil

Suggested Garnishes:
Few lettuce leaves, sprigs of young spinach or watercress, small
    onion rings, anchovy fillets, ham slices, smoked-salmon slices,
    prawns or medium shrimp, bottled or canned mussels, olives,
    sliced cooked carrot, pickled green peppercorns, chilies, canned
    baby sweet-corn cobs, lemon slices, parsley and dill

Cut each egg in half lengthwise. Remove egg yolks; press yolks through a sieve. In a small bowl, combine sieved egg yolks, mayonnaise, salt and pepper. Divide yolk mixture in half. Stir parsley in 1 yolk portion. Place each portion separately in a pastry bags fitted with a star tip. Fill 10 egg whites with plain mayonnaise mixture. Fill remaining 10 egg whites with parsley mayonnaise. Arrange eggs on a platter. Garnish with suggested toppings. Tear lettuce leaves in strips. In a medium bowl, combine lettuce leaves and any remaining garnishes. In a small bowl, beat together lemon juice and oil. Season to taste. Pour lemon-juice mixture over salad ingredients. Toss lightly to coat. Arrange salad in center of platter. Makes 20 servings.

Hard-Cooked Eggs with Sauces

Allow 2 eggs per person

Russian Sauce
1 red bell pepper
1 green bell pepper
1 yellow bell pepper
Large bunch chives
1 cup dairy sour cream
1 teaspoon paprika
Dash Tabasco sauce
1 teaspoon horseradish sauce
1 (2-oz.) jar lumpfish caviar

Dice bell peppers. Finely chop chives. In a medium bowl, combine diced peppers, chopped chives, sour cream, paprika, Tabasco, horseradish sauce and half the lumpfish caviar. Spoon remaining lumpfish caviar on top.

Mushroom Sauce
8 oz. mushrooms
2 leeks
2 onions
4 oz. bacon
1 tablespoon butter

Thinly slice mushrooms and leeks. Peel and finely dice onions. Cut bacon in pieces. Fry until most of fat cooks out of bacon. Add butter, leeks and onions. Cook 4 to 5 minutes. Add mushrooms and continue cooking 6 minutes. Cool and serve.

Cheese Sauce
4 oz. cottage cheese
2 oz. Stilton cheese
Juice of 1 lemon
Salt
1 teaspoon cranberry sauce, if desired

Sieve cottage cheese and Stilton into a bowl. Beat with lemon juice until creamy. Season to taste with salt. Serve garnished with cranberry sauce, if desired.

Capri Sauce
Large bunch fresh mixed herbs
2 canned anchovy fillets
1 tablespoon capers
10 pimiento-stuffed olives
2 egg yolks
1 teaspoon hot mustard
1/4 cup wine vinegar
Salt and pepper
1/2 cup vegetable oil
2 tomatoes

Finely chop herbs, anchovy fillets, capers and olives. In a medium bowl, beat egg yolks with mustard, vinegar, salt and pepper. Beat in oil, a few drops at a time. Stir in chopped herbs, anchovy fillets, capers and olives. Chop tomatoes; stir into sauce.

Cook's Tip

Cottage Cheese with Herbs Spread and Cottage-Cheese Salad Spread, page 35, also make delicious sauces to go with eggs, and are shown above.

Egg Tartlets with Liver Pâté

4 hard-cooked eggs
Bunch fresh mixed herbs (sage, parsley, dill, chives, lovage) or 2
** teaspoons dried mixed herbs**
1/4 cup soft butter
3 tablespoons Dijon-style mustard
Salt and pepper
8 small cooked tartlet shells
4 oz. smooth liver pâté
2 slices canned truffles, if desired
8 small dill sprigs, if desired

Slice each egg in half crosswise. Remove yolks; place in a medium bowl. Finely chop herbs. Add herbs, butter, mustard, salt and pepper to yolks. Beat until smooth and creamy. Place yolk mixture in a pastry bag fitted with a star tip. Pipe mixture in each tartlet shell. Place 1 egg-white half in center of each tartlet. Beat pâté until light and fluffy. Spoon pâté into egg whites. Finely dice truffles, if desired. Sprinkle over pâté. Garnish each tartlet with a sprig of dill, if desired. Makes 8 servings.

Cook's Tip

To make your tartlet shells, see Chicken Tartlets, page 57.

Egg Tartlets with Ham Salad

8 oz. cooked ham
1 crisp apple
1 banana
2 teaspoons lemon juice
1/4 cup mayonnaise
3 tablespoons whipping cream
2 to 3 teaspoons mild curry powder
Pinch each salt and sugar
8 small cooked tartlet shells
4 hard-cooked eggs
4 slices smoked salmon
Few tarragon leaves, if desired

Finely dice ham. Peel apple; cut in thin strips. Dice banana. In a small bowl, combine diced ham and banana and apple strips. Sprinkle ham mixture with 1 teaspoon lemon juice. In a second small bowl, beat together mayonnaise, cream, remaining lemon juice, curry powder, salt and sugar. Adjust seasoning to taste. Pour mayonnaise mixture over ham mixture. Stir to coat well. Spoon salad mixture into tartlet shells. Cut each egg in half lengthwise. Place an egg half on each tart. Cut salmon slices in half lengthwise. Roll salmon pieces. Top each egg half with a salmon roll. Garnish with tarragon leaves, if desired. Makes 8 servings.

Pickled Eggs

2 to 2-1/2 cups vinegar
1 teaspoon mustard seeds
1 teaspoon black peppercorns
3 whole cloves
1 cinnamon stick
2 bay leaves
12 hard-cooked eggs

In a medium saucepan, combine vinegar, mustard seeds, peppercorns, whole cloves, cinnamon stick and bay leaves. Bring to a boil. Cover and simmer over low heat 10 minutes. Place shelled eggs in a tall jar or container with a tight-fitting lid. Slightly cool vinegar mixture. Pour vinegar mixture over eggs. Let stand to cool. Cover jar with a piece of plastic wrap, held in place with a rubber band. Seal jar completely. Place sealed jar in refrigerator. Marinate 2 to 3 days. Eggs will absorb marinade flavor. Serve egg sliced in sandwiches or with a sauce, page 126.

Cook's Tip

Use very fresh eggs for pickling. Eggs should be no more than a week old.

Eggs in Brine with Tomato Chutney

Chutney:
1 lb. tomatoes
2 medium, red bell peppers
3 onions
2/3 cup red-wine vinegar
3/4 cup brown sugar
3/4 teaspoon salt
1 teaspoon Dijon-style mustard
1 teaspoon ground allspice
1/2 teaspoon paprika

Eggs:
1-1/2 qts. water
1/4 cup salt
12 eggs

Peel and quarter tomatoes. Finely chop red peppers and onions. In a medium saucepan, combine tomatoes, chopped red peppers and onions. Add vinegar; bring to a boil. Reduce heat and simmer over low heat until mixture is pulpy and nearly all liquid has evaporated. Stir in sugar, salt, mustard, allspice and paprika. Cook vegetable mixture over high heat, stirring constantly, 8 minutes. Rinse two 1-pint jam jars in boiling water; dry jars well. Ladle hot chutney into jars. Cover jars. Cool and refrigerate. In a medium saucepan, bring water and salt to a boil. Carefully add eggs. Boil 10 to 12 minutes. Remove eggs from salt water, reserving salt water. Plunge eggs in cold water; drain well. Lightly tap shells. Allow salt water to cool. Place eggs in a large jar. Pour cooled salt water over eggs. Cover and refrigerate 2 to 3 days. Serve eggs with chutney.

Eggs with Orange Chutney

Chutney:
1 lb. cooking apples
2 oranges
2/3 cup raisins
1 cup brown sugar
1/4 teaspoon salt
1 teaspoon ground ginger
1/4 teaspoon ground nutmeg
2/3 cup red-wine vinegar
4 oz. cranberry sauce

Eggs:
2 qts. water
8 eggs
1-3/4 oz. loose tea leaves
1 tablespoon salt
1 tablespoon ground mixed spices

Peel and dice apples. Finely grate orange peel. Peel and thinly slice oranges. In a medium saucepan, combine apples, orange peel and slices, raisins, sugar, salt, ginger, nutmeg and vinegar. Bring to a boil. Reduce heat and cook, stirring frequently, 20 to 30 minutes or until reduced to a pulp. Stir in cranberry sauce. Rinse two 1-pint jars with boiling water; dry well. Fill jars with hot chutney. Cover each jar well. Cool and refrigerate. Cook eggs in a medium saucepan in boiling salted water 12 minutes. Drain eggs; plunge in cold water. Place eggs on a board. Roll eggs over board until shells have cracked all over. Bring 2 quarts water to a boil in medium saucepan. Add tea, salt and spices. Place unshelled eggs in water. Cover and simmer over low heat 10 minutes or until eggs have turned brown. Remove from heat. Let eggs stand in water 30 minutes. Drain and let dry. Serve with chutney.

Stuffed Cucumber

1 large cucumber
6 oz. canned golden plums
3/4 celeriac
1 large red apple
8 oz. freshly cooked or canned
 asparagus tips
1/4 cup mayonnaise
1/4 cup plain yogurt
1 teaspoon lemon juice
3/4 teaspoon salt
Pinch sugar
1 bunch lettuce

Cut a wedge from cucumber running down center, lengthwise, leaving a gap measuring one-third of the whole cucumber; reserve wedge. Scoop seeds out of both parts of cucumber. Scoop out cucumber flesh; cut cucumber flesh in pieces. Drain plums; cut in half and remove pits. Peel and finely dice celeriac. Dice apple. Drain canned asparagus. In a medium bowl, combine cucumber pieces, diced celeriac and apple, plum halves and asparagus. In a small bowl, beat together mayonnaise, yogurt, lemon juice, salt and sugar. Pour mayonnaise mixture over cucumber mixture. Toss to coat well. Line cucumber with lettuce leaves. Spoon salad into lettuce-lined cucumber.

Chicken-Salad Tomatoes

4 oz. frozen or canned prawns or medium shrimp
8 tomatoes
Salt and white pepper
1 fresh peach or 2 canned peach halves
1 cooked chicken breast
3 tablespoons mayonnaise
1 tablespoon dairy sour cream
1 tablespoon tomato paste
Dash Worcestershire sauce
Pinch red (cayenne) pepper
1 teaspoon brandy

Thaw and drain frozen prawns or shrimp. Rinse canned prawns or shrimp. Cut a small section off the bottom of each tomato to make a lid. Using a teaspoon, scoop seeds and flesh out of tomatoes. Season inside of tomatoes with salt and pepper. Peel fresh peach. Dice peach or peach halves. Remove skin from chicken breast. Cut chicken breast in small pieces. In a medium bowl, combine diced peach, chicken pieces and prawns or shrimp. In a small bowl, beat together mayonnaise, sour cream, tomato paste, Worcestershire sauce, red pepper and brandy. Stir mayonnaise mixture into peach mixture. Cover and let stand at room temperature 15 minutes. Spoon mixture into tomatoes. Top with tomato pieces. Makes 8 servings.

Cheese & Peppers on Tomato

2 medium, green bell peppers
6 oz. cream cheese, farmer's cheese or ricotta cheese
2 to 3 tablespoons dairy sour cream
Salt and white pepper
1 small onion
4 tomatoes
1/2 teaspoon paprika

Finely dice 1 green pepper. In a small bowl, beat together cheese and sour cream to a smooth creamy paste. Add diced green pepper. Season with salt and white pepper. Cut remaining green pepper in half lengthwise. Remove seeds and pith. Fill green-pepper halves with cheese mixture. Press filled pepper halves together. Wrap in plastic wrap. Refrigerate 30 minutes. Finely dice onion. Thickly slice tomatoes. Sprinkle each tomato slice with salt, pepper and diced onion. Unwrap and separate refrigerated pepper halves. Thinly slice stuffed pepper halves. Place each slice on top of a tomato slice. Sprinkle with paprika. Makes 12 to 14 servings.

Avocado with Shrimp

12 oz. frozen shrimp
2 avocados
3 tablespoons lemon juice
1/4 cup mayonnaise
1/4 cup whipping cream
1 tablespoon whiskey
Salt and white pepper
Bunch fresh mixed herbs (dill, tarragon, salad burnet)
Few sprigs dill, if desired

Thaw and drain shrimp. Cut avocados in half lengthwise, remove pits. Scoop out avocado flesh to within 1/2 inch of shell. Brush each avocado half with lemon juice. Refrigerate or keep in a cool place. Finely dice avocado flesh. In a small bowl, combine diced avocado and shrimp. Sprinkle with some lemon juice. In a small bowl, beat together mayonnaise, cream, whiskey, remaining lemon juice, salt and pepper. Finely chop herbs; stir into mayonnaise mixture. Stir mayonnaise mixture into avocado mixture. Spoon avocado mixture into avocado halves. Garnish each portion with a dill sprig, if desired. Makes 4 servings.

Stuffed Eggplant

1/3 cup rice
2 eggplant
Salt and white pepper
1 shallot
3 tablespoons vegetable oil
8 oz. lean ground beef
1/4 teaspoon curry powder
Generous pinch garlic salt
1/2 teaspoon grated lemon peel
1 tablespoon orange juice
Fresh mint leaves, if desired

Preheat oven to 400F (205C). Cook rice according to package directions; drain well and cool. Cut each eggplant in half lengthwise. Scoop out eggplant flesh to within 1/2 inch of shell. Sprinkle inside each eggplant half with salt. Place halves in an ovenproof dish. Finely chop shallot and eggplant flesh. Heat oil in a medium skillet. Sauté chopped shallot and eggplant until soft. Add ground beef; continue cooking until cooked through, stirring frequently. Stir in cooked rice, curry powder, garlic salt, lemon peel and orange juice. Season to taste with salt and pepper. Cook 1 to 2 minutes. Spoon beef mixture into eggplant halves. Bake 10 to 20 minutes. Cool slightly. Garnish with mint leaves, if desired. Makes 4 servings.

Fennel with Blue-Cheese Dressing

2 fennel bulbs
1 tablespoon lemon juice
Bunch dill
1 tablespoon capers
2 tomatoes
2 oz. soft blue cheese (Roquefort, dolcelatte)
1/2 cup cottage cheese
1/4 cup whipping cream
Salt and black pepper
Pinch garlic salt
Dash vinegar

Wash and trim fennel, reserving tender leaf shoots. Bring 1 cup salted water and lemon juice to a boil in a saucepan. Add fennel bulbs to boiling water. Cover and simmer 15 minutes. Drain and cool slightly. Finely chop dill, reserved fennel leaves and capers. Peel tomatoes; cut each tomato in half. Remove seeds; dice tomato flesh. In a small bowl, crumble blue cheese. Press cottage cheese through a sieve into bowl with blue cheese. Add cream, salt, pepper, garlic salt, vinegar, chopped capers, dill and fennel leaves. Blend all ingredients together. Place cooked fennel flat on a work surface. Slice each fennel in half horizontally along length of head. Top each fennel half with blue-cheese mixture. Garnish with diced tomato. Makes 4 servings.

Stuffed Artichokes

8 canned artichoke bottoms
1 (7-oz.) can tuna
2 hard-cooked eggs
1/4 cup mayonnaise
Salt and pepper
Few drops lemon juice
Generous pinch red (cayenne) pepper
1 (5-oz.) can prawns or medium shrimp
Few lettuce leaves
Few small lemon slices
1 (2-oz.) jar lumpfish caviar

Drain artichoke bottoms and tuna. Finely dice eggs. In a small bowl or blender, combine eggs and tuna. Gradually add mayonnaise. Season with salt, pepper, lemon juice and red pepper. Drain prawns or shrimp; rinse and drain well. Line a serving dish with lettuce leaves. Arrange artichoke bottoms on lettuce leaves. Spoon tuna mixture into center of each artichoke. Top each serving with prawns or shrimp. Garnish with a lemon slice and lumpfish caviar. Makes 8 servings.

Stuffed Leeks

2 large leeks
1 tablespoon lemon juice
2 hard-cooked eggs
5 canned anchovy fillets
2 oz. canned baby sweet-corn cobs or canned whole-kernel corn
1 tablespoon chopped parsley
1/4 cup vegetable oil
1 tablespoon wine vinegar
Pinch salt
Dash Tabasco sauce

Wash and trim leeks; slice each leek in two 4-inch pieces. Bring 2 cups salted water to a boil in a medium saucepan. Blanch leeks 10 minutes. Plunge leeks in cold water; drain well and cool. Slice leek pieces in half lengthwise; sprinkle with lemon juice. Cut a 1/2-inch strip off the end of each leek piece; finely slice strips. Dice eggs. Rinse anchovy fillets in cold water; drain well and finely dice. Drain corn cobs or whole-kernel corn. Cut cobs in thin slices. In a medium bowl, combine leek strips, diced eggs and anchovy fillets, corn and parsley. In a small bowl, beat together oil, vinegar, salt and Tabasco. Pour dressing over leek mixture. Cover and let stand 10 minutes. Spoon leek mixture over leek pieces. Makes 8 servings.

Carrot Boats

4 large carrots
1/4 teaspoon salt
1/2 teaspoon sugar
1 tablespoon lemon juice
2 large apples
10 sweet gherkins
8 oz. ham
Small bunch parsley
1/3 cup dairy sour cream
1/3 cup mayonnaise

Cut each carrot in half lengthwise. In a medium saucepan, bring 1 quart water to a boil. Add salt, sugar and carrot halves. Reduce heat and simmer 15 to 20 minutes. Drain carrots; plunge carrots in cold water. Drain well. Using a teaspoon or point of a vegetable peeler, hollow out a channel along each carrot half. Dice scooped-out carrot flesh; place in a small bowl. Sprinkle cooked carrot halves with lemon juice. Finely dice apples, sweet gherkins and ham. Chop parsley. Stir diced apple, gherkins, ham and parsley into diced carrots. Spoon diced-carrot mixture into carrot halves. Refrigerate 10 to 15 minutes. In a small bowl, blend sour cream and mayonnaise. Season to taste. Serve as a sauce with Carrot Boats. Makes 8 servings.

Stuffed Belgian Endive

2 large Belgian endive
2 tablespoons lemon juice
2 fresh mandarins or 3 tablespoons canned mandarin-orange
   segments
10 pimiento-stuffed olives
4 tomatoes
Salt and black pepper
Generous pinch sugar
3 tablespoons vegetable oil

Trim endive; slice each endive in half lengthwise. Sprinkle
inside each endive with lemon juice. Peel fresh mandarins;
remove skin from orange segments. Drain canned mandarins.
Slice olives. Peel and quarter tomatoes; scoop out seeds and
finely dice flesh. In a small bowl, combine mandarin segments,
olive slices and tomato quarters. In another small bowl, beat
together remaining lemon juice, salt, pepper, sugar and oil.
Pour lemon-juice mixture over mandarin mixture. Cover and
let stand 10 minutes. Spoon mandarin filling in endive halves.
Makes 4 servings.

Celery Rolls

4 celery stalks
8 oz. cream cheese, farmer's cheese or ricotta cheese
1/4 cup whipping cream
1 tablespoon brandy
1 teaspoon paprika
Pinch celery salt
Generous pinch each white pepper and ground ginger
2 sweet gherkins
4 to 8 chilies

Cut each celery stalk in 3-inch pieces. In a small bowl, beat
together cheese, cream, brandy, paprika, celery salt, pepper and
ginger. Place cheese mixture in a pastry bag fitted with a small
star tip. Pipe cheese mixture into celery stalks. Drain and slice
pickles. Arrange on celery rolls together with chilies. Cover with
plastic wrap. Let stand in a cool place 15 to 20 minutes. Makes 4
servings.

Cook's Tip

Serve Celery Rolls as a starter, as cocktail canapés or with wine and
cheese after dinner. If you are serving them as canapés, make them
half the length so they will be easier to eat.

Pastrami with Kumquat Sauce

3 tablespoons mayonnaise
Salt and white pepper
2 teaspoons lemon juice
4 preserved kumquats
2/3 cup whipping cream
8 oz. thinly sliced pastrami

In a small bowl, beat together mayonnaise, salt, pepper and lemon juice. Drain kumquats. Finely dice 3 kumquats; stir into mayonnaise mixture. Thinly slice remaining kumquat. In a medium bowl, whip cream; fold into mayonnaise mixture. Spoon sauce into a serving bowl. Garnish with kumquat slices. Roll pastrami slices. Arrange on a platter. Serve with sauce. Makes 4 servings.

Cook's Tip

If pastrami is not available, smoked ham will taste very good. As a variation, serve smoked ham with fresh-fig sauce or mandarin sauce. Follow the above recipe, but substitute fresh figs or mandarins for kumquats. Any of these combinations are delicious as starters and as side dishes to a main buffet meal.

Avocados with Mussels

2 avocados
2 teaspoons lemon juice
1 small grapefruit
1 (8-3/4-oz.) can mussels
3 tablespoons mayonnaise
1 tablespoon plain yogurt
1 teaspoon ground almonds
Generous pinch each salt, white pepper and curry powder

Cut each avocado in half lengthwise. Remove pits; sprinkle flesh with half the lemon juice. Peel grapefruit; pull into segments and remove skin from each segment. Drain mussels. In a small bowl, combine grapefruit and mussels. Arrange grapefruit mixture in avocado halves. In a small bowl, beat together mayonnaise, yogurt, ground almonds, remaining lemon juice, salt, pepper and curry powder. Spoon mixture over filled avocados. Makes 4 servings.

Cook's Tip

Before arranging grapefruit and mussels in avocado, scoop out some of the avocado flesh with a teaspoon. Mix it into the mayonnaise dressing.

Chicken & Kiwi with Orange Sauce

4 cooked chicken-breast halves
3 kiwi
2 tablespoons butter
3 tablespoons sugar
2/3 cup fresh orange juice
Grated peel of 1/2 orange
1 tablespoon brandy

Skin and bone chicken pieces; cut flesh in thin slices. Arrange chicken in a fan shape on each of 4 individual plates, or on a large platter. Thinly peel and slice kiwi. Arrange slices next to meat slices. Melt butter in a small skillet. Sprinkle sugar over melted butter. Cook over low heat until sugar dissolves. Gradually add orange juice, stirring to blend in juice. Stir in orange peel. Bring to a boil and simmer over low heat, stirring constantly until liquid is reduced by half. Remove from heat and stir in brandy. Cool slightly. Pour a small amount of orange sauce over chicken and kiwi. Serve remaining sauce separately. Makes 4 servings.

Melon with Prosciutto & Mayonnaise

1 tablespoon pickled green peppercorns
1/3 cup mayonnaise
1 teaspoon lemon juice
Pinch salt
1 small honeydew melon
4 oz. thinly sliced prosciutto

Drain peppercorns. Crush half the peppercorns with a fork or mortar and pestle. In a small bowl, beat together crushed peppercorns, mayonnaise, lemon juice and salt. Season to taste. Spoon sauce into a small serving bowl. Sprinkle with remaining peppercorns. Slice melon into wedges; discard seeds. Using a sharp knife, remove rind from each melon wedge. Wrap each melon wedge in slices of prosciutto. Arrange on a platter. Serve with sauce. Makes 4 servings.

Cook's Tip

Honeydew melon is suggested here because it is especially good with prosciutto ham. Crenshaw melon or cantaloupe can also be served.

Stuffed Persimmons

4 persimmons
2 teaspoons lemon juice
1 teaspoon pickled green peppercorns or 1/2 teaspoon freshly ground
    white pepper
8 oz. cream cheese or farmer's cheese
2/3 cup whipping cream
Generous pinch each sugar and salt
4 lemon or orange slices

Wash persimmons in cold water; rub dry. Using a sharp knife, cut a third off each nearest the stalk end. Using a teaspoon, scoop flesh out of persimmons. Finely dice flesh, discarding seeds. Sprinkle persimmon shells and diced flesh with lemon juice. Drain and crush peppercorns with a fork or mortar and pestle. In a small bowl, beat together cheese, cream, sugar, salt and crushed peppercorns or white pepper until smooth. Season to taste. Stir in diced persimmons. Spoon cheese mixture into persimmon shells. Garnish each with a lemon or orange slice. Makes 4 servings.

Lychee Cocktail

1 (11-oz.) can lychees or 1 lb. fresh lychees
12 oz. cooked chicken
1/3 cup mayonnaise
1/4 cup canned lychee juice or apple juice
Salt and white pepper
1/4 cup whipping cream
Grated peel of 1/2 orange
Few lettuce leaves
2 teaspoons lemon juice
1/4 teaspoon red (cayenne) pepper
4 chilies, if desired

Drain canned lychees, reserving juice. Or, peel, halve and pit fresh lychees. Dice chicken. In a small bowl, beat together mayonnaise, canned lychee juice or apple juice, salt, pepper, cream and orange peel. Line 4 individual plates with lettuce. In a medium bowl, combine lychees and diced chicken. Spoon lychee mixture on lettuce. Pour mayonnaise mixture over top. Cover and refrigerate 30 minutes. In a small bowl, combine lemon juice and red pepper. Just before serving, sprinkle lemon-juice mixture over cocktails. Garnish each serving with a chili, if desired. Makes 4 servings.

Papaya Ice Cream

2 papayas
1 cup whipping cream
1/2 cup sugar
1/4 cup Grand Marnier
8 walnut halves

Peel and halve 1 papaya; discard seeds. Press papaya flesh through a sieve or puree in a blender. In a medium bowl, whip cream until stiff, gradually adding sugar. Fold pureed papaya into whipped cream. Spoon papaya mixture into an ice tray. Place in freezer for 1 hour to freeze lightly. Place ice cream in a blender or mixing bowl. Beat or blend thoroughly to prevent ice crystals from forming. Peel and halve remaining papaya; discard seeds. Dice papaya flesh. Stir diced papaya into ice cream. Spoon ice cream into ice tray. Freeze 2 to 3 hours or until firm. To serve, dip base of ice tray in hot water for a few seconds. Turn out ice cream. Cut into squares and arrange in 4 individual glasses or bowls. Sprinkle Grand Marnier over top. Decorate each portion with 2 walnut halves. Makes 2 servings.

Lime Cream

4 or 5 limes
1/4 cup milk
3 egg yolks
3/4 cup sugar
3 tablespoons hot water
1/4 oz. gelatin
1-1/4 cups whipping cream
1 tablespoon Grand Marnier
4 maraschino cherries

Squeeze limes. Measure 2/3 cup lime juice; set aside. In a small bowl or blender, beat together milk, egg yolks and 1/2 cup sugar until frothy. If using a blender, transfer milk mixture to a bowl. Place bowl in a pan of hot water. Beat milk mixture with a whisk until creamy. Remove bowl from water and set aside. In another bowl, pour 3 tablespoons hot water. Stand this bowl in a pan of hot water. Sprinkle gelatin over 3 tablespoons hot water. Stir until dissolved. Pour gelatin mixture into milk mixture. Cool mixture thoroughly. In a medium bowl, whip cream until stiff, gradually adding remaining 1/4 cup sugar. Fold whipped-cream mixture into cooled gelatin mixture. Stir Grand Marnier into lime juice; stir into milk mixture. Spoon Lime Cream into 4 cocktail glasses. Refrigerate 1 hour. To serve, top each serving with a maraschino cherry. Makes 4 servings.

Classic Oysters

For each:
12 to 16 oysters
2 to 3 lemon wedges

Clean oysters under running water; drain well. Hold 1 oyster in a damp cloth, with domed side of shell in palm of your hand. With a sharp movement of an oyster opener or a strong knife, open pointed edge or *hinge* of oyster. Make sure any sea water trapped inside shell does not escape; this adds to flavor. With a kitchen knife, loosen muscle around edge inside shell. Remove top half of shell, leaving oyster in bottom half. Repeat with remaining oysters. Place all half-shells containing oysters on a plate. If you do not have a special oyster plate, sprinkle a layer of rock salt 1/2-inch thick over a regular plate. Arrange oysters on salt. This will prevent oysters from tipping and losing any of their liquid. Eat oysters directly from shells, seasoned to taste with a little lemon juice or freshly ground pepper. Serve with fresh white bread or caraway bread and dry white wine.

Mussels with Saffron Sauce

1 onion
1 small leek
1 cup white wine
1 cup water
2 qts. mussels
3 tablespoons olive oil
1 shallot
1/2 teaspoon powdered saffron
1/4 cup whipping cream
2 lettuce hearts
1 tablespoon lemon juice
1 celery stalk
2 teaspoons chopped chives
Few tarragon leaves, if desired

Dice onion. Cut leek in thin strips. Pour wine and water in a large saucepan. Add diced onion and leek strips. Bring to a boil. Scrub mussels under cold running water. Cut away tufts. Add mussels to boiling liquid. Cover and simmer 10 minutes or until all shells have opened. Remove mussels from liquid, discarding any that have not opened fully. Drain and leave to cool. Shell mussels; place in an ovenproof bowl. Strain mussel juice, reserving 1 cup liquid. Heat oil in a skillet. Dice shallot; add to hot oil. Sauté shallot 1 minute. Add saffron, cream and reserved mussel juice. Boil 1 minute. Pour mussel-juice mixture over mussels. Cool slightly. Cut celery in thin strips. Blanch celery strips in boiling water 2 minutes. Drain; cool slightly. Place half a lettuce heart on each of 4 plates. Sprinkle with lemon juice. Arrange mussel salad around lettuce. Garnish with celery, chives and tarragon, if desired. Makes 4 servings.

Mussels with Mayonnaise

1 small onion
1 small leek
1 cup white wine
1 cup water
2-1/2 qts. mussels
1 cup mayonnaise
1 teaspoon lemon juice
Pinch each salt, white pepper and sugar
1/4 cup whipping cream
Chopped parsley

Chop onion and leek. Pour wine and water in a large saucepan. Add chopped onion and leek. Bring to a boil. Prepare mussels and cook in boiling liquid 10 minutes. Discard any mussels that have not opened fully. Remove mussels; drain and cool. Remove empty mussel shells. Arrange halves containing flesh on 4 individual plates. Continue boiling mussel juice until reduced to about 1/2 cup. Strain liquid and cool slightly. In a small bowl, beat together mayonnaise, mussel juice, lemon juice, salt, pepper and sugar. In a small bowl, whip cream. Fold whipped cream into mayonnaise mixture. Spoon mayonnaise dressing over plates of mussels. Sprinkle with chopped parsley. Makes 4 servings.

Lobster Tartlets

1/3 cup mayonnaise
3 tablespoons whipping cream
Few drops lemon juice
Pinch each salt and sugar
4 small cooked tartlet shells
12 oz. fresh lobster meat or 1 (8-oz.) can lobster
1/2 cup White-Wine Aspic, page 18
4 lettuce leaves
4 teaspoons lumpfish caviar
Few dill sprigs, if desired

In a small bowl, beat together mayonnaise, cream, lemon juice, salt and sugar. Pour mayonnaise mixture into tartlet shells. Drain canned lobster. Slice lobster meat; arrange slices over mayonnaise mixture. Pour aspic over tartlets. Refrigerate until firmly set. Arrange lettuce on 4 individual plates. Place a tartlet on each plate. Top each tartlet with 1 teaspoon lumpfish caviar. Garnish with dill, if desired. Makes 4 servings.

Cook's Tip

Make tartlet shells as in Chicken Tartlets, page 57.

Scampi with Anise Cream

16 fresh or frozen scampi or medium shrimp
1 teaspoon anise seed
1/4 teaspoon salt
2 tablespoons Pernod
1/2 cup clear meat stock
2 teaspoon wine vinegar
2 egg yolks
1/2 cup unsalted butter
1 teaspoon pickled red or green peppercorns, if desired

Rinse fresh scampi or shrimp in cold running water; drain well. Thaw frozen scampi or shrimp; drain well. Crush 1/4 teaspoon anise seed; set aside. Bring 2 cups water to a boil in a medium saucepan. Add remaining anise seed, salt and fresh scampi or shrimp. Simmer 5 minutes. If scampi or shrimp were frozen, place in boiling water. Remove from heat and let stand 5 minutes. Drain well; cool slightly. Remove shells from fresh scampi or shrimp. Bring Pernod, stock and vinegar to a boil in a saucepan. Simmer until reduced to 3 tablespoons. Cool slightly. Beat egg yolks into cooled liquid. Reheat liquid over low heat. Gradually stir in butter to form a thick cream. Stir in crushed anise seed. Season to taste. Crush some ice cubes; place on a large dish. Arrange scampi or shrimp on ice. Pour anise cream into a small bowl. Sprinkle with red or green peppercorns, if desired. Makes 4 servings.

Marinated Prawns with Sole Fillets

1-1/2 lbs. sole fillets
1 to 2 tablespoons flour
1 tablespoon vegetable oil
1 tablespoon currants
2 onions
1/3 cup olive oil
1 cup white-wine vinegar
1 bay leaf
Salt and pepper
1 oz. pine nuts or sliced almonds
8 cooked prawns or medium shrimp

Cut sole in 4 portions; dip each in flour. Heat oil over medium heat in a medium skillet. Fry sole until golden brown on both sides; drain on paper towel. Soak currants in warm water. Cut onions in rings. Heat olive oil in a skillet. Fry onion rings until golden brown. Add vinegar and bay leaf. Season with salt and pepper. Bring to a boil; simmer 2 minutes. Cool vinegar mixture slightly. Drain currants. In a medium bowl, combine sole fillets, pine nuts or almonds, currants and prawns or shrimp. Pour cooled vinegar mixture over fish mixture. Refrigerate 5 to 6 hours. Strain marinade; arrange prawns or shrimp and sole mixture on a flat dish. Sprinkle with a little marinade before serving. Makes 4 servings.

Fish Mousse with Shrimp

1 cup White-Wine Aspic, page 18
4 oz. steamed white fish (pike, whiting, haddock)
1/2 cup white sauce
Pinch each salt and white pepper
6 tablespoons hot meat stock
1-1/2 teaspoons gelatin
1/2 cup whipping cream
1 (7-oz.) can shrimp
Few lettuce leaves
Few dill or parsley sprigs, if desired

Line 4 dariole molds with a thin layer of wine aspic; let stand to set. In a blender or food processor, combine white fish and white sauce; puree mixture. Strain mixture. Season with salt and pepper. Pour meat stock into a large bowl. Place bowl in a pan of hot water. Sprinkle gelatin over meat stock; stir until dissolved. In a medium bowl, whip cream until stiff; fold into stock along with fish puree. Spoon fish mixture into molds. Refrigerate until set. Drain shrimp; rinse in cold water. Drain again. Arrange lettuce on 4 individual plates. Dip molds in hot water for a few seconds. Turn out each mousse on lettuce. Top with shrimp. Pour remaining wine aspic over each mousse. Return to refrigerator until set. Garnish each with a sprig of dill or parsley. Makes 4 servings.

Prawn & Mango Cocktail

2 mangoes
1 red bell pepper
1 (5-oz.) can prawns or medium shrimp
3 tablespoons mayonnaise
1/3 cup dairy sour cream
1 teaspoon sugar
1 teaspoon lemon juice
Few pickled green peppercorns or freshly ground black pepper
1 tablespoon grated fresh horseradish or prepared creamed
   horseradish
Few mint leaves, if desired

Cut each mango in half lengthwise. Remove seeds; discard. Scoop out flesh to within 1/4 inch of shells; finely dice flesh. Cut bell pepper in half; place under broiler until skin breaks. Peel off skin and remove seeds. Slice pepper in thin strips. Drain prawns or shrimp. Rinse in cold water; drain again. In a small bowl, blend together mayonnaise, diced mango, sour cream, sugar, lemon juice, green peppercorns or black pepper, horseradish and prawns or shrimp. Spoon mixture into mango halves. Top with strips of red pepper. Garnish with mint leaves, if desired. Makes 4 servings.

Gravad Lax

3 lbs. fresh salmon
Large bunch dill or parsley
1 tablespoon coarse salt or 1-1/2 teaspoons table salt
1 teaspoon sugar
2 teaspoons white pepper

Remove scales from salmon. Slice salmon in half lengthwise, removing center bone. Rinse each half; drain well. Place 1 fillet, skin-side down, in a large dish. Coarsely chop dill or parsley. Sprinkle over salmon fillet. Combine salt, sugar and pepper. Sprinkle over fish. Top with second fillet, skin side up. Cover fish with foil and weight it down with a kitchen board and 2 full preserving jars or large food cans. Let marinate in refrigerator 3 days. Turn fillets every 12 hours and baste both sides with juices produced by fish. To serve, place salmon fillets separately on a wooden board. Scrape away herbs and seasoning. Cut fish into very thin slices. Serve with wedges of lemon, freshly toasted white bread and a green salad. Makes 6 servings.

Smoked Fish with Gourmet Sauce

1/2 lettuce
1 lb. sliced smoked fish
Generous 1/2 cup whipping cream
1 tablespoon grated fresh horseradish or 2 tablespoons prepared
   creamed horseradish
1/2 cup mayonnaise
1/2 teaspoon salt
2 teaspoons sugar
1/4 cup lemon juice
1/2 lime or lemon
Small bunch parsley

Separate lettuce leaves. Place lettuce on a flat serving dish. Arrange sliced smoked fish on top. In a small bowl, beat together cream, horseradish, mayonnaise, salt, sugar and lemon juice. Place sauce in a scallop shell or glass bowl and set on serving dish. Cut lemon or lime into slices. Garnish serving dish with lime or lemon slices and parsley. Makes 6 servings.

Marinated Sole Fillets

2 cups dry white wine
1/2 cup lemon juice
1 teaspoon salt
1 teaspoon green or black peppercorns
3 fresh sage leaves or a sprinkling of dried sage
3 bay leaves
1-3/4 lbs. fresh sole fillets

Bring wine, lemon juice, salt, peppercorns, sage and bay leaves to a boil in a medium saucepan. Remove from heat; let cool. Rinse sole fillets in cold water; drain well. Cut them in half lengthwise. Place in a bowl. Pour cooled wine mixture over fish. Cover and let marinate in refrigerator 1 to 2 days. Remove fish from refrigerator 2 hours before serving. Lift fillets out of marinade. Drain and arrange on a flat dish. Sprinkle with some of the peppercorns and herbs from marinade. Serve with horseradish and apple cream from Ham & Salad Platter, page 204, and freshly toasted white bread. Makes 4 servings.

Cook's Tip

Only fresh fish is suitable for marinating. Never use frozen fish.

Trout Fillets with Tomato Sauce

2 lbs. fresh trout fillets
Juice of 2 lemons
1/2 cup wine vinegar
Salt and white pepper
2 shallots
4 tomatoes
1 garlic clove
1 teaspoon vegetable oil
1/2 teaspoon dried basil
1 tablespoon tomato paste
1/2 cup red wine
Pinch sugar
1 teaspoon grated lemon peel
Freshly ground black pepper
Few lemon slices

Wash and dry trout fillets. Cut into very thin slices with a sharp knife. Arrange fillets on a flat dish and sprinkle with lemon juice, vinegar, salt and pepper. Cover and let marinate in refrigerator overnight. Dice shallots. Cut a cross in base of each tomato. Dip in boiling water for a few seconds, then remove skin. Halve, seed and dice tomatoes. Crush garlic. Heat oil in a skillet. Sauté shallots until soft. Add tomato, garlic, basil, tomato paste and red wine. Simmer 1 minute, stirring constantly. Season sauce with salt and sugar; cool. Remove trout from marinade. Arrange on a serving dish. Sprinkle with grated lemon peel and black pepper. Garnish with lemon slices. Serve tomato sauce with trout fillets. Makes 4 servings.

Salmon-Trout Niçoise

1 (1-1/4-lb.) fresh salmon trout, cleaned
Salt and pepper
2 cups white wine
1 cup water
5 peppercorns
1 teaspoon kelp, if desired
1 cup Fish Aspic, page 17
1 tablespoon chopped parsley
1 slice stuffed olive
6 thin round slices truffle or 3 black grapes
1 slice cooked carrot
1 hard-cooked egg white
Parsley stalk
3/4 cup whipping cream
1 teaspoon lemon juice
1 tablespoon chopped fresh mixed herbs or 1 teaspoon dried mixed
    herbs

Wash and dry trout. Season with salt and pepper. Place wine,
water and peppercorns in a medium saucepan; add kelp, if
desired. Bring to a boil. Add trout. Simmer over low heat 15
minutes. Lift fish out of liquid. Cut off fins and remove skin.
Cover fish with a damp cloth. Let stand in a cool place 1 hour.
Pour a thin layer of Fish Aspic onto a flat serving dish; let set.
Arrange trout on aspic. Cover with more aspic; let set. Sprinkle
fish's head with parsley. Place olive slice on top for the eye.
Halve grapes, if used, remove seeds. Arrange carrot slice and
round of truffle or grapes on fish. Cut leaf shapes from egg
white. Arrange on either side of a parsley stalk. Pour remaining
aspic over fish; let set. In a small bowl, beat together cream,
lemon juice and mixed herbs. Serve sauce with fish. Makes 4
servings.

Trout with Dill

4 (8-oz.) cleaned trout
Large bunch fresh dill or 1/4 cup dried dill
1 cup salted water
1/2 cup wine vinegar
1 lemon
1/2 cup dry white wine
Pinch salt and sugar
1 teaspoon gelatin
1 cooked carrot, sliced
3/4 cup whipping cream
Grated peel of 1 lemon
1 teaspoon lemon juice
1 tablespoon dry sherry

Wash and dry fish. Place half the dill in stomach cavities of fish.
In a large saucepan, bring salted water and vinegar to a boil. Cut
lemon in half. Squeeze lemon and add juice to vinegar mixture
with a strip of lemon peel. Add trout. Simmer over low heat 10
to 12 minutes. Drain fish. Remove skin. Let fish cool. Pour
wine into a small bowl. Add salt and sugar. Set bowl in a saucepan of water. Place over gentle heat. Sprinkle with gelatin and
stir until gelatin has dissolved. Finely chop remaining fresh dill,
if used. Add dill to gelatin mixture. Place fish on a serving dish.
Decorate with carrot slices. Pour aspic over fish. Let set in refrigerator. In a small bowl, beat together cream, grated lemon
peel, 1 teaspoon lemon juice and sherry. Season to taste. Serve
sauce with fish. Makes 4 servings.

Salmon with Vegetable Salad

1 cup salted water
1/2 cup white wine
1 tablespoon vinegar
2 white peppercorns
8 oz. inexpensive fish pieces
  (coley, whiting)
1 (1-lb.) salmon fillet
1 cup Fish Aspic, page 17
1 lb. fresh mixed vegetables (peas,
  carrots, celery, green beans)
2 to 3 tomatoes
2 tablespoons mayonnaise
1/4 cup whipping cream
1 teaspoon lemon juice
Pinch each salt, white pepper and
  sugar
Few lettuce leaves

Place salted water, wine, vinegar, peppercorns and fish pieces in a medium saucepan. Simmer over low heat 15 minutes; strain. Preheat oven to 425F (220C). Butter a large piece of foil. Wrap salmon in foil, pressing edges together to seal. Place wrapped salmon in a roasting pan. Pour fish stock over salmon. Bake 20 minutes. Remove salmon from oven. Cool in foil, then unwrap and place in refrigerator until completely cold. Pour a thin layer of Fish Aspic over a flat serving dish; let set. Cut salmon into very thin slices with a sharp knife. Arrange slices on dish. Top with remaining aspic. Prepare and dice mixed vegetables. Bring a little salted water to a boil in a saucepan. Add vegetables. Simmer over low heat 15 minutes. Peel tomatoes. Halve, seed and dice them. Add to vegetables and simmer 5 minutes. Drain vegetables; cool. In a small bowl, beat together mayonnaise, cream, lemon juice, salt, pepper and sugar. Stir mixture into vegetables. Arrange lettuce leaves at 1 end of serving dish. Spoon salad on top. Garnish with stuffed eggs, page 124. Makes 4 servings.

Herring with Mixed Peppers

12 pickled-herring fillets
1 red bell pepper
1 green bell pepper
1 yellow bell pepper
4 shallots or 2 small onions
1/4 cup wine vinegar
2 sprigs thyme or 1/2 teaspoon dried thyme
1 sage leaf or a pinch dried sage
Few sprigs basil or 1/2 teaspoon dried basil
2/3 cup vegetable oil
Juice of 1 lemon

If herring are very salty, soak in cold water 1 to 2 hours, changing water several times. Less salty fillets should be washed in cold water and patted dry. Cut fillets into thick strips. Remove cores and seeds from peppers. Cut peppers into thin rings. Finely dice shallots or onions. Bring vinegar to a boil in a small saucepan. Add shallots or onions. Cover. Simmer over low heat 2 minutes; cool. Mix herring and peppers in a large bowl. Pour on vinegar marinade. Finely chop fresh herbs, if used. Add herbs to herring salad. In a small bowl, beat together oil and lemon juice. Pour over salad. Mix thoroughly. Cover and let stand 2 hours in refrigerator. Makes 4 servings.

Herring in Dill Mayonnaise

8 pickled-herring fillets
1/2 cup milk, if desired
1/4 cup water, if desired
1 egg
1/4 cup French mustard
1 teaspoon wine vinegar
Generous pinch each salt and white pepper
1/2 cup vegetable oil
1/3 cup whipping cream
5 oz. pickled cucumbers or dill pickles
Bunch fresh dill or 1 tablespoon dried dill

If herring are very salty, soak in a mixture of milk and water 12 hours. Drain. Cut fillets into thick strips. Place in a bowl or earthenware dish. In a small bowl, beat together egg, mustard, vinegar, salt and pepper. Gradually add oil, a few drops at a time, stirring constantly. Stir in cream. Finely dice pickles. Reserve 1 sprig of fresh dill, if used, and finely chop the remainder. Stir pickles and dill into mayonnaise. Pour mayonnaise over herring and stir in. Cover and refrigerate 1 to 2 hours. To serve, garnish with reserved dill sprig. Makes 4 servings.

Herring in Red-Wine Marinade

8 pickled-herring fillets
2 large red onions
1/2 cup red wine
1/2 cup wine vinegar
3/4 cup sugar
4 black peppercorns
1 cinnamon stick
3 cloves

Rinse herring fillets in cold water. Place in 2 cups water and soak 12 hours. Drain. Cut fillets in half lengthwise and again cross-wise. Arrange fish in layers in a deep earthenware dish. Cut onions into thin rings. Pour red wine and vinegar into a medium saucepan. Add onion rings, sugar, peppercorns, cinnamon and cloves. Bring to a boil. Simmer over low heat 5 minutes. Cool. Pour cold marinade over herring fillets. Cover and refrigerate 3 days. Makes 4 servings.

Cook's Tip

This dish will keep for 2 weeks in a tightly closed screw-top jar in the refrigerator. It is worth making double the quantity and having marinated herring fillets on the menu more than once.

Soused Herring

4 medium onions
1/2 cup vinegar
1/4 cup sugar
1 teaspoon black peppercorns
8 prepared salt-herring fillets
2 hard-cooked eggs

Coarsely chop onions. In a medium bowl, combine vinegar, sugar, peppercorns and onions. Cut herring into equal-size pieces. Place in a deep earthenware dish. Pour vinegar marinade over herring. Cover and refrigerate 4 days. Cut each egg into 8 wedges. To serve, garnish herring with egg wedges. Makes 4 servings.

Cook's Tip

These marinated herring will keep for 2 weeks in a tightly closed screw-top jar in the refrigerator. As a variation, mix diced apple and dairy sour cream into the herring just before serving, photo page 203.

Herring with Apple Salad

1 slice canned pineapple
1 apple
2 carrots
1/2 teaspoon sugar
Juice of 1 small lemon
2 small tomatoes
Bunch chives
1/3 cup mayonnaise
1 tablespoon whipping cream
Generous pinch each salt, black pepper and paprika
8 pickled-herring fillets

Drain pineapple and dice. Peel and core apple. Shred apple and carrots into a medium bowl. In a small bowl, combine sugar and lemon juice. Add pineapple and stir into apple and carrot. Peel tomatoes. Then halve, seed and finely dice. Chop chives. In a small bowl, beat together mayonnaise, cream, salt, pepper, paprika and chives. Fold diced tomato into mayonnaise sauce. Roll up herring fillets. Arrange apple and carrot salad on a flat dish. Top with rolled herring. Drizzle with mayonnaise sauce. Makes 4 servings.

Herring Tartare

8 pickled-herring fillets
1 large onion
3 tablespoons capers
2 teaspoons caraway seeds
2 teaspoons coarsely ground white pepper
1 tablespoon paprika
3 tablespoons chopped parsley
4 egg yolks

If herring are very salty, soak a few hours in cold water, changing water frequently. Pat dry. Finely dice and arrange in the centers of 4 individual plates. Make a well in the middle of each portion. Finely dice onion. On each plate, arrange spoonfuls of diced onion, capers, caraway seeds, pepper, paprika and parsley around herring. Tip 1 egg yolk into the well made in each herring portion. Each guest mixes a portion of herring with seasonings to taste. Serve with fresh whole-wheat bread and butter. Makes 4 servings.

Herring-Salad Platter

1/2 cup wine vinegar
1/4 cup vegetable oil
1 teaspoon sugar
3 tablespoons capers
8 pickled-herring fillets
4 hard-cooked eggs
4 oz. red or black lumpfish caviar
2 small cooked beets
1/3 cup pickled cocktail onions
1 cup chopped cooked carrots

In a medium bowl, beat together vinegar, oil and sugar. Reserve a few capers and lightly crush remainder with a fork. Add to vinegar mixture. Place herring fillets in marinade. Cover and refrigerate 2 hours. Cut eggs in half lengthwise. Top each with 1 teaspoon caviar. Peel and dice beets. Drain cocktail onions. Remove herring fillets from marinade and place on a serving dish. Place eggs around fish. Arrange spoonfuls of beets, onions and carrots around herring. Sprinkle with remaining capers. Makes 4 servings.

Herring Rolls with Corn Salad

1/2 small cauliflower
1 (8-oz.) pkg. frozen peas
1 (10-oz.) can whole-kernel corn
2 small onions
Salt and black pepper
3 tablespoons wine vinegar
1/3 cup vegetable oil
2 small pickled cucumbers or dill pickles
6 to 8 strips canned pimiento
2 cooked carrots
8 pickled-herring fillets.

Break cauliflower into flowerets. Place in a medium saucepan of boiling salted water. Simmer 10 to 15 minutes. Cook peas, following package instructions. Drain cauliflower and peas; cool. Drain corn. Dice onions. In a medium bowl, beat together salt, pepper, vinegar and oil. Stir in onions, cauliflower, peas and corn. Drain pickles and pimientoes. Slice carrots, pickles and pimientoes into thin 2-inch-long strips; combine. Place a few strips across each herring fillet. Roll up fillets and secure with wooden picks. Spoon cauliflower mixture into a large serving dish. Arrange herring rolls alongside. Makes 4 servings.

Mock-Caviar Cream Horns

1 cup whipping cream
1/4 teaspoon salt
Few drops lemon juice
1 (2-oz.) jar lumpfish caviar
4 to 8 cooked puff-pastry horns or patty shells

In a small bowl, whip cream and salt. Fold in lemon juice and caviar. Place cream mixture in a pastry bag. Pipe into pastry horns or patty shells. Serve with ice-cold vodka. Makes 4 servings.

Cook's Tip

You can make your own horns from frozen patty shells. Overlap shells and roll out to a rectangle. Cut into long, 1-inch-wide strips. Make cones from foil. Brush 1 side of the pastry strips with beaten egg yolk. Twist them, egg-side-down, around the cone so coated edges overlap by about 1/4 inch. Press the edges gently together. Brush horn with more egg yolk. Bake in a preheated 400F (205C) oven 15 minutes. Cool and remove foil cones.

Sole Mousse with Mock Caviar

1/2 cup Fish Aspic, page 17
1 cup whipping cream
12 oz. cooked sole fillets
1 cup white sauce
Salt and pepper
1/2 cup hot chicken stock
1/4 oz. gelatin
1/2 (2-oz.) jar lumpfish caviar
6 limes
Few dill sprigs, if desired

Line four 1-1/4-cup molds with a thin layer of Fish Aspic; let set. Whip cream until stiff. Skin fish fillets. Break fish into pieces. Place in a blender or food processor with white sauce. Process until smooth. Season with salt and pepper. Pour chicken stock into a medium bowl. Set in a pan of hot water. Sprinkle with gelatin and stir until dissolved. Fold in half the whipped cream. Let aspic cool slightly, then fold in remaining cream and fish puree. Pour half the sole mousse into aspic-lined molds. Make a small well in center of each and fill with caviar. Top with remaining mousse. Place in refrigerator to set. Thinly slice limes. Arrange lime slices on 4 individual plates. Dip molds in hot water for a few seconds and turn out mousses onto plates. Garnish each portion with dill, if desired. Makes 4 servings.

Trout Toast with Asparagus

4 small slices white bread
4 smoked-trout fillets
24 freshly boiled asparagus spears or 24 canned asparagus tips
1/4 cup Vinaigrette Dressing, page 173
1/2 cup White-Wine Aspic, page 18
1 lemon
8 leaves lemon balm or mint, if desired

Toast bread until golden brown. Cut in half. Remove any skin from fish with a sharp knife. Cut fillets in half crosswise. Top each slice of toast with half a trout fillet. Drain fresh asparagus spears, if used. Cut in half, reserving bottom part for use in a salad. Drain canned asparagus tips. Place asparagus on a flat dish. Pour dressing over asparagus. Cover and marinate 15 minutes. Drain asparagus. Place 3 tips on each trout fillet. Pour wine aspic over asaragus; let set. Cut 3 slices from center of lemon. Cut each slice into 5 or 6 segments. Place 2 lemon segments on each slice of toast. Garnish with a lemon-balm or mint leaf, if desired. Makes 8 servings.

Smoked-Salmon Vols-au-Vent

1 (5-oz.) can prawns or shrimp
1/2 teaspoon lemon juice
4 oz. smoked salmon
1 cup whipping cream
Pinch each salt and white pepper
1/4 cup water
Generous pinch gelatin
8 cooked patty shells
8 thin slices truffle, if desired

Rinse prawns or shrimp in cold water; drain well. Coarsely chop and sprinkle with lemon juice. Cut smoked salmon into small pieces. Place with prawns or shrimp in a blender or food processor. Process until smooth. In a medium bowl, whip cream until stiff. Season with salt and pepper. Gradually fold fish puree into whipped cream. Bring water to a boil in a small saucepan. Remove pan from heat and allow to cool slightly. Sprinkle with gelatin. Stir until gelatin has dissolved. Cool. Stir into fish cream. Cover and refrigerate 30 minutes. Place in a pastry bag fitted with a round tip and pipe into cooked patty shells. Garnish each vol-au-vent with a slice of truffle, if desired. Makes 8 servings.

Party Trout Platter

8 smoked-trout fillets
1 cup White-Wine Aspic, page 18
1 cup whipping cream
Pinch salt
1 tablespoon grated fresh horseradish or 2 tablespoons prepared
   creamed horseradish
4 hard-cooked eggs
1/2 (2-oz.) jar lumpfish caviar
2 lemons
1 (8-1/2-oz.) can asparagus tips
4 thin slices smoked salmon
1 cucumber
Few lettuce leaves
1 stick cold butter
8 slices white bread
Small bunch dill or parsley

Arrange trout fillets in a ring on 1 side of a large flat dish. Pour wine aspic over fish; let set. In a small bowl, whip cream with salt until stiff. Fold in horseradish. Transfer to a glass dish or bowl and place on serving dish. Slice eggs. Place a slice of egg on each trout fillet. Garnish with a spoonful of caviar. Cut 4 thin slices from center of each lemon. Cut through to the center of each lemon slice, twist it and arrange between trout fillets. Drain asparagus tips. Roll a few asparagus tips in each slice of smoked salmon. Wash, dry and thinly slice cucumber. Arrange in a ring on dish next to trout fillets. Top with salmon rolls.

Place lettuce on serving dish. Shave butter into curls with a butter curler and arrange on lettuce. Toast bread. Cut slices in half diagonally and place on the far side of serving dish. Garnish platter with dill or parsley. Makes 8 servings.

Cook's Tip

If you are serving the trout platter when asparagus is in season, fill the smoked salmon rolls with steamed fresh asparagus tips. The stems of the asparagus spears can be reserved and used in a salad.

Smoked-Fish Platter

4 oz. smoked eel
4 oz. smoked conger eel
8 oz. smoked salmon, sliced
1 smoked mackerel
2 smoked-trout fillets
4 oz. canned anchovies
Few dill and parsley sprigs
1 tomato
1 lime

Cut eel into 1-inch pieces. Slice conger eel. Arrange both kinds of eel, salmon, mackerel and trout fillets on a large serving dish. Drain anchovies and place on dish. Garnish fish with dill and parsley. Slice tomato and lime. Arrange on serving dish. Garnish dish with stuffed eggs, page 124. Serve with 1 tablespoon horseradish folded into 2 cups whipped cream, and the following fish salads:

Sweet & Sour Sardines

1/2 (4-oz.) can sardines
1 slice fresh or canned pineapple
1 small mild onion
1 large tomato
1 small melon
1 tablespoon lemon juice
3 tablespoons vegetable oil
Pinch each salt and pepper
Generous pinch mustard powder

Drain sardines and canned pineapple, if used. Slice sardines and pineapple. Slice onion into rings. Peel and dice tomato. Cut melon in half crosswise with a zig-zag motion. Using a melon-baller, scoop out all flesh. In a small bowl, beat together lemon juice, oil, salt, pepper and mustard. Place sardines, pineapple, onion, tomato and melon in a medium bowl. Pour dressing over mixture. Mix well. Arrange salad in one of the melon halves, reserving the other for the Bean Salad.

Herring with Pepper Cream

8 oz. pickled-herring fillets
1/2 red bell pepper
Few lettuce leaves
3 tablespoons dairy sour cream
Pinch each salt and white pepper
Few drops each Worcestershire sauce and lemon juice
1 teaspoon pickled green peppercorns or 1/2 teaspoon freshly ground black pepper

Cut herring fillets into pieces. Remove seeds and core from red pepper. Cut pepper into strips. Combine pepper and herring in a small bowl. Place lettuce on a serving dish. Arrange herring salad on top. In a small bowl beat together sour cream, salt, pepper, Worcestershire sauce, lemon juice and peppercorns or pepper. Spoon over herring salad.

Bean Salad

1/2 (10-oz.) can green beans
1 (8-3/4-oz.) can mussels
1 (5-oz.) can prawns or shrimp
1 tablespoon wine vinegar
3 tablespoons vegetable oil
Pinch each salt and white pepper
1 teaspoon chopped fresh chives, if desired

Drain and chop beans. Drain mussels and prawns or shrimp. Combine mussels, prawns or shrimp, and beans in a medium bowl. In a small bowl, beat together vinegar, oil, salt and pepper. Stir dressing into salad. Arrange salad in second melon half. Garnish with chives, if desired.

Roast Beef with Rémoulade Sauce

2-1/4 lbs. beef sirloin
1 teaspoon salt
1/2 teaspoon black pepper
Generous pinch each onion salt and garlic salt
1 teaspoon hot mustard
3 tablespoons vegetable oil
1 (9-1/2-oz.) jar mixed pickled vegetables

Rémoulade Sauce:
1 canned anchovy fillet
1 onion
2 baby dill pickles
1 tablespoon capers
Bunch chives
Small bunch parsley
3 sprigs each fresh chervil and dill or 1/2 teaspoon each dried chervil
    and dill
1 cup mayonnaise
1 teaspoon hot mustard
Salt and pepper

Preheat oven to 425F (220C). Rinse beef in cold water; pat dry. Cut a lattice pattern into the thin layer of fat surrounding meat. Blend salt, pepper, onion salt and garlic salt. Rub mixture into meat. Brush all over with very thin layer of mustard. Pour oil into a roasting pan. Add meat. Roast 40 to 45 minutes, basting occasionally with pan juices. Let meat cool. Drain pickled vegetables. Cut half the meat into very thin slices. Arrange on a large serving dish with remaining meat and pickled vegetables.

To make Rémoulade Sauce, soak anchovy fillet in water 10 minutes; drain. Finely chop anchovy and onion. Finely dice pickles. Crush capers with a fork. Chop chives, parsley, fresh chervil and dill, if used. In a small bowl, beat together mayonnaise, mustard, salt and pepper. Stir in anchovy, onion, pickles, capers and herbs. Taste and adjust seasoning. Serve with roast beef accompanied by white bread and whole-wheat bread and butter. Makes 6 servings.

Cook's Tip

Instead of mixed pickled vegetables and Rémoulade Sauce, you could serve the roast beef with the vegetable salad given in the recipe for Russian-Salad Platter, page 199. Make double the quantity and omit the ham loaf.

Stuffed Pork with Curry Sauce

2 oz. dried apricots
1 (2-1/4-lb.) pork tenderloin
8 oz. bulk sausage
1/2 onion, finely chopped
1/4 cup chopped parsley
1/2 teaspoon each dried thyme and marjoram
Salt and white pepper
3 tablespoons vegetable oil
1 teaspoon parika
1/3 cup mayonnaise
2 to 3 teaspoons curry powder
1/3 cup whipping cream
Pinch sugar

Soak apricots 2 to 3 hours in warm water. Using a long, thin knife, carefully cut a hole 1-1/2 inches across horizontally through the center of pork but do not cut right through to the other end. Preheat oven to 325F (165C). Scoop out and grind meat. In a medium bowl, blend sausage, onion, 1 tablespoon parsley, thyme, marjoram, salt and pepper. Heat half the oil in a medium skillet. Add sausage mixture. Cook, stirring constantly, until well browned. Remove from heat and stir in ground pork. Stuff pork with sausage mixture. Brush outside with remaining oil and sprinkle with paprika. Cover opening at one end of meat with a piece of foil. Bake 2 hours or until a meat thermometer inserted in pork registers 170F (75C). Sprinkle with remaining parsley. Bake 5 minutes longer. Cool. Drain apricots. Puree in a blender or food processor. In a small bowl, combine apricot puree, mayonnaise, curry powder, cream, sugar and pepper to taste. Serve apricot mayonnaise with ham. Makes 6 servings.

Glazed Fillet of Beef

1 (2-1/4-lb.) beef fillet
1/4 cup vegetable oil
1/2 teaspoon paprika
Pinch dried thyme
Pinch white pepper
1/2 teaspoon salt
4 oz. carrots
8 oz. canned artichoke hearts
3 tablespoons Vinaigrette Dressing, page 173
1/2 cup cool Madeira Aspic, page 18
1/3 cup mayonnaise
1/2 cup whipping cream
1/2 teaspoon hot mustard
3 tablespoons chopped fresh mixed herbs or 2 teaspoons dried mixed
   herbs

Remove any skin from beef. Blend oil, paprika, thyme and pepper. Rub mixture into meat. Wrap meat in foil. Marinate in refrigerator 12 hours. Preheat oven to 425F (220C). Remove foil from meat. Sprinkle meat with salt. Roast 30 to 45 minutes. Meat should be rare. Remove from oven; cool. Cut carrots into strips. Drain and halve artichoke hearts. Cut cooled meat into thick slices. Arrange slices on a flat serving dish. In a small bowl, mix together carrots and artichokes. Sprinkle with Vinaigrette Dressing. Arrange on dish beside meat. Pour Madeira Aspic over meat; let set. In a small bowl, beat together mayonnaise, cream, mustard and herbs. Season to taste. Serve with meat. Makes 6 servings.

Spit-Roast Pork with Herb Mayonnaise

1 (2-1/4-lb.) pork shoulder or pork leg (fresh ham), boned and rolled
1/2 garlic clove
3 tablespoons vegetable oil
1 teaspoon salt
1 tablespoon hot mustard
1/2 teaspoon each dried thyme and marjoram
1 cup mayonnaise
1 dill pickle
Bunch chives and parsley
Small bunch fresh dill or 1 teaspoon dried dill
2 hard-cooked eggs
Asparagus, if desired
1 tablespoon chopped onion

Wash meat in cold water; pat dry. Crush garlic. In a small bowl, beat together oil, salt, garlic, mustard, thyme and marjoram. Rub mixture well into meat. Preheat broiler to 350F (175C). Thread meat onto the spit. Broil 1-3/4 hours or until cooked through. Remove meat from spit; cool. Place meat on a flat serving dish. Pour mayonnaise into a bowl. Finely chop pickle. Finely chop chives, parsley and fresh dill, if used. Chop eggs. Stir pickle, herbs and eggs into mayonnaise. Serve pork with mayonnaise and freshly cooked asparagus, if desired. Garnish with chopped onion. Serves 6.

Braised Veal Mostarda

1 (2-1/4-lb.) veal fillet
1 teaspoon salt
1/4 teaspoon each white pepper, dried rosemary and dried sage
1/2 teaspoon paprika
1 onion
Selection of fresh vegetables in season (carrots, celery, leek)
1/3 cup vegetable oil
1/2 cup hot meat stock
1/2 cup white wine
8 oz. candied fruits

Rinse meat in cold water; pat dry. Blend salt, pepper, herbs and paprika. Rub mixture into meat. Cut onion into quarters. Prepare fresh vegetables; chop coarsely. Preheat oven to 425F (220C). Heat oil in an ovenproof casserole. Add meat. Cook 10 minutes or until browned, turning occasionally. Add onion and mixed vegetables. Cook a few minutes. Pour meat stock and white wine into casserole. Cover with a tightly fitting lid. Braise in oven 60 to 70 minutes, basting often during cooking. Remove from casserole; cool. Before serving, carve meat into thin slices and arrange on a platter. Serve with candied fruits. Makes 6 servings.

Roast Breast of Pheasant

2 young pheasants, dressed
Salt and pepper
Bunch fresh mixed herbs (parsley, rosemary, thyme, marjoram) or
  1 tablespoon mixed dried herbs
2 oz. canned truffles, if desired
8 to 10 bacon slices
3 tablespoons vegetable oil
2 tablespoons brandy
1/2 cup Madeira Aspic, page 18
Sprig watercress

Preheat oven to 425F (220C). Rinse pheasants under cold running water; pat dry. Rub insides of birds with salt and pepper. Divide bunch of fresh herbs in half. Place half the fresh or dried herbs in the cavity of each pheasant. Slice truffles very thinly, if used. Loosen skin over breast of each pheasant with a sharp knife and insert truffle slices underneath. Cover breasts with bacon slices to protect meat from drying out. Rub pheasants all over with oil. Place in a roasting pan. Roast 40 to 45 minutes, basting often. Ten minutes before the end of cooking time, remove bacon slices and pour brandy over pheasants. Return pheasants to oven. Remove roasted pheasants from oven and slice breast off each. Cool. Cut into thick slices. Arrange slices on a dish. Garnish with diced Madeira Aspic and watercress. Makes 4 servings.

Glazed Saddle of Venison

1 (3-lb.) saddle of venison
3 juniper berries
1 bay leaf
Salt and pepper
Generous pinch each allspice, ground ginger and thyme
1 teaspoon paprika
1/3 cup vegetable oil
1/2 cup port
4 shallots
2 tablespoons butter
4 oz. liver sausage
1/2 cup Port Aspic, page 18
5 candied cherries
6 kumquats or 1 (11-oz.) can mandarin-orange segments, drained

Wash meat in cold water; pat dry. In a small bowl, crush juniper berries and bay leaf. Mix in salt, pepper, allspice, ginger, thyme, paprika and oil. Rub mixture into meat. Cover and let marinate 3 hours. Preheat oven to 400F (205C). Place meat in a roasting pan. Roast 1 hour 20 minutes. After 30 minutes of cooking, pour port over meat. Return meat to oven. Remove cooked meat from pan; cool. Carve cooled meat into thick slices. Do not discard carcass. Dice shallots. Sauté in butter until soft. Bring meat juices to a boil in pan on top of the stove. Simmer a few minutes until liquid thickens. Mix liver sausage and diced shallot into liquid. Brush saddle carcass all over with mixture. Arrange meat slices on top. Pour cooled Port Aspic over meat; let set. Garnish with candied cherries and kumquats or mandarin-orange segments. Makes 6 servings.

Turkey Legs with Broccoli

6 tablespoons vegetable oil
2 (12-oz.) turkey legs
1 carrot
1 celery stalk
1 onion
2 tablespoons chopped parsley
Generous pinch dried thyme
2 cups chicken stock
1/2 cup wine vinegar
1/2 cup sherry
Salt and pepper
1 lb. broccoli
2 teaspoons lemon juice
Pinch sugar
Tomato quarters

Heat 1/4 cup vegetable oil in a large casserole. Add turkey and brown all over. Chop carrot and celery. Dice onion. Add carrot, celery, 1/2 tablespoon parsley and thyme to casserole. Continue cooking a few minutes. Pour in chicken stock, vinegar, sherry and salt and pepper to taste. Cover and simmer 30 to 40 minutes. Remove turkey legs; cool. Continue boiling stock until it is reduced to 1 cup; cool. Place broccoli in a medium saucepan. Add enough boiling salted water to cover stalks. Simmer gently 10 to 15 minutes; drain. In a small bowl, beat together lemon juice, sugar and remaining oil. Add salt to taste. Pour mixture over broccoli. Cover and let stand. Arrange turkey legs on a flat serving dish. Sprinkle with remaining parsley. Skim fat from cold stock and pour over meat. Allow to set. Arrange broccoli salad on serving dish. Garnish with tomato quarters. Makes 4 servings.

Poulet-Bresse

2 (2-1/4-lb.) chickens
1 tablespoon vegetable oil
1/4 cup butter
2 onions
1 carrot
1 celery stalk
1 cup wine vinegar
1 cup water
2 sprigs each fresh thyme and parsley or 1/2 teaspoon each dried thyme and parsley
Salt and pepper
6-1/2 cups chicken stock
2 tablespoons all-purpose flour
Juice of 1 lemon
12 shallots
3 tablespoons finely chopped chives

Cut chickens into serving pieces. Heat oil and butter in a large casserole. Add chicken. Cook until browned all over. Dice onions. Chop carrot and celery. Add to casserole and cook until browned. Add vinegar, water and herbs. Season with salt and pepper. Cover and simmer 25 minutes. Remove chicken from casserole. Continue boiling liquid until it is reduced by two-thirds. Add chicken stock and simmer 30 minutes longer. Strain stock. Cool slightly and chill in refrigerator. Combine flour and lemon juice in a medium saucepan. Gradually add 3 cups salted water and bring to a boil. Add peeled shallots and simmer 8 minutes. Drain and let cool. Skim fat from chilled stock. Arrange chicken pieces and shallots on a flat serving dish. Pour over a layer of stock; let set. Add another layer every 30 minutes until all stock is used up. Refrigerate until set. To serve, sprinkle with chives. Makes 6 servings.

Stuffed Turkey Breast

4 oz. carrots
4 oz. bacon slices
3 lbs. boned turkey breast
1/2 teaspoon each salt and white pepper
1 teaspoon paprika
1 tablespoon vegetable oil
1/2 cup butter
1 cup Muscatel Aspic, page 18
Few leaves red endive and 1 fresh or canned whole peach, if desired

Cut carrots and bacon into long strips and freeze solid. Preheat oven to 400F (205C). Using a long skewer, pierce several holes running right through turkey breast near the sides. With the aid of a trussing needle, insert frozen carrot and bacon strips alternately into meat. Blend salt, pepper and paprika. Rub mixture into turkey breast. Place in a roasting pan. Heat oil and pour all over turkey. Roast 65 to 70 minutes. Fifteen minutes before the end of the cooking time, melt butter and sprinkle it over turkey. Return turkey to oven. Let turkey cool. Wrap cooled turkey in foil. Refrigerate until cold. Dice Muscatel Aspic. Carve turkey into thin slices. Arrange slices on a flat plate. Sprinkle with diced aspic. Garnish platter with a salad of red endive and chopped peach, if desired. Makes 6 servings.

Stuffed Quails

8 dressed quails
Salt and pepper
1/4 teaspoon dried basil
6 tablespoons butter
1 tablespoon vegetable oil
3 oz. Madeira Aspic, page 18
1/2 head curly endive
Fresh or canned mandarin-orange segments

Stuffing:
4 oz. chicken livers
1 tablespoon Madeira wine
2 bacon slices
Pinch each salt, white pepper and dried basil
1/2 cup whipping cream
8 slices canned truffle, if desired

Rub quails inside and out with salt, pepper and basil. Heat butter and oil in a medium skillet. Add quails two at a time and cook 10 to 15 minutes or until browned all over. Cool. To make the stuffing, trim chicken livers. Place in a small bowl and sprinkle with Madeira wine. Let stand 30 minutes. Cook bacon until soft in skillet. Add livers and continue cooking 4 minutes. Season with salt, pepper and basil; cool. Place liver mixture in a blender or food processor and puree. Whip cream and stir into liver puree. Place mixture in a pastry bag fitted with a round tip. Half-fill each quail with puree. Add a slice of truffle, if desired, and pipe remaining puree on top. Coat quails several times with aspic, leaving each layer to set before adding the next. Cut endive into strips and arrange on a large serving dish with stuffed quails. Garnish with mandarin-orange segments. Makes 8 servings.

Party Tournedos

1 (1-1/2-lb.) beef fillet
Salt and white pepper
1/2 teaspoon paprika
1/4 cup vegetable oil
1 cup Sherry Aspic, page 18

Garnishes:
1 hard-cooked egg
1-1/2 teaspoons soft butter
2 teaspoons whipping cream
Pinch each salt, pepper and paprika
1 teaspoon chopped fresh mixed herbs or pinch dried mixed herbs
2 tomato wedges

1/2 (12-oz.) can asparagus tips
1/4 cup white wine
1 teaspoon lemon juice
Pinch each salt, sugar and white pepper
Few drops Worcestershire sauce
3 slices cooked carrot

3 canned artichoke bottoms
2 teaspoons lemon juice
1/4 cup white wine
1 tablespoons mayonnaise
Few dill or parsley sprigs
1 teaspoon pickled red or green peppercorns, if desired

2 slices liver pâté
6 grapes
3 tablespoons brandy

Remove any skin from beef. Rinse meat in cold water; pat dry. In a small bowl, beat together salt, pepper, paprika and oil. Rub mixture all over meat. Wrap in foil. Marinate in refrigerator 3 hours. Preheat oven to 425F (220C). Open foil, place meat in foil in oven. Roast 25 to 30 minutes or until tender but rare. Cool. Carve cooled meat into 10 thick slices. Garnish tournedos as follows:

Cut egg in half lengthwise and remove yolk. In a small bowl, blend yolk, butter, cream, salt, pepper, paprika and herbs. Using a pastry bag with a star tip, pipe mixture into egg whites. Top each with a tomato wedge. Arrange eggs on 2 tournedos.

Drain asparagus tips. In a small bowl, beat together white wine, lemon juice, salt, sugar, pepper and Worcestershire sauce. Pour mixture over asparagus. Let marinate 1 hour. Drain and arrange asparagus on 3 tournedos. Garnish with slices of cooked carrot.

Drain artichoke bottoms. Combine lemon juice and white wine. Pour over artichoke bottoms. Let marinate 1 hour; drain. Arrange artichokes on 3 tournedos. Spoon mayonnaise into centers of artichoke bottoms. Garnish tournedos with dill or parsley sprigs and a few pickled red or green peppercorns, if desired.

Place liver pâté on 2 remaining tournedos. Peel grapes. Soak in brandy about 10 minutes; drain. Use to garnish pâté.

Arrange all tournedos on a serving dish. Pour over aspic; let set. Makes 10 servings.

Veal Tournedos with Broccoli Puree

8 thick slices veal fillet
1/4 teaspoon white pepper
Pinch paprika
1/3 cup vegetable oil
1/2 teaspoon salt
8 oz. broccoli
1/4 teaspoon each grated nutmeg, dried thyme and basil
1/4 cup hot meat stock
1/4 oz. gelatin
1 cup whipping cream
1 cup White-Wine Aspic, page 18
8 pickled quail's eggs or slices of hard-cooked egg

Pat veal slices dry. Combine pepper and paprika. Rub mixture over meat. Heat oil in a medium skillet. Cook slices 3 to 4 minutes on each side. Season with salt; let cool. Arrange slices on a serving dish. Trim broccoli. Bring a little salted water to a boil in a medium saucepan. Add broccoli and simmer 10 minutes. Drain and let cool. Place broccoli, nutmeg, thyme and basil in a blender or food processor; puree. Taste and adjust seasoning. Pour meat stock into a small bowl and set in a pan of hot water. Sprinkle with gelatin. Stir until dissolved. Stir into broccoli puree. Whip cream until stiff. Fold into puree. Place in a pastry bag fitted with a star tip. Pipe a rosette onto each tournedos. Spoon aspic over all tournedos. Refrigerate to set. To serve, top tournedos with quail's eggs or slices of hard-cooked egg. Makes 8 servings.

Vitello Tonnato

2-1/4 lbs. leg or loin of veal, boned and rolled
1 garlic clove
6 canned anchovy fillets
1 onion
2 carrots
1 celery stalk
4 cups meat stock
1/2 cup dry white wine
2 bay leaves
5 peppercorns
1 (7-oz.) can tuna
1/3 cup whipping cream
1 egg yolk
3 tablespoons lemon juice
3/4 cup olive oil
3 tablespoons capers
Pinch each salt and pepper
8 oz. candied fruits

Make slits all over veal with a sharp knife. Slice garlic lengthwise. Chop anchovy fillets. Cut onion in half. Coarsely dice carrots. Chop celery. Insert garlic slices and half the anchovy pieces into openings in meat. Place in a large saucepan. Add cold water to cover. Bring to a boil. Simmer 1 minute. Drain and add 1 cup fresh water, onion, carrots, celery, meat stock, wine, bay leaves and peppercorns. Cover and simmer 1-1/2 hours. Cool veal in stock. Dry cooled veal. Strain 1/2 cup stock and reserve. Drain tuna. Place cream, egg yolk, tuna, remaining anchovies and lemon juice in a blender or food processor. Process while gradually adding oil. Place in a bowl. Stir in capers, salt, pepper and enough strained stock to give sauce a thin, creamy consistency. Slice meat. Serve with sauce and candied fruits.

Pork & Turkey-Liver Squares

5 oz. turkey livers
2 tablespoons butter
4 oz. mushrooms
3 tablespoons chopped fresh parsley
2 eggs
1 teaspoon each salt and pepper
2 teaspoons paprika
1/2 teaspoon dried marjoram
1 lb. very finely ground pork
1 lb. bulk sausage
Pie-Crust Pastry, page 14
Beaten egg to glaze

Trim and dice turkey livers. Melt butter in a small saucepan. Add livers. Sauté until browned; cool. Slice mushrooms. In a large bowl, combine parsley, eggs, salt, pepper, paprika, marjoram, ground pork and sausage. Add turkey livers and mushrooms. Preheat oven to 350F (175C). On a lightly floured surface, roll out pastry into 2 squares, one 12-inch and the other 13-inch. Line base and sides of a 12-inch-square baking pan with larger pastry square. Fill with sausage mixture. Lay smaller square on top and press pastry edges firmly together on all sides. Roll out any pastry trimmings and make small decorations. Coat pastry top with beaten egg. Arrange decorations on top and coat with more egg. Pierce top several times with a fork. Bake 45 minutes or until pastry is browned. Cool. Cut into 2-inch squares. Makes 36.

Steak Tartare

2 onions
Bunch parsley
4 fresh sage leaves or a pinch dried sage
6 cornichons
1-1/4 lbs. ground beef sirloin or tenderloin
1 tablespoon capers
3 egg yolks
1/4 teaspoon black pepper
1/2 teaspoon salt
4 canned anchovy fillets

Dice onions. Finely chop parsley and 3 fresh sage leaves, if used. Finely dice cornichons. Combine ground steak, onions, parsley, chopped or dried sage, cornichons, capers, 2 egg yolks, pepper and salt in a large bowl. Arrange steak mixture in a dish. Make a well in the center and pour in remaining egg yolk. Top mixture with anchovy fillets. Garnish with remaining sage leaf, if used. Makes 4 to 6 servings.

Cook's Tip

It is very important to buy and grind the meat for Steak Tartare the same day it will be served.

Steak Tartare Buffet-Style

5 large onions
40 stuffed olives
4 pickled cucumbers or dill pickles
8 canned anchovy fillets
Large bunch each parsley and chives
Salt and white pepper
Paprika
Caraway seeds
Tomato ketchup
Brandy
Capers
9 eggs
3 lbs. ground beef sirloin or tenderloin

Finely dice 4 onions. Cut remaining onion into rings. Chop olives. Finely dice pickles. Cut anchovy fillets in half lengthwise. Chop parsley and chives. Arrange diced onion, olives, pickles, anchovies, parsley, chives, salt, pepper, paprika, caraway seeds, tomato ketchup, brandy and capers in separate small bowls. Break eggs and separate, taking care not to break yolks. Keep whites for another use. Return each yolk carefully to its shell. Sprinkle a dish with rock salt and stand 8 of the filled shells in salt. Place ground steak on a serving platter. Top with onion rings and garnish with remaining egg yolk in its shell. Each guest takes a portion of Steak Tartare and mixes it with the seasonings and accompaniments to taste. Serve with a generous amount of whole-wheat bread. Makes 8 servings.

Individual Steaks Tartare

If you prefer, you can arrange the Steak Tartare on 8 individual plates. Surround each helping with onion rings. Fill rings with diced onion, olives, capers, paprika, salt, white pepper, caraway seeds, chives and parsley. Add brandy and tomato ketchup. Place an egg yolk in a shell on each portion. Serve with separate bowls containing any of the accompaniments listed in the previous recipe and others such as cornichons, canned baby sweet-corn cobs, pickled cocktail onions and mixed pickles.

Cook's Tip

For a variation, you can mix all the spices, herbs, diced ingredients and egg yolks into the Steak Tartare in the kitchen, then serve it on a large serving dish. Be careful not to over-season because guests' tastes are bound to vary. Place extra salt and seasoning on the table so the guests can help themselves.

Giant Cheese Buffet

There is such an enormous range of cheeses on the market that you should have no difficulty in setting up an attractive cheese buffet. Make sure your cheese is fresh and of good quality. Try to balance your selection by including hard, medium and soft cheeses and mild, seasoned or strong varieties. Allow 8 ounces of cheese per person. Arrange your cheeses on platters, as above, slicing only a small amount of each type because cheese stays fresh longer if kept in one piece. You can add variety to your buffet with Gorgonzola Dip, page 175, Cheese & Sausage Salad or Cheese & Fruit Salad. Remember to serve plenty of fresh bread and butter, as well as fruits, nuts, pickles and chutnies. The cheese buffet shown above is made up as follows: on the tray to the left are Edam, Leicester, Emmentaler and Cheshire cheeses, both sliced and in cubes; the cheeseboard in the center holds Tilsit, Livarot, Pont l'Evêque, Reblochon, Camembert, goat cheeses and Gorgonzola Dip; and on the board in the background are samsoe, Jarlsberg, fontina, Gouda and Danish Blue.

Cheese & Sausage Salad

12 oz. ham loaf
8 oz. Edam cheese
4 oz. Emmentaler cheese
1 Spanish onion
1 garlic clove
3 tablespoons wine vinegar
Salt and white pepper
1 teaspoon mild or whole-grain mustard
3 tablespoons chopped fresh mixed herbs (parsley, lovage, thyme, salad burnet, mint) or 2 teaspoons dried herbs
1/2 cup vegetable oil

Cut ham loaf, Edam and Emmentaler into thick slices. Cut slices into strips. Slice onion into thin rings. In a salad bowl, combine ham loaf, cheese and onion. Crush garlic. In a small bowl, beat together vinegar, salt, pepper, mustard, herbs, garlic and oil. Pour dressing over salad. Makes 6 servings.

Cheese & Fruit Salad

1 round honeydew melon
12 oz. Gouda cheese
12 oz. diced mixed fresh fruit (pears, peaches, cherries)
3 tablespoons lemon juice
Pinch salt
1 teaspoon sugar
Pinch each cayenne (red) pepper and ground ginger
1 tablespoon brandy
1/3 cup vegetable oil

Slice a third off stalk end of melon. Scoop out flesh from both parts using a melon-baller. Dice Gouda. Combine melon balls, Gouda and diced fruit in a large bowl. In a small bowl, beat together lemon juice, salt, sugar, red pepper, ginger, brandy and oil. Pour dressing over salad. Cut a pattern around rim of melon shell, if desired. Fill melon with fruit mixture. Makes 6 servings.

Cheese Platter with Gorgonzola Cream

Cheese Platter:
4 oz. Bavarian smoked cheese with ham
4 oz. Tilsit or Havarti cheese
4 oz. Stilton cheese
8 oz. Emmentaler cheese
4 oz. Camembert cheese

Garnishes:
Black olives
Grapes
Shelled walnuts
Small salted pretzels

Gorgonzola Cream:
4 oz. Gorgonzola cheese
2 oz. soft butter
1 egg yolk
1 tablespoon whipping cream
Generous pinch cayenne (red) pepper
1 tablespoon chopped fresh mixed herbs, if desired
4 oz. ham, unsliced

Cut Bavarian smoked cheese, Tilsit or Havarti, Stilton and half the Emmentaler into thin slices. Cut remaining Emmentaler into cubes and Camembert into wedges. Arrange sliced cheese and Camembert wedges on a cheese board. Thread each Emmentaler cube onto a wooden pick with an olive or a grape. Place on cheese board. Arrange walnuts and pretzels over cheese. To make Gorgonzola Cream, place Gorgonzola in a bowl and mash with a fork. Beat in butter, egg yolk, cream, red pepper and herbs, if desired. Finely dice ham and stir into Gorgonzola mixture. Serve with cheese platter. Makes 6 servings.

Country Cheese Board

4 oz. mature Camembert cheese
4 oz. Emmentaler cheese, shredded
1/4 cup soft butter
1 egg yolk
1 teaspoon paprika
Salt and white pepper
1 tablespoon brandy
2 slices pumpernickel bread
1/4 cup chopped pistachio nuts
2 lbs. assorted cheeses (Limburger, Havarti, Gouda, Wensleydale,
  Cheshire, Rambol Poivre)
1 Spanish onion
Bunch radishes

Place Camembert in a large bowl. Mash cheese with a fork. Work in Emmentaler, butter, egg yolk, paprika, salt, pepper and brandy. Let stand in a cool place 2 hours. Crumble pumpernickel into fine crumbs. Form Camembert mixture into balls. Roll half the balls in chopped pistachios and the other half in pumpernickel crumbs. Cut your selection of cheeses into thick slices. Cut onion into rings. Arrange sliced cheese on a large cheeseboard. Garnish with onion rings, radishes and cheese balls. Makes 6 servings.

Mixed-Herb Oil

**Small bunch each parsley and
  chives
2 sprigs sage
2 teaspoons dried thyme
2 teaspoons dried marjoram
2 teaspoons dried lovage, if desired
2 to 2-1/2 cups sunflower oil**

Finely chop parsley, chives and
sage. Place in a preserving jar
with thyme, marjoram and
lovage, if desired. Add enough
oil to cover herbs. Seal jar. Refrigerate 8 to 10 days. Shake oil
well before use and top each
time with fresh oil to keep
herbs covered.

Rosemary Oil

**2 to 3 sprigs rosemary
2 cups olive oil or sunflower oil**

Place rosemary in a tall bottle.
Add enough oil to cover. Cork
the bottle. Refrigerate 2 weeks.
Use oil for salad dressings. Top
with fresh oil after use, to keep
rosemary covered.

Cook's Tip

**You can replace the rosemary with
thyme, as shown, basil, lavender
or sage. Do not keep any herb oil
for more than 6 weeks.**

Lemon Vinegar

Juice and peel of 1 large lemon
1 cup white-wine vinegar
Few lemon-balm leaves, if desired

Pare lemon very thinly, taking care to remove none of the pith with the peel. Squeeze lemon. Measure 6 tablespoons juice and pour into a bottle. Add peel and vinegar. Add lemon balm to mixture, if desired. Cork the bottle and shake well. Refrigerate at least 3 weeks. Strain vinegar through cheesecloth. Return vinegar to bottle and use as required. Store in refrigerator.

Garlic Vinegar

6 garlic cloves
1 sprig thyme
1 teaspoon white peppercorns
2 cups red-wine vinegar

Place garlic, thyme and peppercorns in a bottle. Add vinegar. Cork the bottle. Refrigerate at least 3 weeks. Strain vinegar through cheesecloth. Return to bottle and use as required. Store in refrigerator.

Sage Vinegar

3 sprigs sage
2 cups red-wine vinegar

Place sage in a bottle. Add vinegar. Cork the bottle. Refrigerate at least 3 weeks. Strain vinegar through cheesecloth. Return to bottle and use as required. Store in refrigerator.

Salad-Burnet Vinegar

3 small sprigs salad burnet
2 cups white-wine vinegar

Place salad burnet in a bottle. Add vinegar. Cork the bottle. Refrigerate at least 3 weeks. Strain vinegar through cheesecloth. Return to bottle and use as required. Store in refrigerator.

Savory Butters

Garlic Butter
1 garlic clove
1/2 cup soft butter
1 teaspoon lemon juice
1/2 teaspoon grated lemon peel
1/4 teaspoon white pepper

Crush garlic. In a small bowl, blend garlic, butter, lemon juice, lemon peel and pepper. Shape butter mixture into a square block. Wrap in foil. Refrigerate before slicing.

Green Butter
1/2 cup soft unsalted butter
3 tablespoons juice from cooking spinach
3/4 teaspoon celery salt
Generous pinch white pepper
Pinch grated nutmeg
Chopped parsley

In a small bowl, blend butter, spinach juice, celery salt, pepper and nutmeg. Place in a pastry bag fitted with a star tip. Pipe rosettes onto a sheet of foil. Refrigerate. Serve sprinkled with parsley.

Paprika Butter
3/4 teaspoon sugar
1/2 teaspoon tomato paste
Pinch cayenne (red) pepper
1/2 cup soft butter
1 tablespoon paprika

In a small bowl, blend sugar, tomato paste, red pepper and butter. Spread butter mixture in a 1/2-inch-thick layer on a sheet of foil. Refrigerate. To serve, cut into rectangles and coat with paprika.

Truffle Butter
1 (1/2-oz.) piece truffle
1 teaspoon lemon juice
Salt and cayenne (red) pepper
1/2 cup soft unsalted butter

Finely chop truffle. In a small bowl, combine lemon juice, salt, red pepper, truffle and butter. Shape into a long roll. Wrap in foil. Refrigerate before cutting into slices.

Caper Butter
2 teaspoons capers
1/2 cup soft unsalted butter
1/2 teaspoon each lemon and orange juice
1 (1-3/4-oz.) can anchovy fillets

Drain capers and divide into 2 portions. In a small bowl, crush half the capers into butter. Blend in lemon and orange juice. Drain and chop anchovies. Blend into butter mixture. Shape into small balls. Refrigerate. To serve, top each butter ball with 3 of the remaining capers.

Orange Butter
1 tablespoon orange juice
1 tablespoon grated orange peel
1/2 cup soft unsalted butter
1 tablespoon pickled green peppercorns, if desired

In a small bowl, blend orange juice and peel, butter and peppercorns, if desired. Spread butter mixture in a 1/2-inch-thick layer on a sheet of foil. Refrigerate. To serve, cut into rectangles.

Curry Rosettes
1 teaspoon curry paste or powder
1/4 teaspoon sugar
1/2 cup soft butter

In a small bowl, blend curry paste or powder, sugar and butter. Place butter mixture in a pastry bag fitted with a star tip. Pipe rosettes onto a sheet of foil. Refrigerate until firm.

Sprout Butter
1/2 basket alfalfa sprouts
1/2 cup soft butter
1 teaspoon lemon juice
1 tablespoon dairy sour cream

Snip alfalfa sprouts with kitchen scissors. Wash and drain. Finely chop sprouts. In a small bowl, blend sprouts, butter, lemon juice and sour cream. Spread butter mixture in a 1/2-inch-thick layer on a sheet of foil. Refrigerate. Cut into squares or ovals.

Mustard Butter
1 tablespoon hot mustard
6 drops Tabasco sauce
Dash Worcestershire sauce
1/2 cup soft butter

In a small bowl, beat together mustard, Tabasco, Worcestershire sauce and butter until light and fluffy. Place butter mixture in a pastry bag fitted with a plain tip. Pipe 3 blobs at a time onto a sheet of foil. Refrigerate until firm.

Red-Pepper Rounds
1/2 cup soft butter
Pinch ground ginger
8 drops Tabasco sauce
1/4 cup finely chopped red bell pepper
3 tablespoons chopped parsley

In a small bowl, blend butter, ginger and Tabasco. Mix in chopped pepper. Wrap butter mixture in foil. Shape into a long roll. Refrigerate. To serve, coat with parsley and slice.

Pepper Butter
1 teaspoon freshly ground black pepper
1/4 teaspoon celery salt
Pinch garlic salt
1/2 cup soft unsalted butter

In a small bowl, beat together pepper, celery salt, garlic salt and butter until light and fluffy. Shape butter mixture into a block. Wrap in foil. Refrigerate. To serve, cut into curls.

Ham Butter
2 oz. ham, finely chopped
Generous pinch each white pepper and grated nutmeg
1 tablespoon finely grated Gouda or Cheddar cheese
1/2 cup soft butter

In a small bowl, blend ham, pepper, grated nutmeg, cheese and butter. Shape butter mixture into balls. Refrigerate.

Herb Balls
1/2 cup soft butter
Pinch each pepper and sugar
1 teaspoon lemon juice
1/4 cup chopped fresh mixed herbs

In a small bowl, blend butter, pepper, sugar, lemon juice and half the herbs. Shape butter mixture into balls. Refrigerate. To serve, coat with remaining herbs.

Salmon & Dill Butter
1/2 cup soft unsalted butter
Generous pinch cayenne (red) pepper
1 tablespoon finely chopped onion
3 oz. smoked salmon
1 tablespoon finely chopped dill

In a small bowl, blend butter, red pepper and onion. Chop salmon very finely. Add to mixture. Spread butter mixture in a long 1/2-inch-thick rectangle on a sheet of foil. Refrigerate until firm but not hard. Sprinkle with dill and roll up lengthwise jelly-roll fashion. Refrigerate until firm before slicing.

Horseradish Butter
1/2 cup soft butter
3 tablespoons grated fresh horseradish or prepared creamed horseradish
Pinch sugar

In a small bowl, blend butter, horseradish and sugar. Spread butter mixture in a 1/2-inch-thick layer on a sheet of foil. Refrigerate. To serve, make patterns with a fork and cut into squares.

Mock-Caviar Butter
1/2 cup soft butter
1 teaspoon lemon juice
1 small egg yolk
1-1/2 (2-oz.) jars lumpfish caviar

In a small bowl, blend butter, lemon juice, egg yolk and caviar. Spread butter mixture in a 1/2-inch-thick layer on a sheet of foil. Refrigerate before cutting into rounds.

Ohio Sauce

2 hard-cooked eggs
4 Spanish onions
1/2 cup vegetable oil
1/2 cup vinegar
1 cup water
Salt and pepper
2 garlic cloves
1/2 cup pickled shredded beets
Generous 1/2 cup dairy sour cream
3 tablespoons farmer's cheese or sieved cottage cheese
1-1/2 teaspoons sugar
1 tablespoon chopped chives
1 tablespoon chopped dill, if desired
1 tablespoon chopped borage, if desired

Cut eggs into quarters. Finely chop two of the quarters; set aside. Cut onions into rings. Combine oil, vinegar and water in a medium saucepan. Add onion rings, salt and pepper. Simmer over low heat 5 minutes. Cool. Crush garlic. Drain beets. Place beets, sour cream, farmer's or cottage cheese, sugar, remaining egg quarters, garlic and onion mixture in a blender or food processor; puree. Combine chives, dill and borage, if used. Reserve 1 teaspoon herb mixture. Stir remaining herbs into sauce. Season with salt and pepper to taste. Place sauce in a sauce-boat. Sprinkle with chopped egg and reserved herbs. Makes 6 servings.

Cook's Tip

This sauce is delicious with meat or fish fondue, cold beef and smoked mackerel.

Frankfurt Green Sauce

2 hard-cooked eggs
Bunch parsley
Bunch chives
Large bunch fresh mixed herbs (dill, tarragon, borage, basil)
1 teaspoon sugar
Salt and white pepper
3 tablespoons lemon juice
1/2 cup vegetable oil
1/3 cup mayonnaise
1/4 cup farmer's cheese or sieved cottage cheese
1/3 cup dairy sour cream

Dice eggs; set aside. Place herbs on a chopping board and sprinkle with sugar, salt and pepper. Finely chop with a sharp knife or pound with a mortar and pestle. Place in a small bowl. Combine lemon juice and oil. Pour over herbs. Cover and let stand 5 minutes. In a medium bowl, beat together mayonnaise, farmer's or cottage cheese and sour cream until smooth. Stir in herb mixture and diced eggs. Let stand in a cool place. Makes 6 servings.

Cook's Tip

Try this sauce with boiled beef, chicken or tongue, all kinds of savory jellies and poached eggs.

Sauce Tartare

2 hard-cooked eggs
1 cup mayonnaise
1/3 cup dairy sour cream
Bunch parsley
Bunch each dill and tarragon, if desired
4 dill pickles or 2 dill pickles and 2 tablespoons mixed pickled
**   vegetables**
1 oz. capers

Finely chop eggs. In a medium bowl, beat together mayonnaise and sour cream. Finely chop herbs with a sharp knife or pound with a mortar and pestle. Drain pickles, mixed pickled vegetables, if used, and capers; finely chop. Stir all chopped ingredients into mayonnaise mixture. Thin sauce, if necessary, with a little juice from pickles. Makes 6 servings.

Cook's Tip

A tasty sauce to serve with fish, meat fondue and hard-cooked eggs.

Vinaigrette Dressing

2 small tomatoes
3 green onions
Large bunch fresh mixed herbs (parsley, chives, tarragon, lemon
**   balm, salad burnet)**
2/3 cup vegetable oil
1/4 cup wine vinegar
1 teaspoon lemon juice
1/4 teaspoon sugar
Salt and white pepper

Dip tomatoes briefly into boiling water. Peel and cut into quarters. Discard seeds. Dice flesh. Chop green onions very finely. Finely chop herbs with a sharp knife or pound with a mortar and pestle. In a small bowl, beat together oil, vinegar, lemon juice, sugar, salt and pepper. Stir tomatoes, chopped green onions and herbs into dressing. Makes 6 servings.

Cook's Tip

This dressing is excellent with all kinds of salad. It goes particularly well with fresh asparagus.

Dips for Vegetables

Tomato Dip

1/2 cup tomato paste
Generous 1/2 cup plain yogurt
Pinch each salt, cayenne (red)
   pepper and sugar
1 teaspoon lemon juice
Bunch chives
3 tablespoons pickled green
   peppercorns, if desired

In a small bowl, beat together, tomato paste, yogurt, salt, red pepper, sugar and lemon juice. Finely chop chives. Stir into yogurt mixture. Drain green peppercorns, if used. Crush lightly wth a fork and add to dip.

Herb Dip

Generous 1/2 cup plain yogurt
4 oz. cream cheese
1 tablespoon whipping cream
1/2 garlic clove
1/2 teaspoon celery salt
Pinch white pepper
1/3 cup chopped fresh mixed herbs

In a small bowl, beat together yogurt, cream cheese and cream until smooth. Crush garlic. Add garlic, celery salt, pepper and chopped herbs to yogurt mixture.

Orange Dip

Juice and peel of 1 orange
1/2 cup mayonnaise
3 tablespoons whipping cream
1 tablespoon mild Dijon-style
   mustard
Pinch each salt, white pepper and
   sugar

Set aside a small amount of orange peel. In a small bowl, beat together mayonnaise, cream, orange juice, remaining peel, mustard, salt, pepper and sugar. Place dip in a bowl. Garnish with reserved orange peel.

Cook's Tip

Serve these dips with strips or slices of raw vegetables, such as fennel, celery, red, green and yellow bell peppers, Belgian endive and tomatoes.

Artichoke Dips

Tomato Dip
2 tomatoes
1/2 cup mayonnaise
1/4 cup tomato paste
3 tablespoons whipping cream
5 drops Tabasco sauce
Pinch each salt and sugar
1 tablespoon paprika

Egg Dip
3 hard-cooked eggs
2/3 cup olive oil
1/4 cup wine vinegar
1 teaspoon mild Dijon-style mustard
Salt and white pepper
1 teaspoon capers, drained
1 tablespoon chopped parsley
1 tablespoon chopped lemon-balm leaves, if desired

Mayonnaise Dip
1 cup mayonnaise
2 teaspoons lemon juice
1/4 cup whipping cream, whipped

Peel and quarter tomatoes. Remove seeds. Finely dice flesh. Combine tomatoes, mayonnaise, tomato paste, cream and seasonings.

Halve eggs. Press yolks through a fine sieve. Finely chop whites. Combine yolks, oil, vinegar, mustard, salt and pepper. Crush capers and stir into mixture with parsley and lemon balm, if desired. Add egg whites.

Combine mayonnaise and lemon juice. Fold in whipped cream.

Sausage Dips

Garlic Dip
4 hard-cooked eggs
2 egg yolks
Salt and pepper
Juice of 1 lemon
4 garlic cloves, crushed
Generous 1/2 cup olive oil

Gorgonzola Dip
1/4 cup soft butter
4 oz. Gorgonzola cheese
Generous 1/2 cup plain yogurt

Cream Dip
2 hard-cooked eggs
1/4 cup soft butter
1 tablespoon wine vinegar
Salt and white pepper
Pinch paprika
Few drops Worcestershire sauce
3 tablespoons finely chopped chives
Generous 1/2 cup dairy sour cream
Generous 1/2 cup whipping cream, lightly whipped

Halve eggs. Press cooked yolks through a fine sieve into a small bowl. Blend with raw egg yolks, salt, pepper, lemon juice and garlic. Slowly beat in oil, to make a creamy mayonnaise. Chop cooked egg whites. Stir into dip.

Beat butter until fluffy. Press Gorgonzola through a sieve into a small bowl. Combine butter, cheese and yogurt.

Halve eggs. Press yolks through a sieve into a small bowl. Finely chop whites. Beat butter until fluffy. Blend in vinegar, salt, pepper, paprika, Worcestershire sauce, chives, sour cream, yolks and whites. Fold whipped cream into dip.

Onion Soup

1-1/4 lbs. onions
1 garlic clove
1/2 cup butter
1/2 teaspoon Tabasco sauce
Pinch each cayenne (red) pepper and grated nutmeg
5-1/2 cups meat stock
1 cup dry white wine
4 slices French bread
1/2 cup shredded Emmentaler or Gruyère cheese

Slice onions into thin rings. Crush garlic. Melt butter in a large shallow pan. Add onions and garlic. Sauté until golden brown. Add Tabasco, red pepper, nutmeg and stock. Cover and bring to a boil. Simmer over medium heat 20 minutes. Add wine. Cook a few minutes longer. Remove from heat. Divide soup between 4 individual heatproof bowls. Lightly toast bread. Float 1 slice on each portion of soup. Sprinkle shredded cheese over toast. Place bowls of soup under preheated broiler until cheese has melted. Makes 4 servings.

Consommé with Dumplings

Generous 1/2 cup milk
2 dry bread rolls
5 oz. bacon slices
1 large onion
1 egg
Generous pinch each salt and grated nutmeg
4 cups rich, clarified meat stock, see White-Wine Aspic, page 18
1-1/2 to 2 cups fresh white breadcrumbs
Small bunch parsley

Heat milk in a small saucepan; do not boil. Cut bread rolls into very thin slices. Place in a medium bowl. Pour hot milk over rolls; let stand. Dice bacon as finely as possible. Finely chop onion. Sauté bacon gently in a non-stick skillet until fat runs. Add onion. Cook, stirring constantly, until onion becomes transparent. In a small bowl, beat together egg, salt and nutmeg. Pour over bread mixture. Add bacon and onion. Mix well. Let stand a few minutes. Bring stock to a boil in a medium saucepan. Mix enough fresh breadcrumbs into bread mixture to make a stiff dough. Rinse 2 teaspoons in cold water. Scoop 8 oval dumplings out of the dough, using teaspoons. Place dumplings in boiling stock. Simmer over low heat 10 minutes. Chop parsley. Place 2 dumplings in each of 4 individual soup bowls. Pour consommé over dumplings. Sprinkle with parsley. Makes 4 servings.

Hungarian Goulash Soup

10 oz. pork fillet
8 oz. beef stew-meat
4 onions
2 carrots
2 green bell peppers
1 (8-oz.) can tomatoes
3 tablespoons vegetable oil
2 to 3 teaspoons paprika
Generous pinch garlic salt
Salt and black pepper
4 cups beef stock
Generous 1/2 cup whipping cream

Trim meat and cut into 1-inch cubes. Slice onions into rings. Slice carrots. Quarter green peppers. Remove and discard seeds and pith. Cut flesh into strips. Drain tomatoes, reserving juice. Coarsely chop tomatoes. Heat oil in a large saucepan or casserole. Sauté onions until transparent. Add meat and brown in oil. Stir in carrots and green peppers. Cook 1 to 2 minutes longer. Add chopped tomatoes and reserved juice; stir well. Season to taste with paprika, garlic salt, salt and black pepper. Add beef stock. Cover and bring to a boil. Simmer over low heat 60 to 80 minutes. To serve, stir in cream. Makes 6 to 8 servings.

Oxtail Soup with Meatballs

1 small onion
5 oz. ground pork
l egg, beaten
2 to 3 tablespoons fresh white breadcrumbs
Salt and black pepper
Pinch dried sage
4 oz. mushrooms
Bunch parsley
2 (15-oz.) cans oxtail soup
Generous 1/2 cup red wine
3/4 cup frozen peas
3 tablespoons tomato paste
Pinch each paprika and sugar
Few drops Tabasco sauce
1/3 cup whipping cream

Finely chop onion. In a medium bowl, combine onion, ground pork and beaten egg. Add enough breadcrumbs to make mixture into a stiff dough. Season with salt, pepper and sage. Form dough into walnut-size meatballs. Slice mushrooms as finely as possible. Chop parsley. Place oxtail soup and wine in a medium saucepan. Bring to a boil. Add meatballs. Simmer over low heat 10 minutes. After 5 minutes of cooking, add mushrooms, peas and tomato paste. Season with paprika, sugar and Tabasco. Remove from heat. Stir in cream and sprinkle with parsley. Makes 4 servings.

177

Cream of Cucumber Soup

**1 small or 1/2 European-style
    cucumber
1-1/2 cups whipping cream
2 cups milk or buttermilk
1/2 teaspoon salt
1/2 teaspoon sugar
Juice of 1 lemon
Bunch dill**

Peel cucumber. Cut in half lengthwise. Scoop out seeds with a teaspoon. Finely dice flesh. In a small bowl, combine cream, milk or buttermilk, salt, sugar and lemon juice. Finely chop dill. Stir dill and diced cucumber into soup. Refrigerate before serving. Makes 4 servings.

Chilled Tomato Soup

**2 cups water
2-1/2 lbs. tomatoes
Salt and white pepper
Generous pinch celery salt
Generous 1/2 cup dry white
    vermouth
1 cup plain yogurt
2 oz. mushrooms
Generous 1/2 cup whipping cream
Bunch chives**

Bring water to a boil in a medium saucepan. Quarter tomatoes. Place in boiling water. Cover and simmer over low heat 10 minutes. Remove from heat. Press tomatoes and liquid through a sieve into a medium bowl. Season tomato puree with salt, pepper and celery salt; cool. In a small bowl, blend vermouth and yogurt. Finely slice mushrooms. Beat yogurt mixture, mushrooms and cream into cooled tomato puree. Refrigerate. To serve, finely chop chives and sprinkle over soup. Makes 4 servings.

Iced Borscht

1-1/4 cups dairy sour cream
1-1/2 cups plain yogurt
2 dill pickles
1 onion
1 lb. cooked beets, peeled and diced
Salt and white pepper
Generous pinch sugar
1 tablespoon orange juice
1 tablespoon lemon juice
2 hard-cooked eggs
Few sprigs dill, if desired

Set aside 3 tablespoons sour cream. In a small bowl, blend yogurt and remaining sour cream. Drain and finely dice pickles. Chop onion. Stir pickles, onion and diced beets into yogurt mixture. Season with salt, pepper, sugar, orange and lemon juice. Cover and refrigerate 1 hour. Fill a soup tureen with ice cubes and place in refrigerator. Cut each egg into 8 wedges. Set aside 3 wedges. Dice remaining wedges. Remove ice cubes from tureen. Fill tureen with chilled borscht. Stir in diced eggs. Spoon reserved sour cream into the center of tureen. Garnish with reserved 3 egg wedges and a few dill sprigs, if desired. Makes 4 servings.

Andalusian Gazpacho

1 lb. tomatoes
2 large garlic cloves
3 onions
2 cucumbers
1 large green bell pepper
2 cups fat-free chicken or meat stock
3 tablespoons red-wine vinegar
3 tablespoons olive oil
1 cup fresh white breadcrumbs
2 teaspoons tomato paste
Salt and black pepper
Generous pinch sugar
6 slices stale white bread
1/4 cup butter

Peel and quarter tomatoes. Scoop out seeds. Coarsely chop garlic and 2 onions. Coarsely dice 1 cucumber. Trim and halve green pepper. Remove seeds and pith. Dice flesh. Place tomatoes, garlic, chopped onion, diced cucumber and green pepper in a blender or food processor; puree. Place puree in a soup tureen. Whisk in stock, then vinegar, oil, breadcrumbs and tomato paste. Season with salt, pepper and sugar. Refrigerate 2 hours. Remove crusts from stale white bread. Cut bread into cubes. Melt butter in a skillet. Sauté bread in butter until golden brown; cool. Finely chop remaining onion. Finely dice remaining cucumber. Serve bread croutons, onion and cucumber with gazpacho. Makes 4 servings.

Yogurt & Mixed-Vegetable Soup

1 carrot
1 onion
1 cup salted water
3/4 cup frozen peas
3 tablespoons drained whole-kernel corn
1 garlic clove
Bunch dill
4 cups plain yogurt
3 tablespoons lemon juice
Salt and white pepper
4 mint sprigs, if desired

Dice carrot. Chop onion. Bring salted water to a boil in a medium saucepan. Add carrot, onion, peas and corn. Cover and simmer over low heat 4 minutes. Remove from heat. Let vegetables cool in cooking liquid. Crush garlic. Chop dill. In a small bowl, combine yogurt, garlic, dill and lemon juice. Season to taste with salt and pepper. Stir in vegetables and cooking liquid. Pour soup into 4 individual bowls. Chill throughly. To serve, garnish each bowl with a mint sprig, if desired. Makes 4 servings.

Chilled Fish Medley

8 thawed frozen prawns or medium shrimp
1 cup salted water
1 lb. frozen haddock or cod fillets
12 oz. spinach
Salt and white pepper
4 oz. fresh sorrel, if desired
1 cucumber
1 green onion
1 tablespoon chopped parsley
1 tablespoon chopped dill, if desired
3 cups white wine or dry cider

Drain prawns or shrimp. Bring 1 cup salted water to a boil in a small saucepan. Add frozen fish. Simmer just below boiling point over low heat 10 minutes. Remove from heat. Let fish cool in cooking liquid. Wash spinach; do not dry. Place in a medium saucepan. Add salt. Cover and simmer 15 minutes or until tender. Drain spinach. Cut spinach and sorrel, if used, into strips. Peel cucumber. Cut in half lengthwise. Scoop out seeds with a teaspoon. Dice flesh. Chop green onion. Using a slotted spoon, lift cooled fish out of cooking liquid. Flake fish; set aside. Stir spinach, cucumber, green onion, parsley, seasoning and sorrel and dill, if desired, into fish stock. Add white wine or cider. Add fish pieces and prawns or shrimp. Place soup in a tureen. Refrigerate until ready to serve. Makes 4 servings.

Orange Soup with Vanilla Ice Cream

3/4 cup thawed frozen orange-juice concentrate
2 cups water
Generous 1/2 cup white wine
1/3 cup sugar
1 orange
1 tablespoon cornstarch
8 oz. fresh or frozen raspberries
4 teaspoons Grand Marnier
Vanilla ice cream

Place orange-juice concentrate, water, wine and sugar in a medium saucepan. Bring to a boil. Wash, dry and thinly pare orange. Add peel to soup. Blend cornstarch and a little cold water. Stir into soup. Return to a boil. Simmer over medium heat 1 minute. Add raspberries. Remove from heat. Refrigerate. Remove orange peel from chilled soup with a slotted spoon. Remove pith from orange. Remove skin from each segment. Divide segments between 4 individual bowls. Sprinkle each portion with 1 teaspoon Grand Marnier. Add chilled soup to each bowl. Place a spoonful of vanilla ice cream in the center of each bowl and serve. Makes 4 servings.

Strawberry & Apple Soup

2 medium, sweet apples
3 tablespoons lemon juice
1-1/2 cups water
1/2 cup sugar
1 cup white wine
1 teaspoon grated lemon peel
2 tablespoons cornstarch
8 oz. fresh or thawed frozen strawberries
1 cup chilled sparkling wine
1 tablespoon chopped pistachio nuts, if desired

Peel, quarter and core apples. Slice finely. Sprinkle apple slices with lemon juice. Place water and sugar in a medium saucepan. Bring to a boil, stirring constantly. Add white wine, apples and grated lemon peel. Return to a boil. Blend cornstarch with a little cold water. Stir into soup. Cook a few minutes longer. Remove from heat; cool. Divide strawberries into 2 portions. Press 1 portion through a sieve or puree in a blender or food processor. Stir strawberry puree and whole strawberries into soup. Refrigerate. To serve, add sparkling wine. Divide soup between 4 individual bowls. Sprinkle each serving with chopped pistachios, if desired. Makes 4 servings.

Blackberry & Pineapple Soup

1/2 cup sugar
4 cups water
1 tablespoon lemon juice
Few drops vanilla extract, if desired
8 oz. diced fresh pineapple
1 lb. fresh or thawed frozen blackberries
3 tablespoons cornstarch
Generous 1/2 cup red wine
2 oz. sliced almonds

Set aside 1 teaspoon sugar. Place remaining sugar, water, lemon juice and vanilla, if desired, in a medium saucepan. Bring to a boil. Add pineapple. Cover and simmer over medium heat 5 minutes. Add blackberries. Simmer over low heat 10 minutes longer. Blend cornstarch and wine. Stir into soup. Bring to a boil. Boil 1 minute. Remove from heat; cool. Place soup in a serving bowl. Refrigerate. Place almonds in a small skillet. Sprinkle with reserved 1 teaspoon sugar. Toast until golden brown. Scatter over chilled soup and serve. Makes 4 servings.

Cook's Tip

If using canned pineapple chunks, simmer the blackberries alone for 5 minutes, add the pineapple and continue cooking for 5 more minutes. Then proceed as above.

Lime Soup

2 oz. raisins
3 tablespoons white rum
3 limes
Small piece fresh gingerroot or 1 teaspoon powdered ginger
3 cups water
1 cinnamon stick
4 cloves
1/2 teaspoon vanilla extract
1 cup sugar
1 tablespoon cornstarch
6 tablespoons sweet white wine
2 egg whites

Place raisins in a small bowl. Sprinkle with rum. Marinate 1 hour. Wash and dry limes. Pare very thinly in a spiral shape. Squeeze limes; set aside juice. Finely grate gingerroot, if used. Place water, lime peel, cinnamon stick and cloves in a medium saucepan. Bring to a boil. Cover and simmer over medium heat 8 minutes. Remove lime peel and spices from pan with a slotted spoon. Discard spices; set aside peel. Reduce heat. Stir lime juice, vanilla, grated or powdered ginger and 3/4 cup sugar into soup. Simmer 10 minutes. After 7 minutes of cooking, add raisin and rum mixture. Blend cornstarch and white wine. Stir into soup. Bring to a boil. Continue cooking 1 minute. Remove from heat. Refrigerate. Place a strip of lime peel in each of 4 individual bowls. Add chilled soup. In a medium bowl, whisk egg whites and remaining sugar until stiff. Place spoonfuls on each portion of soup. Makes 4 servings.

Elderberry Soup

2-1/4 lbs. elderberries
4 cups water
2 pears
1/2 cinnamon stick
Grated peel of 1/2 lemon
1/2 cup sugar
Pinch salt
1 tablespoon cornstarch
Generous 1/2 cup sweet white wine
Generous 1/2 cup whipping cream

Strip elderberries from their stalks. Wash in cold water; drain. Bring water to a boil in a medium saucepan. Add elderberries. Cover and simmer over medium heat 15 minutes. Peel, quarter and core pears. Cut into thick slices. Press elderberry mixture through a sieve or puree in a blender or food processor. Return puree to pan. Stir in cinnamon stick, lemon peel, sugar and salt. Bring to a boil. Add sliced pear. Simmer over low heat a few minutes. Remove cinnamon and lemon peel from soup with a slotted spoon. Blend cornstarch and wine. Stir into soup. Bring to a boil. Boil 1 minute. Remove from heat. Refrigerate. In a medium bowl, whip cream until stiff. Pour chilled soup into 4 individual bowls. Decorate each portion with a spoonful of whipped cream. Makes 4 servings.

Cook's Tip

Elderberry Soup is particularly good served on a bed of crushed ice.

Apricot & Cherry Soup

8 oz. cherries
1/2 lemon
3 cups water
1/2 cup sugar
1/2 teaspoon vanilla extract
1/2 cinnamon stick
1 oz. sago
1 lb. apricots
1 cup sweet white wine
4 oz. grated sweet chocolate, if desired

Pit cherries. Slice lemon. Place water, sugar, vanilla, cinnamon stick and lemon slices in a medium saucepan. Bring to a boil. Add sago. Cover and simmer over medium heat 15 minutes. Add cherries. Bring to a boil. Remove from heat. Remove cinnamon stick and lemon slices with a slotted spoon. Dip apricots briefly in boiling water. Plunge into cold water and peel. Quarter apricots and remove pits. Place wine and apricots in a medium saucepan. Bring to a boil. Simmer gently over low heat 5 minutes. Remove from heat. Strain liquid into cherry mixture. Divide apricots into 2 portions. Press 1 portion through a sieve or puree in a blender or food processor. Add pureed and quartered apricots to soup. Refrigerate. Serve chilled soup in 4 individual bowls. Sprinkle with grated chocolate, if desired. Makes 4 servings.

Cheese Spirals

2-1/2 cups all-purpose flour
1 pkg. active dry yeast
2/3 cup warm milk (110F, 45C)
1/4 cup butter or margarine, melted
1 egg, beaten
1/2 teaspoon salt
2 egg yolks
2 teaspoons water
1 cup shredded Emmentaler or Cheddar cheese
1 teaspoon paprika
1 tablespoon caraway seeds
1 tablespoon coarse salt

Lightly grease a baking sheet. Sift flour into a large bowl and form a well in the center. In a small bowl, mix yeast with a little warm milk. Add remaining milk. Pour into well in flour. Sprinkle a little flour over yeast mixture. Cover and let stand in a warm place 15 minutes or until frothy. Add melted butter or margarine, whole egg and salt to yeast mixture. Work in flour. Beat until smooth. Shape dough into a ball. Cover and let rise in a warm place 20 to 30 minutes. Preheat oven to 400F (205C). On a lightly floured surface, roll out dough to a rectangle, 1/4 inch thick. In a small bowl, beat egg yolks with 2 teaspoons water. Brush half the rectangle with egg-yolk mixture. Sprinkle with shredded cheese. Fold over other half of dough. Roll out again 1/4 inch thick. Cut into 1/2-inch-wide strips. Twist strips into spirals. Brush with remaining egg-yolk mixture. Sprinkle spirals with paprika, caraway seeds and salt. Place on prepared baking sheet. Bake 15 to 20 minutes or until golden brown. Makes about 24 servings.

Caraway Bites

2/3 cup all-purpose flour
Pinch each salt, sugar and grated nutmeg
1/4 cup butter or margarine
1 cup finely grated Gouda cheese
1 egg yolk
2 teaspoons water
3 to 4 tablespoons caraway seeds

Grease a baking sheet. Sift flour, salt, sugar and nutmeg into a large bowl. Form a well in the center. Cut butter or margarine into small pieces. Dot around edge of flour. Tip grated cheese into the well. Quickly work all ingredients together to form a dough. Divide dough into 2 portions. Wrap each portion in waxed paper or foil. Refrigerate 30 minutes. Preheat oven to 400F (205C). On a lightly floured surface, roll out both portions of dough separately until thin. Using a pastry cutter, cut dough into squares or rectangles. In a small bowl, beat egg yolk with water. Brush dough with egg-yolk mixture and sprinkle with caraway seeds. Place on prepared baking sheet. Bake 15 minutes or until golden brown.

Cheese Tricorns

2-1/3 cups all-purpose flour
1/2 teaspoon salt
1/2 teaspoon baking powder
6 tablespoons soft butter, cut in pieces
1 egg
1/4 cup dairy sour cream
4 (1/2-oz.) portions processed cheese or 2 oz. Bavarian smoked cheese
1 egg yolk
2 teaspoons water
2 tablespoons sesame seeds

Sift flour, salt and baking powder into a large bowl. Form a well in the center. Place butter in well and mix with a little flour. Add whole egg and sour cream. Knead ingredients together into a smooth dough. Cover and refrigerate 30 minutes. Preheat oven to 400F (205C). Lightly grease a baking sheet. On a lightly floured surface, roll out dough. Cut into 2-inch rounds. Slice processed or smoked cheese. Cut into small cubes, dipping knife frequently into hot water. Place 1 cheese cube on each pastry round. Fold in edges of pastry to form a tricorn. In a small bowl, beat egg yolk with water. Brush tricorns with mixture. Sprinkle with sesame seeds. Place on prepared baking sheet. Bake 15 to 20 minutes or until golden brown. Makes about 32 servings.

Cheese Croissants

2-1/2 cups all-purpose flour
1 pkg. active dry yeast
2/3 cup warm milk (110F, 45C)
1/4 cup butter or margarine, melted
1 egg, beaten
1/2 teaspoon salt
1 (8-oz.) pkg. sliced processed cheese
3 tablespoons chopped parsley
1 egg yolk
1 tablespoon milk
3 to 4 tablespoons sesame seeds

Lightly grease a baking sheet. Sift flour into a large bowl and form a well in the center. In a small bowl, mix yeast with a little warm milk. Add remaining milk. Pour into well in flour. Sprinkle a little flour over yeast mixture. Cover and let stand in a warm place 15 minutes or until frothy. Add melted butter or margarine, whole egg and salt to yeast mixture. Work in flour. Beat until smooth. Shape dough into a ball. Cover and let rise in a warm place 20 to 30 minutes. Preheat oven to 375F (190C). On a lightly floured surface, roll out dough to a 12" x 18" rectangle. Cut into 12 triangles measuring about 6" x 6" x 6" each. Cut each cheese slice into 4 equal triangles. Place 2 triangles on each triangle of dough. Sprinkle with parsley. Starting from a straight side, roll each triangle into a crescent shape. In a small bowl, beat egg yolk with milk. Brush croissants with egg-yolk mixture. Sprinkle with sesame seeds. Place on prepared baking sheet. Bake 15 to 20 minutes or until golden. Makes 12 servings.

Cheese Puffs

Pastry:
1 cup all-purpose flour
1 cup water
Pinch salt
1/2 cup butter or margarine
4 eggs, beaten

Filling:
1/2 teaspoon salt
Pinch each white pepper and celery salt
1-1/4 lbs. cream cheese
1/4 cup dry sherry
1 teaspoon paprika

Sift flour onto a piece of waxed paper. Heat water and a pinch of salt in a medium saucepan. Add butter or margarine and let melt. Bring mixture quickly to a boil. Remove from heat and add flour all at once, stirring vigorously. Return to heat. Beat 1 minute or until dough forms a ball and comes away cleanly from sides of pan. Remove from heat; cool slightly. Grease 2 large baking sheets. Preheat oven to 425F (220C). Gradually beat eggs into dough, making sure each addition is absorbed before beating in the next. Place mixture in a pastry bag fitted with a star tip. Pipe cherry-size blobs of dough onto prepared baking sheets, leaving 1 inch between each. Bake 20 minutes or until golden brown. Slice puffs in half horizontally while still warm. To make the filling, beat together 1/2 teaspoon salt, pepper, celery salt and cream cheese in a small bowl. Divide mixture into 2 portions. Stir sherry into 1 portion; beat paprika into the other. Pipe the 2 flavors of cream cheese alternately into bases of puffs. Arrange top halves to form lids. Makes about 60 servings.

Puff-Pastry Cheese Rings

1 (10-oz.) pkg. thawed frozen patty shells
1 egg yolk, beaten
1 cup shredded Emmentaler or Cheddar cheese
Pinch each salt and white pepper
8 oz. farmer's cheese or cottage cheese
1/4 cup whipping cream
1/4 teaspoon salt
Pinch each white pepper and caraway seeds, crushed

Sprinkle a large baking sheet with cold water. On a lightly floured surface, roll out pastry into a 9" x 15" rectangle. Using a 2-1/2-inch doughnut cutter, cut out 24 rings. Place rings on prepared baking sheet. Brush rings with beaten egg yolk. Sprinkle with shredded cheese, salt and pepper. Let stand on baking sheet about 15 minutes. Preheat oven to 425F (220C). Bake 12 to 15 minutes or until golden brown. Cool on a rack. Place farmer's or cottage cheese, cream, 1/4 teaspoon salt, pepper and caraway seeds in a blender or food processor. Process until smooth. Place cheese mixture in a pastry bag fitted with a star tip. Pipe mixture around 12 rings. Top with remaining 12 rings. Makes 12 servings.

Cook's Tip

If you do not have a doughnut cutter, use a 2-inch cookie cutter inside a 2-1/2-inch one.

Cream-Cheese Layer

1 (10-oz.) pkg. thawed frozen
  patty shells
1 teaspoon pickled green
  peppercorns, if desired
2 lbs. cream cheese or farmer's
  cheese
2 teaspoons mild Dijon-style
  mustard
8 drops Tabasco sauce
1 medium onion, grated
1 teaspoon each salt and
  Worcestershire sauce
2 teaspoons tomato paste
1 teaspoon paprika
3 tablespoons chopped fresh
  mixed herbs or 2 teaspoons
  dried mixed herbs
1 (2-oz.) pkg. sliced almonds
10 chilies
10 pickled cocktail onions
10 thin slices smoked ham

Sprinkle a large baking sheet with cold water. On a lightly floured surface, stack patty shells in 3 piles of 2 shells. Roll out pastry into three 10-inch rounds. Place rounds on baking sheet. Let stand 15 minutes. Preheat oven to 425F (220C). Bake 12 to 15 minutes or until golden brown. Cool. Chop green peppercorns, if used. In a small bowl, beat together cream or farmer's cheese, mustard, Tabasco sauce, onion, salt and Worcestershire sauce until smooth. Divide into 3 portions. Stir tomato paste and paprika into the first portion. Stir green peppercorns, if desired, and herbs into the second portion. Spread first pastry round with tomato mixture. Spread second pastry round with herb mixture. Spread third round with half the remaining cheese mixture. Stack rounds one on top of another, beginning with tomato round, then herb round and topping with plain-cheese round. Lightly toast almonds and press around edge of cake. Place remaining cheese mixture in a pastry bag fitted with a star tip. Pipe 10 rosettes around top of cake. Garnish with chilies, cocktail onions and rolls of ham. Makes 10 servings.

Cheese Pastry Pockets

1 (10-oz.) pkg. thawed frozen patty shells
2 tablespoons butter
1 cup shredded Cheddar, Gruyère or Edam cheese
2 eggs
3 tablespoons chopped parsley
1/4 teaspoon salt
Pinch cayenne (red) pepper
Juice of 1 lemon
1 egg yolk
2 teaspoons water

Place patty shells in an overlapping circle on a lightly floured surface. Roll out dough thinly. Melt butter. In a small bowl, beat together cheese, eggs, parsley, salt, red pepper and lemon juice. Stir in melted butter. Cool. Sprinkle a baking sheet with cold water. Cut pastry into 4-inch rounds. Place 1 tablespoon cheese mixture in the center of each round. Brush around edges of pastry with cold water. Fold rounds in half, pressing edges together to seal. Beat egg yolk with 2 teaspoons water. Brush pastry pockets with egg-yolk mixture. Place pockets on baking sheet. Let stand 10 minutes. Preheat oven to 400F (205C). Bake 12 minutes or until golden brown. Cool. Makes about 15 servings.

Minced-Steak Pasties

Pastry:
2-1/3 cups all-purpose flour
1/2 teaspoon salt
1/2 teaspoon baking powder
6 tablespoons soft butter, cut in pieces
1 egg
1/4 cup dairy sour cream

Filling:
1 onion
2 oz. mushrooms
3 tablespoons butter
8 oz. ground beef sirloin or tenderloin
1/4 teaspoon each salt, pepper and garlic salt
2 hard-cooked eggs
1 egg yolk, beaten

Sift flour, salt and baking powder into a large bowl. Form a well in the center. Place butter in well and mix with a little flour. Add whole egg and sour cream. Knead ingredients together into a smooth dough. Cover and refrigerate 30 minutes. Preheat oven to 400F (205C). To make the filling, finely dice onion. Chop mushrooms. Melt butter in a medium skillet. Sauté onion and mushrooms until golden brown. In a medium bowl, combine onion, mushrooms, ground beef, salt, pepper and garlic salt. Finely dice eggs. Stir into meat mixture. On a lightly floured surface, roll out dough 1/8 inch thick. Cut into 4-1/2-inch rounds. Place 1 tablespoon filling on each round. Brush around edges of pastry with beaten egg yolk. Fold sides over filling, pressing edges together to seal. Brush pastry with remaining egg yolk. Place on a baking sheet. Bake 15 to 20 minutes or until golden brown. Makes about 18 servings.

Cornish Pasties

Pastry:
1-3/4 cups all-purpose flour
Pinch salt
1 egg
1/2 cup soft butter, cut in pieces

Filling:
1 medium potato
1 shallot
5 oz. beef stew-meat
1/3 cup meat stock
1 teaspoon salt
1/2 teaspoon white pepper
1 teaspoon dried thyme
1 egg yolk
2 teaspoons water

Sift flour and salt into a large bowl. Form a well in the center. Tip in whole egg. Dot butter around edge of flour. Quickly knead all ingredients together into a dough. Wrap in foil. Refrigerate 30 minutes. To make the filling, peel potato and shallot; dice finely. Trim beef and cut into very small pieces. In a medium bowl, combine potato, shallot, beef, meat stock, salt, pepper and thyme. Divide mixture into 4 equal portions. Divide pastry into 4 equal portions. Preheat oven to 375F (190C). On a lightly floured surface, roll each portion of pastry into a 7-inch round. Beat egg yolk with 2 teaspoons water. Spoon filling onto centers of pastry rounds. Brush edges of pastry with egg-yolk mixture. Fold rounds in half, pressing edges together to seal. Make a pattern around folded edge with a knife or fork, if desired. Brush tops of pasties with remaining egg yolk. Place on a baking sheet. Bake 25 minutes. Reduce heat to 325F (165C) and bake 20 minutes longer or until golden brown. Makes 4 servings.

Ham Quiches

Pastry:
1-3/4 cups all-purpose flour
1 egg
2 to 3 tablespoons cold water
1/2 cup soft butter, cut in pieces

Filling:
3 medium onions
4 oz. smoked or boiled ham
3 tablespoons vegetable oil
1 cup grated Parmesan or Cheddar cheese
3 tablespoons chopped parsley or basil
4 eggs
Generous 1/2 cup whipping cream
1/4 teaspoon salt
Pinch white pepper

Sift flour into a large bowl. Form a well in the center. Tip in egg and water. Dot butter around edge of flour. Quickly knead all ingredients together to make a dough. Wrap in foil. Refrigerate 1 hour. Preheat oven to 425F (220C). On a lightly floured surface, roll out pastry. Use to line eight 4-inch tartlet cases. Pierce bases several times with a fork. Bake 10 minutes. Cool. Reduce oven heat to 400F (205C). To make the filling, finely dice onions and ham. Heat oil in a skillet. Sauté onions until soft. Cool. In a medium bowl, combine onions, ham, cheese and parsley or basil. Spoon mixture into tartlet shells. In a small bowl, beat together eggs, cream, salt and pepper. Pour over ham mixture. Bake 10 to 12 minutes. Cover with foil, if necessary, to avoid burning. Makes 8 servings.

Asparagus with Smoked Trout

1 lb. fresh asparagus
Pinch sugar
2 smoked-trout fillets
2 hard-cooked eggs
1 tomato
Few sprigs dill, if desired
1 dill pickle
1 small onion
1/4 cup vegetable oil
1 tablespoon wine vinegar
1 teaspoon mild Dijon-style
   mustard
Salt and white pepper
1 tablespoon chopped parsley

Lightly scrape bases of asparagus stalks. Tie asparagus into 2 bundles with cotton thread. Bring 4 cups salted water to a boil in a tall saucepan. Add sugar. Place asparagus bundles upright in pan, so the delicate tips show above the boiling water. Simmer over low heat 20 minutes, or until tender. Drain and cool. Untie cooled asparagus. Arrange on 2 individual plates. Top each portion with a trout fillet. Slice 1 egg. Finely chop remaining egg; set aside. Slice tomato. Garnish each plate with egg and tomato slices and dill sprigs, if desired. Drain and finely chop pickle. Dice onion as finely as possible or shred. In a small bowl, beat together oil, vinegar, mustard, salt, pepper and parsley. Stir in chopped egg, pickle and onion. Spoon dressing over asparagus and trout. Makes 2 servings.

Roquefort Pears with Smoked Ham

5 oz. smoked ham
1 ripe pear
2 oz. Roquefort cheese
1/4 cup soft butter
2 teaspoons port
2 shelled walnut halves
2 lettuce leaves
2 teaspoons red-currant jelly
2 slices whole-wheat bread

Arrange smoked ham on 2 individual plates. Halve pear. Remove and discard core. Using a teaspoon, carefully scoop flesh out of each half to within 1/2 inch of the skin. Place pear flesh in a small bowl; crush pear with a fork. Work in Roquefort. Add butter and port. Beat mixture until smooth and creamy. Place in a pastry bag fitted with a large star tip. Pipe Roquefort cream into pear halves. Top each pear half with a shelled walnut. Place on plates next to ham. Place a lettuce leaf on each plate. Top with a spoonful of red-currant jelly. Lightly toast bread. Cut into fingers and serve with pears. Makes 2 servings.

Cook's Tip

If you find the Roquefort cream too rich, you can replace the butter with farmer's cheese or sieved cottage cheese.

Smoked Eel with Vegetable Salad

1/4 small cauliflower
1 carrot
1/4 leek
1 tablespoon vegetable oil
1 teaspoon cider vinegar
Pinch each salt and pepper
3 tablespoons drained canned whole-kernel corn
8 oz. smoked eel
1 orange
1/2 basket alfalfa sprouts
2 teaspoons grated fresh horseradish or prepared creamed horseradish
Pinch sugar
1 tablespoon whipping cream
2 slices white bread
4 small lettuce leaves
Few sprigs dill, if desired

Break cauliflower into flowerets. Cut carrot and leek into strips. Wrap prepared vegetables separately in foil. Place foil packages in boiling water. Simmer over low heat 15 minutes. Remove foil packages from water. Open packages; let vegetables cool. In a small bowl, beat together oil, vinegar, salt and pepper. In a medium bowl, combine cooked vegetables and corn. Stir in dressing. Cut eel into 4 equal slices. Remove skin. Cut 2 slices from center of orange. Place each on an individual plate. Top with alfalfa sprouts. Squeeze juice from remaining pieces of orange. In a small bowl, beat together orange juice, horseradish, sugar and cream. Spoon over sprouts. Cut bread slices in half; top with lettuce leaves. Place eel pieces on lettuce. Garnish with dill, if desired. Arrange on plates. Place vegetable salad on plates next to eel. Makes 2 servings.

Chicken Breasts with Melon

1/2 head iceberg lettuce
1 small head red endive
2 medium carrots
1/2 basket alfalfa sprouts
2 cooked chicken breasts
1/4 honeydew melon
3 tablespoons plain yogurt
1/4 cup mayonnaise
3 tablespoons French Dressing, page 116

Separate lettuce and endive leaves. Line 2 individual plates with
lettuce. Cut endive leaves into strips. Cut carrots into strips.
Snip alfalfa sprouts with kitchen scissors. Rinse in cold water;
drain. Arrange red endive, carrots and sprouts on lettuce. Slice
chicken. Arrange in a fan shape on plates. Cut melon into 4
wedges. Scoop away seeds. Remove melon rind. Place 2 melon
wedges on each plate next to chicken. In a small bowl, beat
together yogurt and mayonnaise. Place in a small serving bowl.
Pour French Dressing over yogurt mixture in a spiral pattern.
Serve with chicken salad. Makes 2 servings.

Chicken Salad

Pinch each salt and pepper
1 teaspoon paprika
Generous pinch ground ginger
2 chicken legs
3 tablespoons vegetable oil
3 large tomatoes
2 celery stalks
1/3 cup French Dressing, page 116
3 tablespoons mayonnaise
1 teaspoon pickled pink peppercorns, if desired

Blend salt, pepper, paprika and ginger. Rub mixture into chicken
legs. Heat oil in a medium skillet. Cook chicken over high heat
until brown all over. Reduce heat to medium and continue cooking 15 minutes longer. Drain chicken on paper towels; cool.
Slice tomatoes. Cut celery into thin strips including leaves.
Blanch celery in a little boiling salted water 3 minutes. Drain. Arrange on 2 individual plates with chicken legs and tomato slices.
Sprinkle French Dressing over celery. Top each plate with 1 tablespoon mayonnaise. Sprinkle with pink peppercorns, if
desired.

Cream-Cheese Mousse

8 oz. cream cheese
1 teaspoon lemon juice
1 cup less 2 tablespoons whipping cream
Salt and white pepper
Few drops Worcestershire sauce
1 (5-oz.) can prawns or shrimp
1 teaspoon chopped dill
3 tablespoons warm water
1-1/2 teaspoons gelatin
4 to 6 lettuce leaves
2 sprigs dill
Lemon slices

In a small bowl, beat together cream cheese, lemon juice, 1/4 cup cream, salt, pepper and Worcestershire sauce until smooth. Rinse prawns or shrimp in cold water. Drain. Divide into 2 portions. Finely chop 1 portion. Stir into cream-cheese mixture with chopped dill. Pour 2 tablespoons warm water into a bowl. Stand bowl in a saucepan of hot water. Sprinkle with gelatin and stir until dissolved. Mix gelatin liquid into cream-cheese mixture. Refrigerate briefly to cool. Whip remaining cream until stiff. Fold into cheese mixture. Rinse out 2 individual jelly molds with cold water. Pour in cheese mixture. Smooth the surface. Refrigerate molds 3 hours or until completely set. Line 2 individual plates with lettuce leaves. Dip molds into hot water for a few seconds. Turn mousses out onto lettuce. Garnish each plate with a sprig of dill, a few lemon slices and remaining prawns or shrimp. Makes 2 servings.

Cream-Cheese Tartare

8 oz. cream cheese
Generous 1/2 cup whipping cream
1/2 teaspoon salt
Few drops lemon juice
1/2 red bell pepper
1/2 green bell pepper
1 dill pickle
1/2 red onion
1/2 white onion
Small bunch parsley
10 stuffed olives
1 tablespoon pickled green peppercorns, if desired
1 teaspoon each paprika, caraway seeds, capers and freshly ground white pepper

In a small bowl, beat together cream cheese, cream, salt and lemon juice. Arrange in the center of 2 individual plates. Remove seeds and pith from red and green peppers. Finely dice. Drain and chop pickle. Finely dice onions. Finely chop parsley. Slice olives. Drain pickled green peppercorns, if used. Arrange diced peppers, pickle, red and white onion, parsley, sliced olives, green peppercorns, paprika, caraway seeds, capers and white pepper in spoonfuls around cream-cheese mixture on each plate. Mix cream-cheese mixture to taste with the different seasonings and accompaniments at the table. Serve with a choice of breads. Makes 2 servings.

Gourmet Fare

2 large tomatoes
6 tablespoons French Dressing, page 116
1/2 cup cottage cheese
2 cooked chicken breasts
1/4 lettuce
1 tablespoon capers
1/3 cup mayonnaise
2 teaspoons anchovy paste
1/4 cup whipping cream
1 teaspoon hot mustard
Salt and pepper

Slice vertically down center of each tomato, do not cut through base. Scoop out seeds. Sprinkle insides of tomatoes with a little French Dressing. Fill half-open tomatoes with cottage cheese. Slice chicken breasts. Arrange on 2 individual plates with stuffed tomatoes. Cut lettuce into strips. Toss with remaining French Dressing. Arrange lettuce on plates. Drain and chop capers; set aside 1 teaspoon. In a small bowl, beat together mayonnaise, anchovy paste, cream, mustard, salt, pepper and remaining chopped capers. Spoon mayonnaise mixture over sliced chicken. Sprinkle reserved chopped capers on top. Makes 2 servings.

Scandinavian Fare

4 oz. fresh or canned button mushrooms
3 tablespoons vegetable oil
1 tablespoon wine vinegar
1 tablespoon diced onion
Salt and pepper
1-1/2 green bell peppers
1/2 red bell pepper
1 dill pickle
4 oz. ham loaf
1/2 cup mayonnaise
1 teaspoon mustard
3 tablespoons whipping cream
4 thin wedges honeydew melon
Few lettuce leaves
2 smoked-trout fillets
2 hard-cooked eggs, halved
1 teaspoon brandy
1 teaspoon pickled green peppercorns, drained and chopped, if desired

Clean fresh mushrooms or drain canned ones. In a small bowl, beat together oil, vinegar, diced onion, salt and pepper. Pour dressing over mushrooms. Remove and discard seeds and pith from peppers. Finely dice peppers. Stir 1 tablespoon mixed peppers into mushroom salad. Drain pickle. Cut pickle and ham loaf into strips. Place in a small bowl with remaining mixed peppers. In a small bowl, beat together 1/3 cup mayonnaise, mustard and cream. Season and stir into ham mixture. Remove rind and seeds from melon wedges. Divide lettuce between 2 individual plates. Top with ham-loaf salad. Arrange mushroom salad, trout fillets, melon wedges and eggs alongside. In a small bowl, blend remaining mayonnaise, brandy and chopped peppercorns, if desired. Spoon mixture over eggs. Makes 2 servings.

Italian Fare

4 oz. thinly sliced Parma ham or prosciutto
4 oz. salami
4 tomatoes
1/2 small onion
12 black olives
1 small head red endive
2 teaspoons French Dressing, page 116
3 tablespoons mayonnaise
1 teaspoon pickled green peppercorns, if desired

Divide ham and salami slices between 2 individual plates. Slice tomatoes. Cut onion into rings. Arrange tomato slices, onion rings and black olives next to meat. Separate red endive into leaves. Cut into strips. Arrange endive on plates. Sprinkle with French Dressing. Spoon mayonnaise over sliced tomato. Sprinkle with green peppercorns, if desired. Makes 2 servings.

Shepherd's Fare

1/2 cup cottage cheese
1 red bell pepper
1 head Belgian endive
1/2 basket alfalfa sprouts
1/2 (14-oz.) can artichoke hearts
1 hard-cooked egg
1 dill pickle
1/4 cup vegetable oil
1 tablespoon wine vinegar
Pinch each salt, pepper and ground ginger
1 tablespoon chopped fresh mixed herbs (parsley, chives, dill)
6 black olives

Spoon cottage cheese into the centers of 2 individual plates. Remove pith and seeds from pepper. Slice pepper into rings. Separate leaves of Belgian endive. Snip sprouts with kitchen scissors. Rinse in cold water; drain. Drain and halve artichoke hearts. Arrange all salad ingredients in portions around cottage cheese. Finely chop egg. Drain and chop pickle. In a small bowl, beat together oil, vinegar, salt, pepper, ginger, chopped herbs, egg and pickle. Drizzle mixture over salad. Garnish both plates with 3 black olives. Makes 2 servings.

Tongue with Vegetable Salad

8 oz. sliced cooked tongue
1 tomato
3 tablespoons canned whole-kernel corn
1 cucumber
1 strip canned pimiento
Salt and pepper
1/2 head kohlrabi
1 carrot
Small bunch parsley
1 tablespoon wine vinegar
1/4 cup vegetable oil
Pinch dried oregano

Fold tongue slices in half. Arrange in a fan shape on 2 individual plates. Halve tomato. Scoop out seeds; set aside. Drain corn. Cut 2 thick slices from cucumber. Finely dice slices. Drain and chop pimiento. In a small bowl, combine tomato seeds, corn, diced cucumber, pimiento, salt and pepper. Use to fill tomato shells. Place 1 tomato half on each plate. Peel kohlrabi. Cut kohlrabi, carrot and remaining cucumber into strips. In a small bowl, combine vegetable strips. Divide between 2 plates. Finely chop parsley. In a small bowl, beat together vinegar, oil, oregano and chopped parsley. Add salt and pepper to taste. Pour dressing over mixed vegetables. Makes 2 servings.

Pork with Persimmon Cream

6 thin slices cold roast pork
Few lettuce leaves
1 hard-cooked egg
2 teaspoons lumpfish caviar
2 oz. cream cheese
1 ripe persimmon
3 tablespoons whipping cream
Pinch each salt and ground ginger

Arrange pork slices on 2 individual plates. Place lettuce next to meat. Cut egg in half lengthwise. Top each portion of lettuce with an egg half. Garnish egg with lumpfish caviar. Place cream cheese in a small bowl. Wash, dry and quarter persimmon. Hold each persimmon quarter over cream cheese so no juice is lost, using a pointed knife, cut out soft flesh. Slice flesh into strips; set aside. Scrape inside of persimmon over bowl to extract juice. Stir juice into cheese with cream, salt and ginger. Beat cheese mixture until light and fluffy. Place in a pastry bag fitted with a large star tip. Pipe 1 rosette onto each plate. Top rosette with persimmon strips. Makes 2 servings.

Smoked Turkey with Curried Eggs

4 oz. smoked turkey or chicken breast
1/2 mango
Generous pinch cayenne (red) pepper
1 hard-cooked egg
2 oz. cream cheese
3 tablespoons whipping cream
Generous pinch salt
2 slices whole-wheat bread
1 teaspoon curry powder
2 tablespoons soft butter
Generous pinch freshly ground black pepper
1 large tomato
1 tablespoon chopped chives

Slice turkey. Arrange on 2 individual plates. Peel and slice mango. Arrange over turkey. Sprinkle with red pepper. Halve egg and remove yolk. In a small bowl, beat together, cream cheese, cream and salt. Divide mixture into 2 portions. Spread 1 portion over whole-wheat bread. Press egg yolk through a sieve into remaining portion. Add curry powder and butter. Beat until light and fluffy. Place mixture in a pastry bag fitted with a star tip. Pipe curry cream into egg whites. Sprinkle with black pepper. Slice tomato. Place 1 egg half on each piece of bread. Arrange on plates with tomato slices. Sprinkle tomatoes with chopped chives. Makes 2 servings.

Sausage Rolls with Carrot Salad

6 thin bacon slices
12 cocktail sausages
2 medium carrots
1 small apple
1 teaspoon lemon juice
3 tablespoons whipping cream
Salt and white pepper
1/2 teaspoon sugar
Few lettuce leaves
2 slices whole-wheat bread
1 tablespoon butter

Cut bacon slices in half crosswise. Wrap each sausage in a piece of bacon and secure with a wooden pick. Broil sausage rolls under medium heat 8 to 10 minutes or until bacon is crisp, turning once. Place 6 rolls on each of 2 individual plates. Cool. Shred carrots. Peel and coarsely shred apple. In a small bowl, combine carrots and apple. Sprinkle with lemon juice. In a small bowl, blend cream, salt, pepper and sugar. Stir into carrot and apple salad. Divide lettuce between plates. Arrange carrot and apple salad on lettuce. Serve with whole-wheat bread and butter. Makes 2 servings.

Cold Beef with Fruit Salad

2 oranges
4 oz. green grapes
4 oz. black grapes
1 tablespoon chopped almonds
Juice of 1/2 lemon
3 tablespoons Grand Marnier
1/2 teaspoon sugar
8 oz. cold roast beef
1 small grapefruit
1/4 cup cranberry jelly
1 teaspoon grated fresh horseradish or prepared creamed horseradish
2 small lettuce leaves

Cut oranges in half crosswise. Cut out flesh. Remove thin skin between orange segments. Dice flesh, discarding any seeds. Reserve 2 orange shells and discard the other two. Halve grapes and remove seeds. In a small bowl, combine diced orange, grapes and chopped almonds. In a small bowl, blend lemon juice, Grand Marnier and sugar. Pour over fruit salad. Cover and let stand at room temperature 30 minutes. Slice beef very thinly. Arrange on 2 individual plates. Peel grapefruit. Remove thin skin between grapefruit segments. Dice flesh, discarding any seeds. In a small bowl, combine grapefruit, cranberry jelly and horseradish. Place 1 lettuce leaf on each plate. Top with grapefruit mixture. Fill 2 reserved orange shells with marinated fruit salad. Arrange next to lettuce. Serve with fresh French bread. Makes 2 servings.

Duck with Artichoke Salad

1 boned duck breast
Salt and white pepper
1 tablespoon vegetable oil
1/4 cup butter
1 teaspoon pickled pink or green peppercorns, if desired
1/2 (14-oz.) can artichoke hearts
1/2 onion
1 small tomato
2 teaspoon chopped parsley
1 tablespoon wine vinegar
1/4 cup olive oil
Few lettuce leaves

Rub duck breast with a little salt and pepper. Brush with 1 tablespoon vegetable oil. Cover and let stand at room temperature 2 hours. Melt butter in a medium skillet. Cook duck breast over medium heat 7 minutes, stirring constantly. Duck will be rare; if you prefer it cooked through, continue cooking 7 minutes longer. Cool. Cut into slices. Arrange on 2 individual plates. Drain pink or green peppercorns, if used. Sprinkle over duck. Drain and halve artichoke hearts. Cut onion into rings. Quarter tomato. Remove seeds. Dice flesh. In a small bowl, combine artichoke, onion, tomato and chopped parsley. In a small bowl, blend vinegar and oil. Add salt and pepper to taste. Pour dressing over artichoke salad. Divide lettuce leaves between plates. Arrange salad on top. Makes 2 servings.

Russian-Salad Platter

1 cup frozen mixed vegetables
8 oz. ham loaf, unsliced
1 celery stalk
3 tablespoons mayonnaise
Pinch each salt, celery salt and
    white pepper
1/2 teaspoon soy sauce
6 tomatoes
1 teaspoon coarsely ground black
    pepper
3 tablespoons whipping cream
3 hard-cooked eggs
3 teaspoons lumpfish caviar

Cook frozen vegetables following package instructions. Drain and cool. Cut ham loaf into thin strips. Trim celery. Slice into strips. In a small bowl, combine meat and vegetables. In a small bowl, beat together mayonnaise, salt, celery salt, white pepper and soy sauce. Pour over salad ingredients. Thinly slice tomatoes. Arrange tomato slices in a ring on 2 individual plates. Spoon salad into center of rings. Sprinkle tomatoes with coarsely ground black pepper. Whip cream until stiff. Halve eggs. Place 3 halves on each portion of salad. Top with whipped cream. Garnish egg halves with lumpfish caviar. Makes 2 servings.

Children's Lunch Party

Children have seemingly insatiable appetites, so offer your young guests plenty to eat and a variety of different fruit juices to drink. You can buy many prepared foods, such as cold meats, continental sausages, various kinds of bread and bread rolls, mixed pickles, sauces, chips and candies. Brightly colored paper plates, cups and napkins add a festive note, and have the added bonus of no washing up. Here are some suggestions for homemade party dishes. All make 10 to 12 servings.

Meat-Loaf Sandwiches
2 onions
1 cup fresh white breadcrumbs
3 lbs. ground beef, lamb or pork
4 eggs
1 teaspoon paprika
Salt and white pepper
3 tablespoons chopped parsley
12 lettuce leaves
24 slices white bread
3 tomatoes
2 hard-cooked eggs

Preheat oven to 400F (205C). Dice onions. In a medium bowl, combine breadcrumbs, ground meat, eggs, paprika, salt, pepper and parsley. Shape into a long loaf. Bake 40 to 45 minutes. Cool. Cut cooled loaf into 12 thick slices. Place 1 lettuce leaf on each of 12 slices of bread. Top with a slice of meat loaf. Slice tomatoes. Slice eggs. Arrange tomato and egg slices on top of meat loaf. Top each sandwich with a second slice of bread.

Potato & Cucumber Salad
2-1/4 lbs. new potatoes
2 onions
1 cucumber
1/2 cup mayonnaise
1/3 cup plain yogurt
1/4 cup wine vinegar
Salt and pepper
Bunch chives

Wash potatoes. Place in a medium saucepan of boiling salted water. Simmer over medium heat 20 to 25 minutes or until tender. Drain and cool. Peel cooled potatoes and slice. Finely dice onions. Cut cucumber into very thin slices. In a medium serving bowl, combine potato, onion and cucumber. In a small bowl, beat together mayonnaise, yogurt, vinegar, salt and pepper. Pour over salad before serving.

Spicy Rice Salad
Generous 1 cup rice
1 tablespoon curry powder
1 lb. boned cooked chicken
2 pears
3 slices canned pineapple
1/2 (15-oz.) can mandarin-orange segments
1 tablespoon chopped pistachio nuts, if desired
1/4 cup lemon juice
Salt and pepper
6 tablespoons vegetable oil

Cook rice following package instructions, adding curry powder to cooking water. Rinse cooked rice through with cold water; drain. Remove skin from chicken. Dice meat. Peel, halve, core and dice pears. Drain and chop pineapple and mandarin-orange segments. In a medium serving bowl, combine rice, chicken, pears, pineapple and mandarin-orange segments. Garnish with pistachios, if desired. In a small bowl, blend lemon juice, salt, pepper and oil. Pour over rice salad.

Pasta Salad

1 lb. lunch meat
8 oz. Cheddar or Tilsit cheese
8 oz. dill pickles
1 red bell pepper
1-1/2 cups cooked peas
1-1/4 lbs. cooked pasta shells or
  noodles
1/4 cup wine vinegar
Salt and white pepper
Generous 1/2 cup vegetable oil

Dice lunch meat and cheese. Drain and slice pickles. Quarter red pepper. Remove seeds and pith. Dice flesh. In a medium serving bowl, combine lunch meat, cheese, pickles and red pepper. Add cooked peas and pasta shells or noodles. In a small bowl, blend vinegar, salt, pepper and oil. Stir into salad.

Stuffed French Bread

2 long French loaves
2/3 cup mayonnaise
4 oz. mortadella or cervelat
  sausage
4 oz. salami
4 oz. smoked cheese
3 large tomatoes
3 hard-cooked eggs
Parsley sprigs
Few lettuce leaves
4 oz. blue cheese (Danish Blue,
  dolcelatte)
1 lb. meat salad (bought
  ready-made, or use any meat
  salad from salad section)

Cut loaves in half lengthwise. Spread insides with mayonnaise. Slice mortadella or cervelat, salami and smoked cheese. Fold slices in half. Arrange at intervals along bottom half of 1 loaf. Cut 2 tomatoes and 2 eggs into slices and remaining tomato and egg into wedges. Arrange sliced tomatoes and eggs in the intervals between cold meat and cheese slices.

Garnish loaf with sprigs of parsley. Cover with top half of loaf. Line bottom half of second loaf with lettuce. Slice blue cheese. Arrange meat salad in spoonfuls on lettuce leaves, alternating with slices of blue cheese and remaining tomato and egg wedges. Cover with top half of loaf.

Summer Fruit Dessert

8 oz. morello or other tart cherries
8 oz. raspberries
8 oz. red currants
2 cups water
1 cup sugar
Scant 1/2 cup cornstarch
1 cup whipping cream
1/4 teaspoon ground cinnamon

Pick over fruit. Pit cherries. Place fruit in a medium saucepan with water, bring to a boil and simmer 5 minutes. Press fruit through a sieve. Add enough water to puree to makes 4 cups. Set aside 2 tablespoons sugar. Add remaining sugar to fruit puree. Return puree to saucepan. Bring to a boil. Blend cornstarch with a little cold water. Stir cornstarch mixture into fruit puree. Simmer 3 minutes, stirring constantly. Pour fruit mixture into a medium serving bowl. Let set in refrigerator. To serve, whip cream with reserved sugar until stiff. Spoon onto dessert and sprinkle with cinnamon.

Giant Meat Platter

8 oz. boiled ham
8 oz. smoked ham
4 oz. smoked Parma ham or prosciutto
4 oz. salami
8 oz. tongue sausage or cooked tongue
8 oz. ham loaf or mortadella
4 oz. meat loaf
4 oz. liver sausage
1 lb. head cheese
14 oz. finely ground beef sirloin or tenderloin
2 onions
Salt and white pepper
1/2 teaspoon paprika
2 egg yolks
Few lettuce leaves
3 tablespoons vegetable oil
2 teaspoons wine vinegar
1 tablespoon caraway seeds
2 hard-cooked eggs
2 to 4 tomatoes
Bunch radishes
Coarsely ground black pepper
Parsley sprigs
Selection of pickled vegetables such as baby gherkins, canned
    pimiento, canned baby sweet-corn cobs and olives

Arrange all cold meats except head cheese on a large serving platter or board. Place ground beef in a medium bowl. Dice 1 onion and mix half into beef with salt, white pepper, paprika and 1 egg yolk. Arrange lettuce in 1 corner of meat platter. Top with ground-beef mixture. Make a well in the center of the meat and carefully tip in second egg yolk. Place remaining diced onion next to egg. Sprinkle with a little paprika. Arrange head cheese on a separate flat dish. Slice remaining onion into rings. Arrange over head cheese. In a small bowl, blend oil and vinegar. Pour over head cheese. Sprinkle with caraway seeds. Slice hard-cooked eggs. Cut each tomato into 8 wedges. Arrange sliced eggs and a few tomato wedges on platter. Sprinkle eggs with coarsely ground black pepper. Serve remaining tomato wedges and radishes separately. Garnish platter with parsley and a selection of pickled vegetables. Serve with various kinds of bread, rolls and crispbreads. Makes 8 to 10 servings.

Cook's Tip

You can serve any kind of cold meat at a buffet and the ones listed are intended only as suggestions. The Steak Tartare can be replaced with a meat or sausage salad, a Waldorf or even a crab salad. Slices of pâté, terrine or cold roast meat can be substituted for the head cheese. You can also vary the garnishes with sliced cucumber, celery and red and green bell peppers, depending on what is in season.

Gourmet Platters

Sausage & Meat Platter
2 heads Belgian endive
1/3 cup salad dressing, pages 116 to 117
1 tomato, sliced
8 oz. garlic sausage
4 oz. smoked ham
6 Veal Tournedos with Broccoli Puree, page 163

Cheese Platter
8 oz. Stilton cheese
8 oz. Emmentaler cheese, sliced
Cheese Balls from Country Cheese Board, page 167
2 red bell peppers
3 stuffed olives
8 oz. cream cheese
1/4 teaspoon celery salt
1 tablespoon brandy
1 shallot, minced

Cut endive into fine strips. Toss in a salad dressing of your choice. Place endive salad in the center of a large serving platter. Garnish with tomato slices. Arrange garlic sausage, smoked ham and tournedos on platter.

Cut Stilton into wedges. Arrange on a platter with Emmentaler and Cheese Balls. Slice peppers into wedges. Remove seeds and pith. Slice olives. In a small bowl, beat together cream cheese, celery salt, brandy and minced shallot. Place in a pastry bag fitted with a star tip. Pipe onto pepper wedges. Garnish each with a slice of olive. Arrange on platter. Makes 6 servings.

Cook's Tip

Serve with a herring salad and a cheese and salami salad.

Country Sausage Platter

4 oz. tongue sausage or cooked tongue
4 oz. garlic sausage
8 oz. ham
10 oz. smoked or cold roast pork
4 oz. liver sausage
8 oz. mortadella
8 oz. salami, unsliced
Few lettuce leaves
10 oz. meat salad (bought ready-made, or use any meat salad of your choice)
Pickles, canned baby sweet-corn cobs, sliced tomato, radishes, parsley

Arrange sliced cold meats on 1 or 2 flat serving dishes. Top 1 platter with unsliced salami. Arrange lettuce leaves on top of the other platter. Place 3 tablespoons meat salad on lettuce. Serve remaining meat salad in a separate bowl. Garnish platters with baby gherkins, baby corn cobs, tomato slices, radishes and parsley. Serve with an assortment of breads, rolls and crispbreads. Makes 6 servings.

Cook's Tip

Cold-meat platters can be prepared several hours in advance, if you cover them with plastic wrap and store in a cool place.

Ham & Salad Platter

Generous 1 cup frozen peas
1 large avocado
1 teaspoon lemon juice
1/2 red bell pepper
1 dill pickle
4 oz. ham loaf, unsliced
1/3 cup mayonnaise
Salt and white pepper
1/2 teaspoon curry powder
Few sprigs dill
1 crisp sweet apple
2 tablespoons grated fresh horseradish or prepared creamed
  horseradish
1 cup whipping cream
Generous pinch sugar
14 oz. smoked or boiled ham
1 lb. smoked or cold roast pork

Garnishes:
2 hard-cooked eggs
2 tomatoes
1/2 honeydew melon
5 dill pickles
Black grapes
5 chilies
Canned baby sweet-corn cobs
Parsley sprigs

Cook peas following package instructions. Drain and cool. Cut avocado in half lengthwise and remove pit. Scoop flesh out of each half to within 1/4 inch of the shell. Dice flesh. Sprinkle diced avocado and inside of shells with lemon juice. Remove seeds and pith from red pepper. Cut flesh into strips. Drain pickle. Cut pickle and ham loaf into strips. In a medium bowl, combine peas, diced avocado, red pepper, pickle and ham loaf. In a small bowl, beat together mayonnaise, salt, pepper and curry powder. Stir into salad. Fill avocado halves with salad. Garnish each with a sprig of dill. Peel, quarter, core and finely shred apple. Place in a small bowl with horseradish. Whip cream with sugar until stiff. Fold into horseradish and apple mixture. Taste and adjust seasoning. Place mixture in a pastry bag fitted with a large plain tip. Cut 6 slices from smoked or boiled ham. Roll up slices. Pipe horseradish cream into each roll. Cover a large serving platter with smoked or roast pork. Arrange stuffed ham rolls on top. Cut a few more slices of ham, fold in half and place at 1 end of platter with remaining uncut piece of ham. Arrange stuffed avocado halves at the other end of platter. Slice eggs. Quarter tomatoes. Cut melon into wedges and remove seeds. Drain pickles. Slice into a fan-shape, if desired. Garnish platter with eggs, grapes, tomato quarters, melon wedges, pickles, chilies, baby corn cobs and parsley. Serve with toasted white bread, whole-wheat bread, rye bread and butter. Makes 6 to 8 servings.

Cheese Platters with Camembert

6 puff-pastry horns, page 152
2 egg yolks, beaten
3 tablespoons shredded Cheddar
   cheese
8 oz. cream cheese
Pinch cayenne (red) pepper
Salt and white pepper
1 teaspoon lemon juice
2 stuffed olives, sliced
Few lettuce leaves
4 oz. Brie cheese
8 oz. Camembert cheese
3/4 cup soft butter
1/2 garlic clove
1 small onion
1/2 teaspoon caraway seeds
1 teaspoon paprika
Few sprigs parsley
4 oz. Danish Blue cheese
8 oz. Gruyère cheese, sliced
8 oz. Bavarian smoked cheese
   with ham, sliced
8 oz. cervelat sausage

Preheat oven to 425F (220C). Brush pastry horns with half the beaten egg yolk. Sprinkle with shredded Cheddar cheese. Bake a few minutes until cheese begins to melt. In a small bowl, beat together cream cheese, red pepper, salt, pepper and lemon juice. Place in a pastry bag fitted with a star tip. Pipe mixture into pastry horns. Garnish with olive slices. Arrange stuffed horns on 1 side of a serving platter. Arrange lettuce and Brie on platter. In a small bowl, mash Camembert with a fork. Beat in butter and remaining beaten egg yolk. Crush garlic. Cut onion in half crosswise. Slice 1 half into rings. Shred other half into Camembert mixture. Blend in garlic, half the caraway seeds, paprika and salt and pepper to taste. Pile in a bowl and top with onion rings, parsley and caraway seeds. Cut Danish Blue into wedges. Arrange all remaining cheeses and cervelat sausage on another large serving platter. Serve with radishes, stuffed eggs, pages 124 to 125, fresh bread and scoops of butter. Makes 6 to 8 servings.

Fish Platter

8 oz. thawed frozen prawns or shrimp
1 medium pineapple
1/4 cup mayonnaise
6 tablespoons whipping cream
1 teaspoon lemon juice
1 teaspoon sugar
Generous pinch salt
1 teaspoon pickled green peppercorns or capers, if desired
Trout with Dill, page 146
Salmon with Vegetable Salad, page 147

Garnishes:
Stuffed eggs, pages 124 to 125, horseradish and apple cream from
Ham & Salad Platter, page 204, apple slices, lettuce, asparagus tips

Rinse prawns or shrimp in cold water; drain well. Cut a wedge out of pineapple lengthwise, leaving a gap measuring one-third of the whole pineapple. Remove peel from wedge. Dice flesh, discarding any hard parts of the core. In a small bowl, beat together mayonnaise, cream, lemon juice, sugar and salt. In a medium bowl, combine diced pineapple and prawns or shrimp. Stir in mayonnaise mixture. Spoon seafood salad into pineapple shell. Sprinkle with pickled green peppercorns or capers, if desired. Arrange stuffed pineapple, Trout with Dill, Salmon with Vegetable Salad on serving platters. Garnish with any of the suggested garnishes. Makes 6 to 8 servings.

Copenhagen Platter

1 (5-oz.) can prawns or shrimp
3 strips canned red pimiento
1 tablespoon chopped fresh or canned pineapple
1/4 cup mayonnaise
8 oz. sliced ham
8 tomatoes
Few sprigs dill
Salt and white pepper
1 cup whipping cream
2 to 3 tablespoons grated fresh horseradish or prepared creamed
  horseradish
Pinch sugar
4 oz. thin bacon slices
Few lettuce leaves
14 oz. liver pâté
Parsley sprigs
6 hard-cooked eggs
8 oz. meat salad (bought ready-made)

Rinse prawns or shrimp in cold water; drain well. Chop coarsely. Drain and dice pimiento. In a medium bowl, combine chopped prawns or shrimp, pimiento, pineapple and mayonnaise. Spread ham slices with mixture. Roll up and arrange on a serving platter. Slice 2 tomatoes. Place a slice on each ham roll and garnish with dill. Cut end opposite stalk off each remaining tomato. Scoop out seeds. Sprinkle insides with salt and pepper. In a medium bowl, whip cream until stiff. Fold in horseradish and sugar. Fill tomatoes with horseradish mixture. Place next to ham rolls. Broil bacon until crisp. Arrange lettuce with bacon and liver pâté. Top with parsley. Halve eggs. Mix yolks into meat salad. Spoon mixture into egg whites. Garnish with parsley. Makes 6 servings.

Meat Platters with Pineapple Salad

3-1/4 lbs. assorted sliced cold meats (tongue, meat loaf, roast pork, liver sausage, tongue sausage, garlic sausage, roast beef)
Generous 1 cup frozen peas
1 red bell pepper
8 oz. mortadella
8 oz. Edam cheese
3 tablespoons sliced almonds, toasted
1/3 cup mayonnaise
1/3 cup plain yogurt
3 tablespoons vinegar
Salt and pepper
1 small onion
1 pineapple
1 maraschino cherry

Garnishes:
Tomato wedges, green-pepper rings, stuffed olives, sliced hard-cooked egg, lettuce, canned baby sweet-corn cobs, pickles, pickled cocktail onions, canned pimiento strips, parsley

Arrange cold cuts on several serving platters. Cook peas following package instructions. Drain and cool. Trim and quarter red pepper. Remove seeds and pith. Slice red pepper, mortadella and Edam into strips. Combine in a medium bowl with peas and almonds. In a small bowl, beat together mayonnaise, yogurt, vinegar, salt and pepper. Shred onion into dressing. Stir dressing into salad. Cut a wedge out of the pineapple lengthwise. Remove rind from wedge. Dice flesh. Stir into salad. Spoon salad into pineapple shell. Top with maraschino cherry. Place on 1 of the serving platters. Garnish platter with any of the suggested garnishes. Serve with Seasonal Sausage Salad, page 80. Makes 8 to 10 servings.

Country Buffet

A country buffet calls to mind fresh whole-grain bread, rolls, country butter, crisp radishes, fresh fruit and several varieties of cheese, such as Cheddar, Cheshire, Wensleydale, Stilton, Camembert and Emmentaler. You can also serve a selection of cold meats. Seen here are roast pork, smoked ham, liver sausage and salami. A mixed salad and a herring dish make a lively contrast. Draft beer and cider are both favorite accompaniments to country fare. Here are some additional recipe ideas. They make 6 to 8 servings.

Cheese & Onion Dip

1 large onion
1 garlic clove
Generous 1/2 cup milk
1-1/2 lbs. farmer's cheese or
    sieved cottage cheese
Salt
Few sprigs fresh mixed herbs
    (parsley, dill, chives)

Finely dice onion and garlic. In a medium bowl, combine farmer's cheese or sieved cottage cheese, diced onion, garlic and salt. Place cheese dip in a bowl. Garnish with sprigs of fresh herbs.

Camembert Pâté

1/2 teaspoon caraway seeds
1 small onion
8 oz. mature Camembert cheese
1 cup soft butter
1 teaspoon paprika
1/4 teaspoon white pepper
1 hard-cooked egg
Sprig parsley

Grind caraway seeds with a mortar and pestle. Finely dice onion. Place Camembert in a medium bowl. Mash with a fork. Beat in butter, caraway, diced onion, paprika and white pepper. Arrange Camembert Pâté on a plate. Slice egg. Garnish pâté with sliced egg and parsley.

Red-Currant Dessert Soup

4 cups water
1 cup sugar
1-3/4 lbs. red currants
1 tablespoon cornstarch

Bring water and sugar to a boil in a medium saucepan, stirring constantly. Add red currants. Cover and simmer over low heat 3 minutes. Blend cornstarch in a little cold water. Stir into red-currant mixture. Bring to a boil. Simmer gently 1 minute. Remove from heat. Pour soup into a large shallow bowl. Chill thoroughly. Serve with cream.

Swiss Buffet Party

A Swiss buffet party will obviously include a wide variety of real Swiss cheeses such as Appenzeller, Emmentaler, Gruyère, Sbrinz and Vacherin. Add a touch of color with slices of salami and ham and a crisp lettuce or endive salad. You could even serve thinly sliced Bündnerfleish (Swiss smoked beef), if you can buy it, as a very special party delicacy. Try the following authentic Swiss recipes. They make 6 to 8 servings.

Emmentaler Salad
Few lettuce leaves
14 oz. Emmentaler cheese, unsliced
8 oz. cooked chicken
1 large red bell pepper
1 large sweet apple
1 slice canned pineapple
3/4 cup cooked peas
1/2 cup canned pineapple juice
1/4 cup dairy sour cream
Pinch white pepper
1/2 teaspoon curry powder

Line a large salad bowl with lettuce. Slice Emmentaler and chicken into thin strips. Cut red pepper in half. Remove seeds and pith. Dice flesh. Peel, quarter, core and dice apple. Drain pineapple, reserving juice. Cut pineapple into pieces. In a medium bowl, combine cheese, chicken, red pepper, apple, pineapple and peas. In a small bowl, beat together, mayonnaise, pineapple juice, sour cream, white pepper and curry powder. Stir dressing into salad. Arrange on the bed of lettuce.

Swiss Ham Tarts
4 oz. ham, unsliced
1 onion
2 oz. bacon slices
2 tablespoons shredded Emmentaler cheese
Generous 1/2 cup whipping cream
1 egg
Salt and white pepper
1 tablespoon chopped parsley
6 to 8 small cooked tartlet shells, page 57

Preheat oven to 425F (220C). Finely dice ham. Finely chop onion. Cut bacon into small pieces. In a small skillet, sauté bacon until transparent; set aside. Fry onion in bacon drippings until golden brown. In a medium bowl, combine ham, bacon, onion and Emmentaler. In a small bowl, lightly whip cream, egg, salt, pepper and parsley. Spoon ham filling into cooked tartlet cases. Pour in whipped-cream mixture. Bake 10 minutes. Cool.

Smörgåsbord

Meat Platter
2-1/4 lbs. assorted cold meats
1 hard-cooked egg

Arrange sliced cold meats on a serving platter or board. Quarter egg and use to garnish platter.

Herring Platter
10 pickled-herring fillets
5 small cooked carrots
Bunch dill
8 maatjes herring fillets
2 tomatoes
1 onion

Drain pickled-herring fillets. Cut carrots in half crosswise. Wrap each half in a herring fillet. Garnish with a sprig of dill. Arrange in a circle round the edge of a flat dish. Drain maatjes herring. Place in the center of the dish. Quarter tomatoes. Slice onion into rings. Garnish dish with tomatoes and onion.

Red Herring Salad
10 maatjes herring fillets
2 cups milk
16 oz. pickled beets
2 crisp sweet apples
Generous 1/2 cup dairy sour cream
3 tablespoons mayonnaise
1 lemon slice, sprig dill

Soak salted herring fillets in milk 30 minutes. Drain and cut into pieces. Drain and chop beets. Quarter, core and dice apples. In a medium bowl, combine herring, beets and apples. In a small bowl, beat together sour cream and mayonnaise. Stir into herring mixture. Garnish with a slice of lemon and a sprig of dill.

Green Herring Salad
10 maatjes herring fillets
1/4 cup chopped dill or parsley
Juice of 2 lemons
1/2 cup vegetable oil
2 green bell peppers
1 (10-oz.) can green beans
16 oz. pickled cocktail onions
10 oz. canned pimiento

Chop herrings. Place in a bowl with dill or parsley, lemon juice and oil. Quarter green peppers. Remove seeds and pith. Dice flesh. Drain and chop beans, cocktail onions and pimiento. Stir green peppers, beans, cocktail onions and pimiento into herring mixture. Let stand.

Meatballs
1/4 cup butter
1 onion
1 tablespoon chopped parsley
1 lb. ground beef
1 egg
1/2 cup fresh breadcrumbs
Salt
1/2 teaspoon dried marjoram
1 teaspoon paprika
1/3 cup vegetable oil

Melt butter in a medium skillet. Finely dice onion. Sauté in butter with parsley. Place in a medium bowl with ground beef, egg, breadcrumbs, salt, marjoram and paprika. Mix well and shape into small balls. Heat oil in skillet. Cook meatballs 8 to 10 minutes, turning constantly. Place in a serving bowl and cool. Makes 10 to 12 servings.

Add interest to a Smörgåsbord by serving a variety of stuffed eggs, pages 124 to 125, stuffed tomatoes, page 35, and Gravad Lax, page 144. Round off the buffet with a crisp cucumber salad, assorted sliced cheeses and plenty of fresh rolls and butter. Makes 10 to 12 servings.

Danish Buffet

Red-Cabbage Salad
20 dried pitted prunes
1-1/4 lbs. pickled red cabbage
1 onion, cut in rings

Soak prunes 12 hours in enough cold water to cover. Place prunes with juice in a medium saucepan. Bring to a boil. Drain red cabbage. Add to prunes. Simmer over low heat 20 to 30 minutes or until prunes are tender. Place prunes and cabbage in a serving bowl. Garnish with onion rings.

Prawn Salad
Few lettuce leaves
1 lb. thawed frozen prawns
Juice of 1 small grapefruit
3 tablespoons whipping cream, whipped
1 teaspoon lumpfish caviar

Line a bowl with lettuce. Top with prawns. Sprinkle with grapefruit juice. Garnish with whipped cream and lumpfish caviar.

Herring Salad
6 pickled-herring fillets
6 cooked carrots
Few lettuce leaves
2 oz. lumpfish caviar
4 egg yolks
1 onion, cut in rings

Drain pickled-herring fillets. Cut into pieces. Slice carrots. Line half of a large flat dish with lettuce. Top with lumpfish caviar. Place egg yolks in their shells on top. In a medium bowl, combine herring, carrots and onion. Arrange on dish.

Deep-Fried Sole
6 sole fillets
1/2 teaspoon salt
1/3 cup all-purpose flour
2 egg yolks, beaten
1/2 cup dried breadcrumbs
Oil for deep-frying
Rémoulade Sauce, page 13

Rub sole with salt. Coat in flour then in beaten egg yolk and finally in breadcrumbs. Heat oil in a deep-fat fryer to 375F (190C). Fry fillets 3 to 4 minutes or until golden brown. Serve with Rémoulade Sauce.

Meat & Fish Platter
1-3/4 lbs. cold roast pork
1-1/2 lbs. cold roast beef
8 oz. smoked eel

Garnishes:
Parsley, dill, tomatoes, radishes, lemon slices and grapes

Arrange cold meats and skinned eel on separate platters. Finish your Danish buffet with Gravad Lax, page 144, and a selection of Danish cheeses. Garnish dishes with any of the suggested garnishes. Makes 10 to 12 servings.

Danish Almond Rings
2-1/4 lbs. almond paste or marzipan
1 cup granulated sugar
1 lb. sifted powdered sugar
5 egg whites
Grated peel of 1 lemon
1 teaspoon lemon juice

Preheat oven to 300F (150C). Knead almond paste or marzipan to a dough with granulated sugar, half the powdered sugar, 3 egg whites, grated lemon peel and juice. Roll mixture into 10 finger-thick rolls of varying lengths. Join ends to make rings. The largest ring should be 7 inches across and each successive ring should measure 1/2 inch less than the previous one. Line 2 baking sheets with waxed paper. Lay rings separately on sheets. Bake 20 minutes or until pale golden. Cool. Stack cooled rings in a tree shape as shown. In a small bowl, beat together remaining powdered sugar and egg whites. Pipe a fine pattern on rings.

Italian Buffet

One of the best-known Italian delicacies must be prosciutto ham with melon, so it would be appropriate to serve it for an Italian buffet with some salami and mortadella sausage. As the centerpiece of your buffet, why not serve Italian Veal Galantine, page 67, or Braised Veal Mostarda, page 158, accompanied by different salads? You can also incude a selection of creamy Italian cheeses, such as Gorgonzola, provolone, goat cheese, Bel Paese and dolcelatte. Also serve fresh fruit, olives, white bread, Italian bread sticks, fruit juices and Italian wines. And finally, no Italian buffet would be complete without pizzas; some recipes are given here. They make 6 to 8 servings.

Party Pizzas
Dough:
1 teaspoon sugar
1-1/4 cups warm water (110F, 45C)
2 teaspoons active dry yeast
4 cups all-purpose flour
1 teaspoon salt

Toppings:
6 large tomatoes
4 oz. canned artichoke hearts
3 cups shredded Gruyère, mozzarella or Cheddar cheese
16 oz. mixed canned shellfish (mussels, prawns, shrimp)
4 oz. mushrooms
4 oz. salami
6 stuffed olives, halved
10 to 12 pitted black olives
3 tablespoons chopped fresh mixed herbs
1/3 cup olive oil

In a small bowl, dissolve sugar in warm water. Stir in yeast. Let stand in a warm place about 10 minutes or until frothy. Sift flour and salt into a large warmed bowl. Make a well in the center and pour in yeast liquid. Mix to a soft but not sticky dough. Turn out onto a lightly floured surface. Knead dough 10 minutes or until smooth and elastic. Shape into a ball. Place in a bowl. Cover with a damp cloth. Let stand in a warm place until doubled in size. Preheat oven to 425F (220C). To make the toppings, peel tomatoes. Slice 2 tomatoes. Cut remaining tomatoes into wedges. Drain and halve artichoke hearts. Divide shredded cheese into 3 portions. Drain shellfish. Slice mushrooms. Grease three 7-inch layer-cake pans. Knead dough quickly 1 to 2 minutes. Divide into 3 equal portions. Pat 1 portion in each pan. Cover the first with tomato slices, artichoke halves and salami. Sprinkle stuffed olives over the top, followed by 1 portion shredded cheese. Arrange shellfish, black olives and half the remaining tomato wedges on the second pizza. Top with second portion of cheese. Cover the third pizza with sliced mushrooms, remaining tomato wedges and shredded cheese. Scatter chopped herbs over the top. Sprinkle each pizza with olive oil. Bake 30 to 40 minutes or until browned.

Olive Appetizers
2 celery stalks
2 garlic cloves
3 shallots
14 oz. black olives
4 mint leaves
1/2 cup olive oil

Cut celery in half lengthwise. Slice into 2-inch pieces. Finely chop garlic. Cut shallots into thin rings. Arrange celery, garlic, shallots and olives in layers in a preserving jar. Chop mint leaves and sprinkle over contents of jar. Pour in olive oil. Seal jar. Let stand in a cool place 2 hours.

Tomato & Mozzarella Salad

6 large tomatoes
6 oz. mozzarella cheese
Salt and freshly ground black pepper
1 teaspoon each fresh oregano and basil or 1/2 teaspoon each dried oregano and basil
6 tablespoons olive oil

Slice tomatoes. Thinly slice mozzarella. Arrange tomatoes and cheese in layers on a plate. Sprinkle with salt, pepper and herbs. Pour oil over salad.

Vegetable Salad with Italian Green Sauce

8 oz. frozen peas
8 oz. frozen diced carrots
12 oz. frozen broccoli
12 oz. frozen green beans
1/2 (14-oz.) can artichoke hearts
1 small head red endive
2 hard-cooked eggs
Few romaine-lettuce leaves
10 black olives

Sauce:
2/3 cup chopped fresh mixed herbs (parsley, chives, dill, basil, marjoram)
4 green onions
1 garlic clove
4 canned anchovy fillets
1 mild chili, if desired
1/2 cup olive oil
1/4 cup wine vinegar
Salt and pepper

Cook all frozen vegetables separately, following package instructions. Drain and cool. Drain and halve artichoke hearts. Separate endive leaves. Slice eggs. Line half of a large salad platter with lettuce and the other half with red endive. Arrange vegetables in portions on lettuce and endive. Garnish with sliced eggs and olives. To make the sauce, place mixed herbs in a small bowl. Slice green onions. Finely chop garlic. Drain anchovy fillets. Cut chili, if used, in half. Remove seeds and pith. Finely chop chilies and anchovies. Combine green onion, garlic, chili, anchovy and herbs. In a small bowl, beat together oil, vinegar, salt and pepper. Pour over anchovy mixture. Place sauce in a sauce-boat. Serve with salad.

Italian Fruit Salad

2 to 3 lbs. mixed fresh fruit (pear, melon, persimmon, peach, grapes, figs)
3 tablespoons amaretto liqueur or peach brandy
4 oz. candied cherries
Vanilla ice cream
3 tablespoons chopped pistachio nuts

Prepare fruit. Cut into thin slices. Mix together in a large bowl. Add amaretto or peach brandy. Cover and let stand 30 minutes. Arrange fruit salad in individual bowls. Add cherries. Top each portion with a scoop of vanilla ice cream. Sprinkle with pistachios before serving.

Classic Cold Buffet

For more formal occasions, serve Veal Terrine, page 67, with preserved kumquats, Stuffed Pork with Curry Sauce, page 157, and 6 Trout with Dill, page 146. Offer 2 or 3 salads, a cheese platter and a light dessert. Recipes make 6 servings.

Waldorf Salad
2 medium, sweet apples
3 to 4 celery stalks
1 (8-oz.) can pineapple pieces, drained
1 cup chopped walnuts
Juice of 1/2 lemon
1/2 cup mayonnaise
Salt, white pepper and sugar

Peel, quarter and core apples. Cut into fine strips. Cut celery into strips. In a medium bowl, combine apples, celery, pineapple and walnuts. Add lemon juice. Season mayonnaise with salt, pepper and sugar. Stir into salad.

Mediterranean Salad
1 head iceberg lettuce
3 hard-cooked eggs, quartered
3 tomatoes, quartered
2 onions, cut in rings
1/2 (10-oz.) can green beans, drained
1 cucumber, sliced
8 black or green olives
1/3 cup olive oil
Juice of 1 lemon
1 teaspoon mild Dijon-style mustard
Salt and pepper
1 tablespoon chopped fresh mixed herbs

Separate lettuce leaves. In a medium bowl, combine eggs, tomatoes, onions and beans. Add cucumber and olives. In a small bowl, beat together oil, lemon juice, mustard, salt and pepper. Pour dressing over salad. Sprinkle with chopped herbs.

Summer Bavarois
1 lb. Summer Fruit Dessert, page 201, (half quantity of recipe)
2 cups milk
1 vanilla pod
6 egg yolks
3/4 cup sugar
2 tablespoons warm water
1/4 oz. gelatin
1-1/4 cups whipping cream

Prepare Summer Fruit Dessert. Pour into 6 glasses or bowls to set. Place milk in a medium saucepan with vanilla pod. Bring to a boil. Cover and remove from heat. Let stand 10 minutes. In a medium bowl, beat egg yolks with sugar until thick. Gradually pour in milk, beating constantly. Return to saucepan with vanilla pod. Heat very gently. Do not let custard become too hot or it will curdle. Stir over low heat 5 to 8 minutes or until custard thickens enough to coat the back of a spoon. Strain into a chilled medium bowl. Let cool slightly, stirring occasionally. Pour warm water into a small bowl. Set in a saucepan of hot water. Sprinkle with gelatin and stir until dissolved. Add to custard. Cool completely, stirring frequently. Lightly oil 6 small jelly molds. Whip cream until thick. Gently fold into custard. Refrigerate 1 to 2 hours or until set. To serve, dip each mold briefly in hot water and turn out on top of each Summer Fruit Dessert.

Sunday Buffet

Here is a light summer lunch to serve as a change from the traditional Sunday roast. Have 1 main cold-meat dish such as Vitello Tonnato, page 163, a salad platter, assorted cheeses and fruit. Recipes make 6 servings.

Salad Platter

1 small head red endive
4 oz. mushrooms
1/2 cup vegetable oil
3 tablespoons lemon juice
Pinch sugar, salt and pepper
1 tablespoon chopped parsley
2 oz. young spinach or watercress
1/2 onion
1 tablespoon wine vinegar
1 (5-oz.) can prawns or shrimp
3 tablespoons dairy sour cream
1 tablespoon chopped dill
1 large lettuce leaf
2 hard-cooked eggs

Separate endive leaves. Cut into narrow strips. Slice mushrooms. In a small bowl, combine 1/3 cup oil with 2 ta-blespoons lemon juice. Divide into 2 portions. Season 1 portion with sugar, salt and pepper. Toss endive in dressing. Arrange in 1 corner of a large serving dish. Mix parsley into remaining portion. Season to taste. Pour dressing over sliced mushrooms. Arrange on platter next to endive. Thoroughly wash spinach or watercress; drain. Finely chop onion. In a small bowl, beat together remaining oil, vinegar, onion, salt and pepper. Toss young spinach or watercress with dressing. Place on platter. Drain prawns or shrimp. Rinse under cold water; dry well. In a small bowl, combine sour cream, remaining lemon juice, dill and salt and pepper to taste. Pour over prawns or shrimp. Arrange lettuce on platter. Top with prawns or shrimp. Cut eggs into wedges. Add to salad platter.

Cheese Platter
with Cheese Salad

8 oz. Stilton Cheese
8 oz. Brie cheese or Bavarian Brie with herbs
8 oz. Cheddar cheese
8 oz. fresh Gouda cheese
1 kiwi
4 oz. strawberries
1/4 cup canned mandarin-orange segments
1 tablespoon lemon juice
3 tablespoons plain yogurt
1/2 teaspoon sugar
Pinch salt
Generous pinch cayenne (red) pepper

Cut Stilton and Brie into wedges. Dice Cheddar. Arrange cheese on a board. To make the cheese salad, cut Gouda into strips. Thinly peel kiwi. Cut into slices and halve each slice. Reserve 1 strawberry. Hull and quarter remaining strawberries.

Drain mandarin oranges. In a medium bowl, combine Gouda, kiwi, strawberries and mandarin oranges. In a small bowl, beat together lemon juice, yogurt, sugar, salt and red pepper. Pour over cheese salad. Cover and refrigerate. Garnish salad with reserved strawberry before serving.

Food for a Feast

The choice of dishes for entertaining large numbers of guests spans the whole spectrum of food, from canapés to desserts. A large buffet would consist of several smaller ones, including cold-meat platters, a cheeseboard, 1 or 2 cold roasts, several light salads, a pâté or terrine or two, a choice of desserts, fresh fruit and a plentiful supply of bread and rolls. This buffet is centered around Spit-Roast Pork with Herb Mayonnaise, page 158, Glazed Saddle of Venison, page 159, and Pâté d'Escargots, page 64, served here with horseradish and apple cream from Ham & Salad Platter, page 204. You can find ideas for the cheeseboard on previous pages, for stuffed eggs on pages 124 to 125, and for canapés on pages 38 to 51—or you may like to try the special Party Canapés shown here. Allow 2 stuffed eggs and 4 to 5 canapés per person. All the other recipes given below serve 6 to 8.

Party Canapés
12 slices white bread
6 tablespoons butter
12 small slices cold roast pork
6 canned pineapple segments
6 slices banana
1/4 cup mayonnaise
1 teaspoon curry powder
6 slices truffled liver pâté
1/4 cup diced Madeira Aspic, page 18
6 orange segments
1/3 cup Cottage Cheese with Herbs, page 35
6 thin slices smoked salmon
6 sprigs dill
1/3 cup Waldorf Salad, page 214
12 small slices cold roast beef
6 walnut halves

Remove crusts from bread. Cut each slice in half to make squares or triangles, or into 2 rounds. Spread with butter.

Arrange pork, pineapple and banana on each of 6 bread triangles. Blend mayonnaise and curry powder. Pipe a rosette on top of pork and fruit.

Place 1 slice liver pâté on each of 6 bread squares. Top with Madeira Aspic and orange segments.

Spread 6 bread squares with Cottage Cheese with Herbs. Roll up salmon slices and place on top. Garnish with dill.

Spoon Waldorf Salad onto remaining bread pieces. Top with beef. Garnish with walnuts.

Artichoke Salad
1 (14-oz.) can artichoke hearts
3 tomatoes
2 shallots
6 tablespoons vegetable oil
3 tablespoons wine vinegar
Salt and white pepper
6 tablespoons chopped fresh mixed herbs

Drain and halve artichoke hearts. Peel and quarter tomatoes. Scoop away seeds. Dice flesh. Cut shallots into rings. In a medium bowl, lightly mix all ingredients. In a small bowl, beat together oil, vinegar, salt and pepper. Mix dressing into salad. Sprinkle herbs over the top.

Apple & Rice Salad
Generous 1 cup rice
2 sweet apples
2 small oranges
Generous 1/2 cup whipping cream
1/4 cup dry sherry
3 tablespoons lemon juice
Generous pinch each sugar and
  ground ginger

Cook rice in boiling salted water following package instructions; drain. Wash, quarter, core and dice apples. Peel oranges. Remove skin from orange segments. Discard seeds. In a medium bowl, combine rice and fruit. In a medium bowl, whip cream, sherry, lemon juice, sugar and ginger. Stir into salad.

Corn & Pepper Salad
2 (12-oz.) cans whole-kernel corn
6 bell peppers, red, green and
  yellow
3 onions
2/3 cup vegetable oil
1/4 cup wine vinegar
Salt and black pepper
1 tablespoon chopped fresh mixed
  herbs

Drain corn. Quarter peppers. Remove seeds and pith. Slice flesh into fine strips. Cut onions into rings. In a medium bowl, combine all ingredients. In a small bowl, beat together oil, vinegar, salt and pepper. Pour over salad. Sprinkle with herbs.

Mixed-Salad Bowl
2 lettuces
2 heads red endive
4 oz. young spinach or watercress
2 onions
Generous 1/2 cup vegetable oil
1/4 cup wine vinegar
Pinch each salt, white pepper and
  sugar
Bunch chives

Separate lettuce and red endive leaves. Thoroughly wash young spinach or watercress; shake dry. Cut onions into rings. In a medium bowl, combine all ingredients. In a small bowl, beat together oil, vinegar, salt, pepper and sugar. Stir dressing into salad. Chop chives. Sprinkle over salad.

Rich Chocolate Mousse
Generous 3/4 cup sugar
4 egg yolks
3 tablespoons Cointreau
7 oz. unsweetened chocolate
1-1/2 teaspoons gelatin
2 tablespoons warm water
3 cups whipping cream
1/4 teaspoon vanilla extract
1 tablespoon chopped nuts

In a medium bowl, beat together 1/2 cup sugar, egg yolks and Cointreau. Set bowl in a saucepan of hot water. Whisk until frothy. Place chocolate in a small bowl. Set bowl in a saucepan of hot water until melted. Stir into yolk mixture. Dissolve gelatin in warm water. Stir into chocolate mixture. In a medium bowl, whip cream with remaining sugar and vanilla until stiff. Reserve 3 tablespoons. Fold remaining cream mixture into chocolate mixture. Place in a large bowl to set. Pipe on reserved whipped cream before serving. Sprinkle with nuts.

Index

A

Almond Rings, Danish 211
Anchovy Mayonnaise 13
Andalusian Gazpacho 179
Angelo's Chicken Salad 105
Anise Cream, Scampi with 142
Antipasti from Italy 54
Antipasto Platter 55
Appetizers, Olive 212
Apple & Celery Salad 102
Apple & Orange Salad 110
Apple & Quail's-Egg Salad 78
Apple & Rice Salad 217
Apple Juice, Carrot & 7
Apple Salad, Carrot & 69
Apple Salad, Herring with 150
Apple Salad, Potato & 102
Apple Salad with Rum Dressing 109
Apple Soup, Strawberry & 181
Apple, Cottage Cheese with 35
Apricot & Cherry Soup 183
Artichoke Dips 175
Artichoke Salad 216
Artichoke Salad, Duck with 198
Artichokes, Stuffed 133
Artichokes with Vegetable Julienne 56
Asparagus & Sprout Salad 94
Asparagus Crispbread 28
Asparagus Salad 76
Asparagus Salad, Chicken & 96
Asparagus, Trout Toast with 153
Asparagus with Smoked Trout 190
Aspic Dishes 118-123
Aspic, Madeira 18
Aspic, Muscatel 18
Aspic, Port 18
Aspic, Prawns in 122
Aspics, Basic Fish Stock for 17
Aspics, Light Meat Stock for 17
Aspic, Sherry 18
Aspic, Shrimp in 118
Aspic, White-Wine 18
Avocado & Ham Salad 105
Avocado Cocktail 60
Avocado Fruit Salad 115
Avocado Salad, Celery & 69
Avocado with Shrimp 132
Avocados with Mussels 136

B

Bacon, Pâté & 26
Baked Roquefort Slices 24
Balkan Salad 85
Balkan Tomato Salad 72
Bamboo-Shoot Salad 74
Banana & Tomato Salad 108
Basic Fish Stock for Aspics 17
Basic Recipes 10
Bavarian Cornets 30
Bavarois, Summer 214
Bean Salad 155
Bean Salad, Lima- 87
Bean Salad, Piquant Eggs with 125
Bean Salad, Shrimp & Green- 79
Bean-Sprout Salad, Mussel & 73
Beccafico Sardines 55
Beef Mayonnaise 29
Beef Salad, Piquant 86
Beef with Fruit Salad, Cold 198
Beef with Rémoulade Sauce, Roast 156
Beef, Glazed Fillet of 157
Blackberry & Pineapple Soup 182
Blue Cheese & Walnut 26
Blue-Cheese Dressing 116
Blue-Cheese Dressing, Fennel with 133
Boats, Endive 104
Borscht, Iced 179
Braised Veal Mostarda 158
Bread, French 11
Bread, Garlic 11

Bread, Homemade 10
Bread, Rye 12
Bread, Stuffed French 201
Bread, Whole-Wheat 11
Breakfast Special 28
Brioche Pastry 14
Broccoli Puree, Veal Tournedos with 163
Broccoli Salad 90
Broccoli, Turkey Legs with 160
Brunch Slices 24
Buffet Party, Swiss 209
Buffet with Assorted Dressings, Salad 116
Buffet, Classic Cold 214
Buffet, Country 208
Buffet, Danish 211
Buffet, Italian 212
Buffet, Sunday 215
Butter, Caper 170
Butter, Garlic 170
Butter, Green 170
Butter, Ham 171
Butter, Horseradish 171
Butter, Mock-Caviar 171
Butter, Mustard 171
Butter, Orange 170
Butter, Paprika 170
Butter, Pepper 171
Butter, Salmon & Dill 171
Butter Slices, Savory 38
Butter, Sprout 170
Butter, Truffle 170
Butters, Savory 170
Butters with Herbs & Spices 170

C

Cabbage Salad, Chinese- 70
Cabbage Salad, Red- 103, 211
Cabbage Salad, Savoy- 103
Cabbage Salad, White- 103
Camembert Cocktail 101
Camembert Pâté 208
Camembert, Cheese Platters with 205
Canapés & Snacks 38
Canapés Tartare, Salmon 43
Canapés, Melon & Ham 43
Canapés, Party 44, 216
Canapés, Smoked-Fish 39
Caper Butter 170
Capri Sauce 126
Caraway Bites 184
Caribbean Salad 113
Carrot & Apple Juice 7
Carrot & Apple Salad 69
Carrot Boats 134
Carrot Salad, Celery & 71
Carrot Salad, Sausage Rolls with 197
Caviar Butter, Mock- 171
Caviar Cream Horns, Mock- 152
Caviar, Prawn & Mock 26
Caviar, Sole Mousse with Mock 152
Celeriac Rounds 47
Celeriac Salad 77
Celery & Avocado Salad 69
Celery & Carrot Salad 71
Celery Juice, Tomato & 7
Celery Rolls 135
Celery Salad, Apple & 102
Cervelat Salad 89
Champagne, Mock 9
Chanterelle Salad 93
Chanterelle Tartlets 56
Chaudfroid, Dark 19
Chaudfroid, Light 18
Chaudfroid, Making 18
Cheese & Fruit Salad 166
Cheese & Herb Crackers 45
Cheese & Onion Dip 208
Cheese & Peppers on Tomato 131
Cheese & Salami Salad 99
Cheese & Sausage Salad 166
Cheese Board, Country 167

Cheese Bonnets 38
Cheese Buffet, Giant 166
Cheese, Chicken Salad with Ham & 85
Cheese Croissants 185
Cheese Fritters 42
Cheese Pastry Pockets 188
Cheese Platter with Cheese Salad 215
Cheese Platter with Gorgonzola Cream 167
Cheese Platters with Camembert 205
Cheese Puffs 186
Cheese Rings, Puff-Pastry 186
Cheese Salad 20
Cheese Salad, Cheese Platter with 215
Cheese Salad, Corn & 83
Cheese Salad, Corned-Beef & 101
Cheese Salad, Feta- 97
Cheese Salad, Swiss- 21
Cheese Sauce 126
Cheese, Smoked Eel & Danish 48
Cheese Spirals 184
Cheese Sticks 40
Cheese Tricorns 185
Cheese from Many Lands 166-167
Cheese with Apple, Cottage 35
Cheese with Ginger & Honey, Cottage 35
Cheese with Herbs, Cottage 35
Chef's Salad Platter 95
Cherry Soup, Apricot & 183
Chicken & Asparagus Salad 96
Chicken & Kiwi with Orange Sauce 137
Chicken & Red-Endive Salad 79
Chicken & Vegetable Mold 120
Chicken & Vegetable Salad 96
Chicken Breasts with Melon 192
Chicken Cocktail 59
Chicken Livers, Spicy 27
Chicken Salad 192
Chicken Salad, Angelo's 105
Chicken Salad, Exotic 82
Chicken Salad with Ham & Cheese 85
Chicken Tartlets 57
Chicken-Salad Tomatoes 131
Children's Lunch Party 200
Chilled Fish Medley 180
Chilled Tomato Soup 178
Chinese Fruit Salad 112
Chinese-Cabbage Salad 70
Chocolate Mousse, Rich 217
Chutney, Eggs in Brine with Tomato 129
Chutney, Eggs with Orange 129
Classic Cold Buffet 214
Classic Mayonnaise 12
Classic Oysters 140
Club Sandwich 24
Cocktail, Avocado 60
Cocktail, Camembert 101
Cocktail, Chicken 59
Cocktail, Hearts-of-Palm 60
Cocktail, Lobster 58
Cocktail, Lychee 138
Cocktail, Mushroom 59
Cocktail, Mussel 61
Cocktail, Prawn & Mango 143
Cocktail, Prawn 58
Cocktail, Spicy Melon 61
Cold Beef with Fruit Salad 198
Cold Buffet, Classic 214
Cold Meats 156-165
Cold Platters 202
Cold Savory Soups 178
Consommé with Dumplings 176
Cooking a Galantine 17
Copenhagen Platter 206
Corn & Cheese Salad 83
Corn & Pepper Salad 217
Corn Salad, Herring Rolls with 151
Corned Beef & Egg 23
Corned-Beef & Cheese Salad 101
Cornets, Bavarian 30
Cornish Pasties 189
Cottage-Cheese Salad 35

Cottage Cheese with Apple 35
Cottage Cheese with Ginger & Honey 35
Cottage Cheese with Herbs 35
Country Buffet 208
Country Cheese Board 167
Country Sausage Platter 203
Country Terrine 65
Crackers, Cheese & Herb 45
Cream Cheese, Curried Peaches with 32
Cream Dip 175
Cream Dressing, Potato Salad with 87
Cream Horns, Mock-Caviar 152
Cream-Cheese Layer 187
Cream-Cheese Mousse 193
Cream, Cheese Platter with Gorgonzola 167
Cream-Cheese Tartare 193
Cream, Herring with Pepper 155
Cream, Lime 139
Cream of Cucumber Soup 178
Cream, Pork with Persimmon 196
Crisp Savories 184
Crispbread, Asparagus 28
Croissants, Cheese 185
Croquettes, Curried 40
Croquettes, Game & Mushroom 41
Croquettes, Prawn 42
Crostini, Tuscan 25
Croûte, Pork Fillet en 62
Crudités 68
Crudités 68
Cucumber & Dill Salad 77
Cucumber & Prawn Salad 82
Cucumber Cocktail 7
Cucumber, Danish Salami & 23
Cucumber Salad, Potato & 200
Cucumber Soup, Cream of 178
Cucumber, Stuffed 130
Cup, Pineapple 9
Cup, Strawberry 9
Curried Cream, Royal Sole with 51
Curried Croquettes 40
Curried Eggs, Smoked Turkey with 197
Curried Peaches with Cream Cheese 32
Curry Mayonnaise 13
Curry Rosettes 170
Curry Sauce, Stuffed Pork with 157

D
Danish Almond Rings 211
Danish Buffet 211
Danish Cheese, Smoked Eel & 48
Danish Macaroni Salad 98
Danish Salami & Cucumber 23
Danish Sandwiches 31
Dark Chaudfroid 19
Deep-Fried Sole 211
Delicatessen Meat Salads 33
Dessert Soup, Red-Currant 208
Dessert Soups 181
Dessert, Summer Fruit 201
Dill Butter, Salmon & 171
Dill Mayonnaise, Herring in 148
Dill Salad, Cucumber & 77
Dill, Trout with 146
Dips 174
   Artichoke Dips 175
   Cheese & Onion Dip 208
   Cream Dip 175
   Egg Dip 175
   Garlic Dip 175
   Gorgonzola Dip 175
   Herb Dip 174
   Mayonnaise Dip 175
   Orange Dip 174
   Sausage Dips 175
   Tomato Dip 174, 175
Dips for Vegetables 174
Dominoes 45
Dressings:
   Blue-Cheese Dressing 116
   Egg & Herb Dressing 116
   French Dressing 116

   Sherry Dressing 117
   Thousand Island Dressing 117
   Vinaigrette Dressing 173
   Yogurt Dressing 117
Duck with Artichoke Salad 198
Dumplings, Consommé with 176

E
Eel & Danish Cheese, Smoked 48
Eel & Salmon, Smoked 30
Eel Salad, Smoked- 32
Eel with Vegetable Salad, Smoked 191
Egg & Herb Dressing 116
Egg & Pepper Spread 34
Egg & Tongue 26
Egg Dip 175
Egg Dishes 124-129
Egg Platter, Party 125
Egg Salad, Apple & Quail's- 78
Egg Salad, Salami & 20
Egg Specialties 126
Egg Tartlets with Ham Salad 127
Egg Tartlets with Liver Pâté 127
Egg Tarts, Quail's- 48
Egg, Corned Beef & 23
Egg, Ham & 20
Egg, Mushroom with 22
Egg, Roast Beef & 26
Eggplant, Stuffed 132
Eggs in Brine with Tomato Chutney 129
Eggs with Bean Salad, Piquant 125
Eggs with Endive Salad, Stuffed 53
Eggs with Orange Chutney 129
Eggs, Iceberg Lettuce with Garnished 81
Eggs, Party 124
Eggs, Pickled 128
Eggs, Smoked Turkey with Curried 197
Eggs with Sauces, Hard-Cooked 126
Elderberry Soup 183
Emmentaler Salad 209
Emmentaler Spread 34
Endive & Fruit Salad 73
Endive Boats 104
Endive Salad, Stuffed Eggs with 53
Endive, Stuffed Belgian 135
Escargots, Pâté d' 64
Exotic Chicken Salad 82
Exotic Fruits 136-139

F
Fall Fruit Salad 111
Fennel Salad 70
Fennel with Blue-Cheese Dressing 133
Feta-Cheese Salad 97
Fig, Prosciutto & 28
Fish 140-155
Fish & Pea Salad 91
Fish Canapés, Smoked- 39
Fish Medley, Chilled 180
Fish Mold, Tomato & 118
Fish Mousse with Shrimp 143
Fish Platter 206
Fish Platter, Meat & 211
Fish Platter, Smoked- 155
Fish Specialties 144
Fish Stock for Aspics, Basic 17
Fish with Gourmet Sauce, Smoked 144
Fish, Sauerkraut & Smoked 88
Fish, Tomato & 21
Food for a Feast 216
For Cocktail Parties 38-51
For Fall 103
For Two 190-199
For the Epicure 162
For the Gourmet 136
Frankfurt Green Sauce 172
French Bread 11
French Bread, Stuffed 201
French Dressing 116
French-Style Hors d'Oeuvres 52
Fritters, Cheese 42
From the Smörgåsbord 26

Fruit Dessert, Summer 201
Fruit Salad in Pineapple 114
Fruit Salad, Avocado 115
Fruit Salad, Cheese & 166
Fruit Salad, Chinese 112
Fruit Salad, Cold Beef with 198
Fruit Salad, Endive & 73
Fruit Salad, Fall 111
Fruit Salad, Italian 213
Fruit Salad, Jamaican 107
Fruit Salads 106
Fruit Salad, Spicy 109
Fruit Salad, Summer 114
Fruit, Sauerkraut & 88

G
Galantine, Cooking a 17
Galantines, Pâtés, Terrines & 14
Game 159
Game & Mushroom Croquettes 41
Garlic Bread 11
Garlic Butter 170
Garlic Dip 175
Garlic Vinegar 169
Gazpacho, Andalusian 179
Giant Cheese Buffet 166
Giant Meat Platter 202
Ginger & Honey, Cottage Cheese with 35
Ginger Salad, Plum & 110
Glazed Fillet of Beef 157
Glazed Saddle of Venison 159
Gorgonzola Cream, Cheese Platter with 167
Gorgonzola Dip 175
Gourmet Fare 194
Gourmet Platters 203
Gourmet Sauce, Smoked Fish with 144
Gourmet's Delight 31
Grape & Walnut Salad 111
Grapefruit Salad 106
Gravad Lax 144
Green Butter 170
Green Herring Salad 210
Green Sauce, Frankfurt 172
Green-Bean Salad, Shrimp & 79

H
Haddock & Salmon Pasty 64
Haddock Mold 119
Ham & Cheese, Chicken Salad with 85
Ham & Egg 20
Ham & Salad Platter 204
Ham & Vegetable Mold 121
Ham Butter 171
Ham Canapés, Melon & 43
Ham Mousse 52
Ham Quiches 189
Ham Rolls with Horseradish Cream 43
Ham Rolls, Hawaiian 33
Ham Salad, Avocado & 105
Ham Salad, Egg Tartlets with 127
Ham Tarts, Swiss 209
Ham, Hearts of Palm in 57
Ham, Roquefort Pears with Smoked 191
Ham, Sauerkraut & 88
Hard-Cooked Eggs with Sauces 126
Hawaiian Ham Rolls 33
Hearts of Palm in Ham 57
Hearts-of-Palm Cocktail 60
Heartwarming Soups 176
Herb Balls 171
Herb Crackers, Cheese & 45
Herb Dip 174
Herb Dressing, Egg & 116
Herb Mayonnaise 13
Herb Mayonnaise, Spit-Roast Pork with 158
Herb Oil, Mixed- 168
Herb Oils & Vinegars 168
Herbs, Cottage Cheese with 35
Herring Platter 210
Herring, Rollmop 26
Herring Rolls with Corn Salad 151
Herring Salad 211

Herring Salad, Green 210
Herring Salad, Pepper & 99
Herring-Salad Platter 151
Herring Salad, Red 210
Herring, Soused 149
Herring Tartare 150
Herring in Dill Mayonnaise 148
Herring in Red-Wine Marinade 149
Herring with Apple Salad 150
Herring with Mixed Peppers 148
Herring with Pepper Cream 155
Homemade Bread 10
Honey, Cottage Cheese with Ginger & 35
Horseradish Butter 171
Horseradish Cream, Ham Rolls with 43
Hungarian Goulash Soup 177
Huntsman's Salad 84

I
Ice Cream, Orange Soup with Vanilla 181
Ice Cream, Papaya 139
Ice Cream, Vanilla 19
Iceberg Lettuce with Garnished Eggs 81
Iceberg Salad with Port Dressing 74
Iced Borscht 179
Individual Steak Tartare 165
Introduction 5
Italian Buffet 212
Italian Fare 195
Italian Fruit Salad 213
Italian Green Sauce, Vegetable Salad with 213
Italian Salad 97
Italian Veal Galantine 67

J
Jamaican Fruit Salad 107
Juice, Apple & Carrot 7
Juice, Tomato & Celery 7

K
Kiwi Salad with Orange Cream 107
Kiwi Salad, Raspberry & 112
Kiwi with Orange Sauce, Chicken & 137
Kumquat Sauce, Pastrami with 136

L
Lax, Gravad 144
Layer, Cream-Cheese 187
Leeks, Stuffed 134
Lemon Vinegar 169
Lettuce with Garnished Eggs, Iceberg 81
Light Chaudfroid 18
Light Meals 190
Light Meat Stock for Aspics 17
Light Salads 71
Lima-Bean Salad 87
Lime Cream 139
Lime Soup 182
Lining & Cooking a Terrine 16
Lining a Pâté Pan 15
Liver Pasties 63
Liver Pâté, Egg Tartlets with 127
Liver Squares, Pork & Turkey- 164
Liver-Sausage Snacks 46
Liver-Sausage Swirls 50
Livers, Spicy Chicken 27
Loaf, Luxury Party 36
Loaf, Mosaic 37
Lobster Cocktail 58
Lobster Tartlets 141
Lunch Party, Children's 200
Luting Paste 17
Luxury Party Loaf 36
Lychee Cocktail 138

M
Macaroni Salad, Danish 98
Mackerel Salad, Rice & 93
Mackerel, Smoked 27
Madeira Aspic 18
Making Chaudfroid 18
Mango Cocktail, Prawn & 143

Marinade, Herring in Red-Wine 149
Marinated Prawns with Sole Fillets 142
Marinated Sole Fillets 145
Mariner's Breakfast 26
Mayonnaise Dip 175
Mayonnaise Variations 12
Anchovy Mayonnaise 13
Beef Mayonnaise 29
Classic Mayonnaise 12
Curry Mayonnaise 13
Herb Mayonnaise 13
Mushroom Mayonnaise 13
Olive Mayonnaise 13
Quick Mayonnaise 12
Tomato Mayonnaise 13
Meat & Fish Platter 211
Meat & Vegetable Salad 98
Meat Pasty 63
Meat Platter 210
Meat Platter, Giant 202
Meat Platters with Pineapple Salad 207
Meat Salad, Seville 89
Meat Salads, Delicatessen 33
Meat Stock for Aspics, Light 17
Meat-Loaf Sandwiches 200
Meat-Salad Rolls 46
Meatballs 210
Meatballs, Oxtail Soup with 177
Mediterranean Salad 214
Melon & Ham Canapés 43
Melon, Chicken Breasts with 192
Melon Cocktail, Spicy 61
Melon Salad 108
Melon with Prosciutto & Mayonnaise 137
Minced-Steak Pasties 188
Mixed-Herb Oil 168
Mixed-Pepper Salad 71
Mixed-Salad Bowl 217
Mixed-Vegetable Soup, Yogurt & 180
Mock Caviar, Sole Mousse with 152
Mock Champagne 9
Mock-Caviar Butter 171
Mock-Caviar Cream Horns 152
Mold, Chicken & Vegetable 120
Mold, Haddock 119
Mold, Ham & Vegetable 121
Mold, Summer Salad 123
Mold, Tomato & Fish 118
More Party Canapés 47
Mosaic Loaf 37
Mousse, Cream-Cheese 193
Mousse, Ham 52
Mousse, Rich Chocolate 217
Mousse, Tomato 52
Mousse with Mock Caviar, Sole 152
Mousse with Shrimp, Fish 143
Mozzarella Salad, Tomato & 213
Mulled Wine 10
Muscatel Aspic 18
Mushroom Cocktail 59
Mushroom Croquettes, Game & 41
Mushroom Mayonnaise 13
Mushroom Salad 78
Mushroom Salad in Tomato Rings 78
Mushroom Sauce 126
Mushroom Terrine 66
Mushroom with Egg 22
Mussel & Bean-Sprout Salad 73
Mussel Cocktail 61
Mussels & Sprouts 21
Mussels, Avocados with 136
Mussels with Mayonnaise 141
Mussels with Saffron Sauce 140
Mustard Butter 171

N
New Yorker 29
Niçoise, Salmon-Trout 146
Nouvelle Cuisine 78

O
Ohio Sauce 172

Oil, Mixed-Herb 168
Oil, Rosemary 168
Olive Appetizers 212
Olive Mayonnaise 13
Onion Dip, Cheese & 208
Onion Soup 176
Open Sandwiches 20
Orange Butter 170
Orange Chutney, Eggs with 129
Orange Cream, Kiwi Salad with 107
Orange Dip 174
Orange Salad 106
Orange Salad, Apple & 110
Orange Sauce, Chicken & Kiwi with 137
Orange Soup with Vanilla Ice Cream 181
Oxtail Soup with Meatballs 177
Oyster Salad 53
Oysters, Classic 140

P
Papaya Ice Cream 139
Paprika Butter 170
Party Baking 184-189
Party Buffets 200
Party Canapés 44, 216
Party Dishes 122
Party Drinks 7
Party Egg Platter 125
Party Eggs 124
Party Extras 168-175
Party Nests 39
Party Pizzas 212
Party Sandwiches 20-33
Party Slices 47
Party Specials 95
Party Starters 56
Party Tournedos 162
Party Trout Platter 154
Party, Children's Lunch 200
Party, Swiss Buffet 209
Pasta Salad 201
Paste, Luting 17
Pasties, Cornish 189
Pasties, Liver 63
Pasties, Minced-Steak 188
Pastrami with Kumquat Sauce 136
Pastry Cheese Rings, Puff- 186
Pastry Pockets, Cheese 188
Pastry, Brioche 14
Pastry, Pie-Crust 14
Pastry, Puff 15
Pasty, Haddock & Salmon 64
Pasty, Meat 63
Pâté & Bacon 26
Pâté, Camembert 208
Pâté d'Escargots 64
Pâté, Egg Tartlets with Liver 127
Pâté Pan, Lining a 15
Pâtés & Pies 62-67
Pâtés en Croûte 62
Pâtés, Terrines & Galantines 14
Pea Salad 90
Pea Salad, Fish & 91
Peaches with Cream Cheese, Curried 32
Pears with Smoked Ham, Roquefort 191
Pepper & Herring Salad 99
Pepper Butter 171
Pepper Cream, Herring with 155
Pepper Rounds, Red- 171
Pepper Salad, Corn & 217
Pepper Salad, Mixed- 71
Pepper Spread, Egg & 34
Peppers, Herring with Mixed 148
Peppers on Tomato, Cheese & 131
Peppers, Sausage & 20
Persimmon Cream, Pork with 196
Persimmons, Stuffed 138
Pheasant, Roast Breast of 159
Pickled Eggs 128
Pie-Crust Pastry 14
Pies & Pastries 186
Pineapple Cup 9

Pineapple Salad, Meat Platters with 207
Pineapple Soup, Blackberry & 182
Pineapple, Fruit Salad in 114
Pinwheels 22
Piquant Beef Salad 86
Piquant Dressing, Red-Endive Salad with 72
Piquant Eggs with Bean Salad 125
Pizzas, Party 212
Plum & Ginger Salad 110
Pork & Turkey-Liver Squares 164
Pork Fillet en Croûte 62
Pork with Curry Sauce, Stuffed 157
Pork with Herb Mayonnaise, Spit-Roast 158
Pork with Persimmon Cream 196
Port Aspic 18
Port Dressing, Iceberg Salad with 74
Potato & Apple Salad 102
Potato & Cucumber Salad 200
Potato & Sausage Salad 83
Potato Salad with Cream Dressing 87
Poulet-Bresse 160
Poultry 160
Prawn & Mango Cocktail 143
Prawn & Mock Caviar 26
Prawn Cocktail 58
Prawn Croquettes 42
Prawn Salad 211
Prawn Salad, Cucumber & 82
Prawn-Tartare Slices 49
Prawns in Aspic 122
Prawns with Sole Fillets, Marinated 142
Prosciutto & Fig 28
Prosciutto & Mayonnaise, Melon with 137
Puff Pastry 15
Puff-Pastry Cheese Rings 186
Puffs, Cheese 186
Punches 9

Q

Quail's-Egg Salad, Apple & 78
Quail's-Egg Tarts 48
Quails, Stuffed 161
Quiches, Ham 189
Quick Mayonnaise 12

R

Rabbit Terrine 66
Radish Salad, Strawberry & 104
Raspberry & Kiwi Salad 112
Red Herring Salad 210
Red-Cabbage Salad 103, 211
Red-Currant Dessert Soup 208
Red-Endive & Spinach Salad 75
Red-Endive Salad with Piquant Dressing 72
Red-Endive Salad, Chicken & 79
Red-Pepper Rounds 171
Red-Wine Marinade, Herring in 149
Rémoulade Sauce 13
Rémoulade Sauce, Roast Beef with 156
Rice & Mackerel Salad 93
Rice & Tuna Salad 86
Rice Salad 84
Rice Salad, Apple & 217
Rice Salad, Spicy 200
Rich Chocolate Mousse 217
Riesling, Salmon in 119
Riviera Salad Platter 94
Roast Beef & Egg 26
Roast Beef with Rémoulade Sauce 156
Roast Breast of Pheasant 159
Roast Meats 156
Rollmop Herring 26
Rolls, Stuffed Party 37
Roquefort Boats 51
Roquefort Pears with Smoked Ham 191
Roquefort Slices, Baked 24
Rosemary Oil 168
Royal Sole with Curried Cream 51
Rum Dressing, Apple Salad with 109
Russian Sauce 126
Russian-Salad Platter 199
Rye Bread 12

S

Saddle of Venison, Glazed 159
Saffron Sauce, Mussels with 140
Sage Vinegar 169
Salads 68-117
  Angelo's Chicken Salad 105
  Apple & Celery Salad 102
  Apple & Orange Salad 110
  Apple & Quail's-Egg Salad 78
  Apple & Rice Salad 217
  Apple Salad with Rum Dressing 109
  Artichoke Salad 216
  Asparagus & Sprout Salad 94
  Asparagus Salad 76
  Avocado & Ham Salad 105
  Avocado Fruit Salad 115
  Balkan Salad 85
  Bamboo-Shoot Salad 74
  Banana & Tomato Salad 108
  Bean Salad 155
  Broccoli Salad 90
  Caribbean Salad 113
  Carrot & Apple Salad 69
  Celeriac Salad 77
  Celery & Avocado Salad 69
  Cervelat Salad 89
  Chanterelle Salad 93
  Cheese & Fruit Salad 166
  Cheese & Salami Salad 99
  Cheese & Sausage Salad 166
  Cheese Salad 20
  Chef's Salad Platter 95
  Chicken & Asparagus Salad 96
  Chicken & Red-Endive Salad 79
  Chicken & Vegetable Salad 96
  Chicken Salad 192
  Chicken Salad with Ham & Cheese 85
  Chinese Fruit Salad 112
  Chinese-Cabbage Salad 70
  Corn & Cheese Salad 83
  Corn & Pepper Salad 217
  Corned-Beef & Cheese Salad 101
  Cottage-Cheese Salad 35
  Cucumber & Dill Salad 77
  Cucumber & Prawn Salad 82
  Danish Macaroni Salad 98
  Delicatessen Meat Salads 33
  Emmentaler Salad 209
  Endive & Fruit Salad 73
  Exotic Chicken Salad 82
  Fall Fruit Salad 111
  Fennel Salad 70
  Feta-Cheese Salad 97
  Fish & Pea Salad 91
  Fruit Salad in Pineapple 114
  Grape & Walnut Salad 111
  Grapefruit Salad 106
  Green Herring Salad 210
  Ham & Salad Platter 204
  Herring Salad 211
  Herring-Salad Platter 151
  Huntsman's Salad 84
  Iceberg Salad with Port Dressing 74
  Italian Fruit Salad 213
  Italian Salad 97
  Jamaican Fruit 107
  Kiwi Salad with Orange Cream 107
  Lima-Bean Salad 87
  Meat & Vegetable Salad 98
  Mediterranean Salad 214
  Melon Salad 108
  Mixed-Pepper Salad 71
  Mushroom Salad 76
  Mussel & Bean-Sprout Salad 73
  Orange Salad 106
  Oyster Salad 53
  Pasta Salad 201
  Pea Salad 90
  Pepper & Herring Salad 99
  Piquant Beef Salad 86
  Plum & Ginger Salad 110
  Potato & Apple Salad 102

Potato & Cucumber Salad 200
Potato & Sausage Salad 83
Potato Salad with Cream Dressing 87
Prawn Salad 211
Raspberry & Kiwi Salad 112
Red Herring Salad 210
Red-Cabbage Salad 103, 211
Red-Endive & Spinach Salad 75
Red-Endive Salad with Piquant Dressing 72
Rice & Mackerel Salad 93
Rice & Tuna Salad 86
Rice Salad 84
Riviera Salad Platter 94
Russian-Salad Platter 199
Salad Buffet with Assorted Dressings 116
Salad Platter 215
Salad Supreme 100
Salami & Egg Salad 20
Sauerkraut Salads 88
Savoy-Cabbage Salad 103
Seasonal Sausage Salad 80
Seville Meat Salad 89
Shrimp & Green-Bean Salad 79
Sicilian Salad 113
Sicilian Seafood Salad 54
Smoked-Eel Salad 32
Spicy Fruit Salad 109
Spicy Rice Salad 200
Spring Salad 75
Strawberry & Radish Salad 104
Summer Fruit Salad 114
Summer Salad Mold 123
Summerhouse Salad 95
Swiss Salad 84
Swiss-Cheese Salad 21
Tomato & Mozzarella Salad 213
Tuna Salad 81
Vegetable Salad with Italian Green Sauce 213
Vegetable-Salad Platter 92
Waldorf Salad 214
White-Cabbage Salad 103
Salads as Main Meals 80
Salad-Burnet Vinegar 169
Salami & Cucumber, Danish 23
Salami & Egg Salad 20
Salami Salad, Cheese & 99
Salmon & Dill Butter 171
Salmon Canapés Tartare 43
Salmon Pasty, Haddock & 64
Salmon Platter, Smoked- 91
Salmon Vols-au-Vent, Smoked- 153
Salmon in Riesling 119
Salmon with Vegetable Salad 147
Salmon, Smoked Eel & 30
Salmon-Trout Niçoise 146
Sandwich, Club 24
Sandwich Snacks 32
Sandwiches & Rolls 23
Sandwiches, Danish 31
Sandwiches, Meat-Loaf 200
Sangria 10
Sardines, Beccafico 55
Sardines, Stuffed 55
Sardines, Sweet & Sour 155
Sauces:
  Capri Sauce 126
  Cheese Sauce 126
  Frankfurt Green Sauce 172
  Mushroom Sauce 126
  Ohio Sauce 172
  Rémoulade Sauce 13
  Russian Sauce 126
  Sauce Tartare 173
  Sweet-Wine Sauce 19
Sauerkraut & Fruit 88
Sauerkraut & Ham 88
Sauerkraut & Smoked Fish 88
Sauerkraut Salads 88
Sausage & Peppers 20
Sausage Dips 175
Sausage Platter, Country 203
Sausage Rolls with Carrot Salad 197

Sausage Salad, Cheese & 166
Sausage Salad, Potato & 83
Sausage Salad, Seasonal 80
Sausage Snacks, Liver- 46
Sausage Swirls, Liver- 50
Savory Butter Slices 38
Savory Butters, 170
Savory Tidbits 41
Savoy-Cabbage Salad 103
Scampi with Anise Cream 142
Scandinavian Fare 194
Seafood Molds 118
Seafood Salad, Sicilian 54
Seafood in Aspic 119
Seasonal Sausage Salad 80
Seville Meat Salad 89
Shellfish 140
Shepherd's Fare 195
Sherry Aspic 18
Sherry Dressing 117
Shrimp & Green-Bean Salad 79
Shrimp in Aspic 118
Shrimp, Avocado with 132
Shrimp, Fish Mousse with 143
Sicilian Salad 113
Sicilian Seafood Salad 54
Smoked Eel & Danish Cheese 48
Smoked Eel & Salmon 30
Smoked Eel with Vegetable Salad 191
Smoked Fish, Sauerkraut & 88
Smoked Fish with Gourmet Sauce 144
Smoked Ham, Roquefort Pears with 191
Smoked Mackerel 27
Smoked Trout 21
Smoked Trout, Asparagus with 190
Smoked Turkey with Curried Eggs 197
Smoked-Eel Salad 32
Smoked-Fish Canapés 39
Smoked-Fish Platter 155
Smoked-Salmon Platter 91
Smoked-Salmon Vols-au-Vent 153
Smörgåsbord 210
Smörgåsbord Favorites 26
Snacks, Liver-Sausage 46
Soft Drinks 7
Sole Fillets, Marinated 145
Sole Fillets, Marinated Prawns with 142
Sole Mousse with Mock Caviar 152
Sole with Curried Cream, Royal 51
Sole, Deep-Fried 211
Soup Selection 176-183
   Apricot & Cherry Soup 183
   Blackberry & Pineapple Soup 182
   Chilled Tomato, Soup 178
   Cream of Cucumber Soup 178
   Elderberry Soup 183
   Hungarian Goulash Soup 177
   Lime Soup 182
   Onion Soup 176
   Orange Soup with Vanilla Ice Cream 181
   Oxtail Soup with Meatballs 177
   Red-Currant Dessert Soup 208
   Strawberry & Apple Soup 181
   Yogurt & Mixed Vegetable Soup 180
Soused Herring 149
Special Fillings 36
Special-Occasion Buffets 200-217
Special Sauces 172
Spicy Chicken Livers 27
Spicy Fruit Salad 109
Spicy Melon Cocktail 61
Spicy Rice Salad 200
Spinach Salad, Red-Endive & 75
Spit-Roast Pork with Herb Mayonnaise 158
Spread, Egg & Pepper 34
Spread, Emmentaler 34
Spread, Stilton 34
Spreads & Fillings 34-37
Spring Salad 75
Sprout Butter 170
Sprout Salad, Asparagus & 94
Sprout Salad, Mussel & Bean- 73

Sprouts, Mussels & 21
Steak Pasties, Minced- 188
Steak Tartare 164
Steak Tartare Buffet-Style 165
Steak Tartare, Individual 165
Steak-Tartare Rounds 49
Sticks, Cheese 40
Stilton Spread 34
Stock for Aspics, Basic Fish 17
Stock for Aspics, Light Meat 17
Strawberry & Apple Soup 181
Strawberry & Radish Salad 104
Strawberry Cup 9
Stuffed Artichokes 133
Stuffed Belgian Endive 135
Stuffed Cucumber 130
Stuffed Eggplant 132
Stuffed Eggs 124
Stuffed Eggs with Endive Salad 53
Stuffed French Bread 201
Stuffed Leeks 134
Stuffed Party Rolls 37
Stuffed Persimmons 138
Stuffed Pork with Curry Sauce 157
Stuffed Quails 161
Stuffed Sardines 55
Stuffed Tomatoes 40
Stuffed Turkey Breast 161
Stuffed Vegetables 130
Stuffed Watermelon 115
Summer Bavarois 214
Summer Fruit Dessert 201
Summer Fruit Salad 114
Summer Salad Mold 123
Summerhouse Salad 95
Sunday Buffet 215
Super Spreads 34
Sweet & Sour Sardines 155
Sweet-Wine Sauce 19
Swiss Buffet Party 209
Swiss-Cheese Salad 21
Swiss Ham Tarts 209
Swiss Salad 84

T
Tartare Buffet-Style, Steak 165
Tartare, Cream-Cheese 193
Tartare, Herring 150
Tartare, Individual Steak 165
Tartare Rounds, Steak- 49
Tartare, Salmon Canapés 43
Tartare, Sauce 173
Tartare Slices, Prawn- 49
Tartare, Steak 164
Tartlets with Ham Salad, Egg 127
Tartlets with Liver Pâté, Egg 127
Tartlets, Chanterelle 56
Tartlets, Chicken 57
Tartlets, Lobster 141
Tarts, Quail's-Egg 48
Tarts, Swiss Ham 209
Terrine, Country 65
Terrine, Lining & Cooking a 16
Terrine, Mushroom 66
Terrine, Rabbit 66
Terrine, Veal 67
Terrines & Galantines 65
Terrines & Galantines, Pâtés, 14
The Cheeseboard 166
The Cold Table 208
The First Course 52-61
Thousand Island Dressing 117
Tomato & Celery Juice 7
Tomato & Fish 21
Tomato & Fish Mold 118
Tomato & Mozzarella Salad 213
Tomato, Cheese & Peppers on 131
Tomato Chutney, Eggs in Brine with 129
Tomato Dip 174, 175
Tomato Mayonnaise 13
Tomato Mousse 52
Tomato Rings, Mushroom Salad in 78

Tomato Salad, Balkan 72
Tomato Salad, Banana & 108
Tomato Sauce, Trout Fillets with 145
Tomato Soup, Chilled 178
Tomatoes, Chicken-Salad 131
Tomatoes, Stuffed 40
Tongue, Egg & 26
Tongue with Vegetable Salad 196
Tonnato, Vitello 163
Tournedos Elysée, Veal 50
Tournedos with Broccoli Puree, Veal 163
Tournedos, Party 162
Tricorns, Cheese 185
Trout, Asparagus with Smoked 190
Trout Fillets with Tomato Sauce 145
Trout Niçoise, Salmon- 146
Trout Platter, Party 154
Trout Toast with Asparagus 153
Trout with Dill 146
Trout, Smoked 21
Truffle Butter 170
Tuna Salad 81
Tuna Salad, Rice & 86
Turkey Breast, Stuffed 161
Turkey Legs with Broccoli 160
Turkey with Curried Eggs, Smoked 197
Turkey-Liver Squares, Pork & 164
Tuscan Crostini 25

V
Vanilla Ice Cream 19
Vanilla Ice Cream, Orange Soup with 181
Veal Galantine, Italian 67
Veal Mostarda, Braised 158
Veal Terrine 67
Veal Tournedos Elysée 50
Veal Tournedos with Broccoli Puree 163
Vegetable Dishes 130-135
Vegetable Julienne, Artichokes with 56
Vegetable Mold, Chicken & 120
Vegetable Mold, Ham & 121
Vegetable Molds 120
Vegetable Salad, Chicken & 96
Vegetable Salad, Meat & 98
Vegetable-Salad Platter 92
Vegetable Salad, Salmon with 147
Vegetable Salad, Smoked Eel with 191
Vegetable Salad, Tongue with 196
Vegetable Salad with Italian Green Sauce 213
Vegetable Soup, Yogurt & Mixed- 180
Vegetables, Dips for 174
Vegetarian Special 22
Venison, Glazed Saddle of 159
Vinaigrette Dressing 173
Vinegar, Garlic 169
Vinegar, Lemon 169
Vinegar, Sage 169
Vinegar, Salad-Burnet 169
Vitello Tonnato 163
Vols-au-Vent, Smoked-Salmon 153

W
Waldorf Salad 214
Walnut, Blue Cheese & 26
Walnut Salad, Grape & 111
Watermelon, Stuffed 115
White-Cabbage Salad 103
White-Wine Aspic 18
Whole-Wheat Bread 11
Wine 8
Wine Aspic, White- 18
Wine, handling 8
Wine, Mulled 10
Wine Sauce, Sweet- 19
Wine, serving 8

Y
Yogurt & Mixed-Vegetable Soup 180
Yogurt Dressing 117

5.725309461 18